CHRISTIANS

IN

JAPAN

NI HON
Japan

NI
in

IKIRU
*to live,
living*

KIRISUTO
Christ

日本に生きるキリスト者たち

SHA
people

TACHI
*plural,
many*

Carolyn Bowen Francis
John Masaaki Nakajima

Friendship Press
New York

Book design and typesetting by Patricia Kellis
Kanji (characters) for titles by Moromizato Hideko, Okinawa
Map by Sean Grandits

©1991 by Friendship Press, Inc.
Editorial Offices: 475 Riverside Drive, Room 772, New York, NY 10115
Distribution Offices: P.O. Box 37844, Cincinnati, OH 45222-0844

Manufactured in the United States of America

Library of Congress Cataloging-in-Publication Data

Francis, Carolyn Bowen and Nakajima, John Masaaki.
Christians in Japan / Carolyn Bowen Francis and John Masaaki Nakajima.
    p. cm.
    ISBN 0-377-00216-X
    1. Protestant churches—Japan—History—20th century. 2. Japan—
Church history—1945- 3. Japan—Religion—1945- 4. Christianity and
other religions—Japanese. I. Francis, Carolyn. II. Nakajima, John, 1928-
BR1309.C47 1991   90-21016
275.2—.dc20   CIP

Contents

Facts About Japan

LOCATION: The Japanese archipelago consists of four main islands and about 3,900 smaller islands located off the east coast of the Asian continent. It stretches from 20 degrees to 45 degrees north latitude, approximately the same latitude as Santiago, Cuba or Mexico City in the south, and Montreal, Canada or the Oregon-Washington border of the U. S. in the north.

SIZE: 378,000 square kilometers (slightly larger than the state of California).

POPULATION: 122,610,000 (U.S., 246,330,000; Canada, 25,950,000).*

POPULATION DENSITY: 324 people per square kilometer (U. S., 26 per sq. km.; Canada, 3 per sq. km.).

FORM OF GOVERNMENT: Parliamentary democracy.

LEGISLATURE: The parliament, called the National Diet, is composed of the 512-seat House of Representatives, elected every 4 years, and the 252-seat House of Councillors, elected every 6 years.

EXECUTIVE: The prime minister, elected by the political party in power, appoints the members of the 20-member Cabinet.

JUDICIARY: The court system consists of the Supreme Court, 8 high courts, 50 district courts, and many summary courts.

POLITICAL PARTIES: Liberal Democratic Party, Japan Socialist Party, Komeito (Clean Government Party), Democratic Socialist Party, Japan Communist Party, United Social Democratic Party.

LOCAL GOVERNING UNIT: Japan is divided into 47 prefectures, equivalent to states or provinces in other countries.

HISTORICAL PERIODS:

8000 B.C.	Jomon	1338 A.D.	Muromachi
300 B.C.	Yayoi	1573 A.D.	Momoyama
300 A.D.	Yamato	1603 A.D.	Edo (Tokugawa)
593 A.D.	Asuka	1868 A.D.	Meiji
710 A.D.	Nara	1912 A.D.	Taisho
794 A.D.	Heian	1926 A.D.	Showa
1192 A.D.	Kamakura	1989 A.D.	Heisei

Some of the names of historical eras are derived from place names (usually the center of power). Others are especially chosen at the end or beginning of an emperor's reign, expressing in two Japanese characters of especial beauty a quality of or hope for that period.

---

*Statistics concerning population are from 1988.

Foreword

JAPAN:

Snow-capped Mt. Fuji rising above cherry trees in bloom,
Kimono-clad women bowing deeply in greeting,
Stately pageantry of ancient drama, music, and dance,
Painstaking practice of flower arrangement and tea ceremony,
Personal kindness lavished on family and guests.

JAPAN:

Disregard and destruction of natural resources and beauty,
Emergence of vibrant women as political leaders,
Eager acceptance of the new, the modern, the foreign,
Impatient people on the go — in work and play,
Public avoiding of the misfit, the outsider.

Which is the true Japan? Both are—thus describing Japan briefly is a difficult task.

We are inviting you to meet both of these Japans by meeting individual Christians--a small minority in Japanese society engaged in the daily struggle to be faithful witnesses to God's loving plan for all creation.

Because Japanese society has traditionally stressed the importance of the small group rather than the individual as the basic unit of society, we introduce Japan and the Christian community through the theme of a group-oriented society. We invite readers to observe some of the security and the constraints experienced by those people who are "insiders," in Japanese society, to listen to the pain and suffering of those people who are "outsiders," and then to glimpse ways in which the Christian community is engaging in mission to both.

We begin our journey to Japan by looking at Christian beginnings. We end the journey by joining sisters and brothers in the Christian community in Japan to explore new ways to join hands across land and sea for our common mission in Jesus Christ.

Japanese names appearing in the book are written in the traditional Japanese order, with the surname appearing first and the personal name last. The surname is capitalized the first time for clarity.

Marks over certain vowels in Japanese words to indicate a long vowel sound have been omitted in the interest of printing.

Japanese words have been italicized and defined the first time they appear and not marked thereafter. Most Japanese words also appear in the glossary (page 158).

In Japanese the form of a noun does not change when it is plural, the practice also followed in this book.

The exchange rate of U.S. $1 = Y140 has been used throughout the book, despite occasional fluctuations.

Deep appreciation is expressed to Christian colleagues throughout Japan for being the subjects, the storytellers, and the co-laborers in the joy of sharing one part of the story of the Christian community in Japan with brothers and sisters across the peaceful Pacific. Their valuable contributions are listed on pages 159-160. Special gratitude goes to missionary colleague Margaret Warren, whose valuable liaison, legwork, and support enabled communication between Tokyo and Okinawa. Much needed advice on content and style was gratefully received from Friendship Press director Audrey Miller and editor Carol Ames, and from longtime colleague in mission Pat Patterson, coordinator, Japan-North America Commission on Cooperative Mission. The calligraphy that appears throughout the book is by Ms. MOROMIZATO Hideko, Koza Church (Kyodan), Okinawa City, Okinawa.

Introduction

On June 14, 1864, a young man of twenty-one left Hakodate, Hokkaido, after sneaking aboard an American ship. At that time to leave the country was strictly forbidden by the Japanese government. Such an attempt, if discovered, was punishable by death. Influenced by seeing huge Dutch warships in the harbor, by reading Chinese translations of such books as a history of the United States, *Robinson Crusoe*, and the Bible, NIISIMA Shimeta (later renamed Joseph Hardy Neesima in the U.S. and NIIJIMA Jo in Japan) dared to break the law to realize his aspiration of studying abroad in order to better serve his country.

After a little over a year-long journey, Niisima arrived at Boston, where he met Mr. and Mrs. Alpheus Hardy, prominent lay leaders in the Congregational Church and major benefactors also of the American Board of Commissioners for Foreign Missions. The couple became Niisima's lifetime sponsors. After ten years of study in an atmosphere that owed much to its Puritan heritage, Niisima was able to return to Japan, because a policy change by the new Japanese government lifted the ban on foreign travel.

The American Board appointed Niisima as its missionary to Japan to work alongside American missionaries already in Japan. Just before leaving the U.S., Niisima appealed to the General Assembly of the American Board concerning his fervent desire to establish a Christian school in Japan. Immediately U.S. $5,000 was collected. Thus one of the earliest Christian schools in Japan, the Doshisha, was established in Kyoto in 1875.

This was the first time North American Christians sponsored a Japanese to be trained in the U.S. as a worker for Christ in Japan. Similar cooperation in Christian mission has continued for more than one hundred years since that time.

In 1890, Niisima died at age forty-six. Five years previously, in 1885, twelve-year-old NAKAJIMA Suteo accompanied his father Buhei to immigrate from Choshu (now Yamaguchi Prefecture) to Hokkaido. As Japan's new era dawned with the Meiji Restoration in 1868, key government positions were dominated by high-ranking officers of the Choshu clan. But for low-ranking *samurai* (feudal warriors) like Buhei, Japan's modernization meant the loss of everything—both the prestige and the stipends accorded them as samurai. As compensation, the government devised the *Shizoku Imin* (special

1

samurai immigration) project. Many samurai who had lost their livelihood were sent en masse to the "undeveloped" barren lands of Hokkaido. Whatever land they cultivated there became their own. Whether they realized that their presence deprived the native Ainu people (see page 64-68) of their homeland is unclear.*

During the Meiji era, the government also made Hokkaido a dumping place for major-offense criminals, including political dissidents, and a number of prisons were established there. Many of the early wardens were kindly disposed toward Christianity and sought to use it as an ethical principle to reform prisoners. Christian evangelists were often invited to be prison chaplains. Among them were early Doshisha graduates, who did not limit their Christian ministry to the prison but also made their homes places of worship and Bible study.

Niisima spent the summer of 1887 in Sapporo, Hokkaido, and while there preached at a house-church meeting. When he returned to Kyoto, he appealed to the Congregational Church headquarters in Osaka to send a full-time pastor to that area of Hokkaido.

Nakajima Suteo was attracted to that house-church meeting and was later baptized there. He became one of the founding members of Iwamizawa Church, Hokkaido, in 1899. In 1924, Suteo's son Masayoshi entered the Theological Department of Doshisha University.

In the 1880s, ODAWARA Jotaro and Miyo left Noto Peninsula (Ishikawa Prefecture) to establish a small lacquer-ware workshop in downtown Kyoto. Among their customers were the Rev. and Mrs. Niisima. Partly under their influence, Jotaro and Miyo became Christians. While their youngest daughter, Shizue, was studying at the Doshisha Girls' High School, she and Masayoshi sang together in the Kyoto Church choir. They were married in 1928, upon Masayoshi's graduation.

After serving several years as pastor at Otsu Church, near Kyoto, Masayoshi and Shizue in 1933 accepted a call to pastor a tiny Japanese congregation in Manila, the Philippines. Although evangelism among the four thousand Japanese residents of Manila was difficult, the couple was accepted and their Sunday School flourished.

The Philippines, then a colony of the U.S., was invaded by Japanese forces in December, 1941, because of the U.S. military bases

---

*In the post-World War II land reform, when Suteo's heir, his grandson, was living outside Hokkaido, all of the family land was confiscated by the government. In return, the heir (this writer, heir because his father had died), received the price of a much-needed pair of shoes.

there. In the Philippines, the Nakajimas experienced Pearl Harbor Day, and there Masayoshi was drafted into the Japanese Army in late 1944. He was killed two months later in a strafing attack by U.S. fighter planes. In late 1945, after nearly a year of wandering around the mountains of Luzon as refugees, Shizue and their children came back to Japan. Shizue remained an active participant in many anti-war movements until partially paralyzed by a stroke in late 1988.

Masayoshi and Shizue's son Masaaki (this writer, also known as John) met KINUGASA Aiko, whose parents taught at Doshisha, while he was a student at Doshisha Graduate School of Theology. They married in 1953 after he graduated from seminary and she graduated from the Department of English Literature. The couple had sung together in a Kyoto church choir.

Thus Masaaki's life experience includes the Philippines, where he spent the whole of his boyhood; Doshisha, from middle school through graduate school; Hokkaido, where he served as pastor for six years and as Hokkai District director of evangelism for three years; Toronto, Canada, where he did graduate study; and New Jersey, USA, where he worked as a fraternal worker in a Presbyterian church. His several ecumenical experiences, including serving as general secretary of the National Christian Council in Japan (NCCJ) and subsequently of the United Church of Christ in Japan (*Nihon Kiristo Kyodan*, called *Kyodan* hereafter) led to his becoming chair of Japan-North America Commission on Cooperative Mission (JNAC) and to serving as co-author and editor, with Carolyn Bowen FRANCIS, of this book.

This writer's reason for beginning this study book with a personal story is to help readers realize that behind the accounts of Christianity in Japan recorded here there are many other untold stories. We feel that an invisible cord binds all these human stories together. Yes, that cord is the story of God's work. God has been at work in raising up Christian people in Japan. God has been at work in binding North American and Japanese Christians together in mission. To tell the story of Christianity in Japan is to tell the story of how God has been at work among us.

This book seeks to introduce the Japan that Christians in Japan confront today. As editors, we have emphasized Christian witness and the challenge Japanese society imposes upon Christians there, rather than institutional and statistical aspects.

During the time of the "post-war Christian boom," the pastor of the church I attended in Kyoto repeatedly appealed to the congregation to build a sanctuary capable of seating one thousand worshipers. It was a grand vision for a pastor who regularly preached to a congregation of one hundred each Sunday morning. The vision never was realized. The church was rebuilt a few years ago to accommodate one hundred fifty worshipers. Sunday morning worship attendance has shrunk to about seventy now. But we don't consider the church a failure. At the time, the churchgoers were mostly young people who had lost their self-identity in wartime defeat; they were attracted to Christianity as a new fad with a certain tint of American democracy. Today, this church has become a center of genuine Christian witness, actively engaged in human rights and anti-war movements and other programs, while preaching in depth the gospel of Jesus Christ.

In the course of world history, there have been many "Christian nations" that have not succeeded in making a true Christian witness. Many have been ruled by military dictatorships. Many have exploited other nations. Many have started wars. Many profit by selling weapons for the ruthless destruction of human life.

"Not everyone who says to me 'Lord, Lord,' will enter the kingdom of heaven, but only the one who does the will of my Father in heaven. On that day, many will say to me, 'Lord, Lord, did we not prophesy in your name, and cast out demons in your name, and do many deeds of power in your name?' Then I will declare to them, 'I never knew you; go away from me, you evildoers'" (Matthew 7:22-23).

Churches in Japan are trying not to be like this "many." Japanese churches will always be in the minority, as long as they truly follow Christ's way. This book tells the story of such Christian witness. We believe readers will feel the strong hands of God, who has led Christians in Japan as they have struggled to be faithful in this task. We invite readers to join us in affirming the power of God as we move into the future engaging in our common mission.

Thus, our exploration of Christian witness in Japan begins with a look at Christian beginnings, followed by a look at life on the inside and the outside of Japanese society as the arena for Christian witness. Finally, we examine Japan's role in the world today and our common task in mission.

Let me close by sharing with you some reflections from my 1988 Easter message, which commemorated the fourth anniversary of the signing of the covenant of mission cooperation between United Church of Christ in Japan (*Kyodan*) and the Korean Christian Church in Japan (KCCJ).

The words "suffered under Pontius Pilate" in the Apostle's Creed point clearly to the historical reality that Jesus Christ lived during the reign of Pontius Pilate, Roman Procurator of Judea from A.D. 26 to 36. Thus, we can know that Jesus did not suddenly appear out of nowhere, but was born and lived during a particular period in history. The opening paragraph of the Letter to the Hebrews also stresses the importance of locating an event in a particular point in history: "God spoke to our ancestors in many and various ways long ago by the prophets, but in these last days God has spoken to us by a Son."

How has the Japanese church lived under "Pontius Pilate"?

In his Gospel account, Luke goes to great length to vindicate Pontius Pilate. In the same way in Acts, Luke tries to ingratiate himself with the Roman authorities, declaring that it was the Jews who were to blame for Jesus' death, not Pilate or Rome. This rationale can be seen as Luke's appeal to the authorities to recognize the new faith.

It pains me to reflect on the reality that we Japanese Christians have long adopted an attitude toward *our* "Pontius Pilate" that closely resembles the attitude of Luke. In 1910 the vast majority of Japanese churches declared that Japan's annexation of Korea was God's will, and they supported "Pontius Pilate's" national policy. One church even quickly accepted financial assistance from the Japanese Governor-General of Korea in order to launch a flourishing program of evangelism in Korea.

Over six thousand Korean residents in Tokyo were massacred on the occasion of the Great Kanto Earthquake in 1923. I have heard that some Christians joined citizens' patrols at that time, being misguided by wild rumors which accused Korean residents of insurrection. Unfortunately, I have never heard of any Christians giving aid to the Korean victims.

From the time of the Sino-Japanese War in 1894-95* to World War II and Japan's invasion of other Asian countries, Christians not only approved the national policy and actively promoted and backed the war effort; they also cooperated with the state policy which declared that *Shinto*** was not a religion. It became the duty of all citizens, including Christians, to worship at Shinto shrines; and even Kyodan leaders were dispatched to Korea to promote this policy.

---

*Japanese forces drove the Chinese out of Korea, defeated the Chinese naval fleet, and captured part of China. As victor, Japan received Formosa (Taiwan), which marks the beginning of Japanese colonization there.

**The indigenous Japanese religion declared the offical state religion during World War II. See pages 16-17.

Thus, the Japanese church aligned itself with state power to protect its own life. When those in our midst who resisted the state were oppressed, the church did as the state dictated, cutting off and casting away brothers and sisters in the faith, all in the interest of self-survival.

The Japanese church, then, has not "suffered under Pontius Pilate," but instead has in many ways submitted to, sided with, and obeyed Pontius Pilate.

Now imperial succession of Japan's new emperor has occurred. The two-year period mourning the death of the previous emperor and accession of the new emperor has been used to strengthen the power of Pontius Pilate, as many people feared. As Christians in Japan, we must never relax our vigilance!

Recently a well-known Kyodan minister has raised the question of whether the church can successfully engage in evangelism without hoisting the Rising Sun flag on holidays and revering the emperor. I would like to pose the question whether an evangelism that so ingratiates itself with the state can really be called mission which communicates the Good News.

We are encouraged by the words in Hebrews 13:12-13: "Therefore Jesus also suffered outside the city gate in order to sanctify the people by his own blood. Let us go forth to him outside the camp and bear the abuse he endured."

God does not expect us to shut ourselves up within the four walls of the church, having fellowship only with kindred spirits and receiving the grace of salvation.

Outside the gate rushes the swiftly flowing stream of history. Whether we like it or not, Pontius Pilate's powerful authority is swirling all around us. Jesus shed blood and suffered in the midst of such power and authority. May we, too, be those who "suffer under Pontius Pilate," that we might also, then, experience the grace of resurrection!

NAKAJIMA Masaaki (John)

Part One

Christianity in Japan

DAI-ICHI
Part One

NIHON
Japan

NIOKERU
in

KIRISUTOKYO
Christianity

第一 日本におけるキリスト教

Christian Beginnings: The Catholic Period

カトリック

KATORIKKU
Catholic

"If I went to Japan, would the people become Christian?"

"My people would not immediately become Christians; but they would first ask you a multitude of questions, weighing carefully your answers and your claims. Above all, they would observe whether your conduct agreed with your words. If you should satisfy them on these points—by suitable replies to their inquiries and by a life above reproach—then, as soon as the matter was known and fully examined, the king [*daimyo*], the nobles, and the educated people would become Christians. Six months would suffice; for the nation is one that always follows the guidance of reason."

The questioner was Francis Xavier, Portuguese priest and one of six founding members of the Society of Jesus. Answering Xavier's query was Anjiro, a thirty-six-year-old Japanese who in 1548 fled his country after killing a man and boarded a Portuguese ship en route to India. There he met Xavier, sent by the king of Portugal as missionary to Europeans and Indians in Malacca, a Portuguese territory.

Anjiro's reply filled Xavier with the desire to take Christianity to Japan. Accompanied by Anjiro, newly baptized and serving as interpreter, and two other Jesuits, Xavier arrived in Kagoshima, Anjiro's home province in southern Japan, on August 15, 1549. He was the first Christian missionary to reach Japan, six years after the first Europeans, Portuguese traders, arrived in Japan.

Appeal to the powerful

The Japan that Xavier entered was not a unified political entity but was severed by conflict among the *daimyo* (local feudal lords), all trying to maintain and extend their territorial domains. The daimyo paid nominal allegiance to the emperor residing in the capital city of Kyoto, but it was the *shogun*, the strongest military general, who claimed real leadership over all the daimyo.

Some daimyo initially welcomed the missionaries as representatives of Portugal, hoping to attract Portuguese trade and military aid.

ODA Nobunaga, the general who unified Japan by 1578, later extended favor to the missionaries in a ploy to control the militant Buddhist forces threatening his political control.

Xavier's method of proselytizing was accepted missionary policy at that time: evangelizing individual Japanese while seeking to gain the favor of the daimyo and an audience with the emperor. Xavier believed that gaining the leaders' support would result in the conversion of the masses they controlled. He also felt it natural to use his position as a representative of politically and economically powerful Portugal in his mission endeavors.

Xavier was ultimately denied an audience with the emperor, and he and his missionary colleagues encountered both ridicule and opposition. Nevertheless, several local daimyo did give him permission to teach Christianity, and he soon baptized the first converts.

After two years Xavier left his colleagues and the infant Christian community in Japan, returning to India to recruit new workers for Japan and prepare for beginning mission work in China as an aid in furthering mission work in Japan. Today we question Xavier's reliance on Portuguese political power and his emphasis on mass conversions of the people through winning their leaders. Nevertheless, we must applaud his zeal in propagating Christianity and his enthusiastic leadership, which attracted both colleagues and converts during the initial mission period in Japan.

Following Xavier's departure, the growth of Christianity in Japan was uneven. The conversion of daimyo and their followers was followed by persecution of Christians by some non-Christian daimyo and Buddhist priests who were threatened by Christianity's increasing strength and the political favor shown missionaries.

An annual report to the church in Portugal reported that in 1581, 30 years after Xavier's departure, there were 150,000 Christians and 200 churches in Japan, the majority in Kyushu, the southern island. Japan's total population was then about 16 million.

A general's threats

TOYOTOMI Hideyoshi, the skillful general who succeeded ODA Nobunaga, initially appeared to favor the missionaries. But in 1587, he suddenly issued an edict calling for the expulsion of all missionaries within twenty days. While this decree was not enforced, it signified the end of the top authorities' show of support for the foreign religion and missionaries. These instruments of profit and political control were now seen as a threat to Japanese sovereignty and as the vanguard of European incursion and conquest. Japanese authorities made it clear, however, that they wished to maintain trade relations with the Portuguese.

Individual and mass conversions continued, as did schools and charitable institutions, but missionaries deemed it wise to adopt a lower profile in evangelism. Most withdrew to a small island off Kyushu where they once again set up schools and a printing press.

In 1593 Spanish Franciscan priests from the Philippines arrived in Japan, encouraged by the Spanish government, which sought to establish trade relations with Japan. Their arrival both angered and threatened the Jesuits, who feared that Hideyoshi's wrath would now be directed at all Christians. Distrust and competition between the two religious orders heightened Japanese authorities' mistrust of missionary motives.

In 1596 a Spanish galleon from Manila washed ashore off the coast of the island of Shikoku. The captain attempted to gain Hideyoshi's permission to continue on to Mexico. Seeking to impress a Japanese official with the Spanish king's power, he explained Spain's successful method of extending its empire:

The kings of Spain begin by sending out teachers of our religion, and when these have made sufficient progress in gaining the hearts of the people, troops are dispatched who unite with the new Christians in bringing about the conquest of the desired territory.

In response, Hideyoshi ordered troops to surround Jesuit and Franciscan establishments in Kyoto and Osaka and officials to secure the names of churchgoers in those cities. Twenty-four Christians—three Franciscan fathers, three brothers, a Japanese Jesuit lay brother, two Jesuit novices and fifteen persons employed by the missionaries including young teenage boys—were arrested, paraded through the streets, and taken to Nagasaki. There, with two other Christians who had tried to minister to the prisoners en route, they were crucified in February 1597.

Successive government edicts forbade any daimyo to become Christian and ordered all missionaries to Nagasaki for deportation. Some of the 125 Jesuits remaining in Japan went into hiding and others followed Hideyoshi's order. In 1598, 137 churches, a college, a seminary, and many Jesuit residences in southern Kyushu were destroyed, and many Christians there were persecuted. After Hideyoshi's death in 1598, his successor, TOKUGAWA Ieyasu, eased the persecution of Christians for a time. Missionaries came out of hiding and new ones arrived, churches and charitable institutions were rebuilt, and 70,000 baptisms were recorded within a two-year period.

From 1602, Jesuit and Franciscan missionaries in Japan were joined by Spanish Dominicans and Augustinians from the Philippines. The rivalry among the four orders rekindled Japanese suspicion and distrust of Christianity.

Suspicion leads to persecution

Neither Ieyasu, who declared himself shogun in 1603, nor his son, Hidetada, declared shogun in 1605, actively persecuted Christianity at first, although some local daimyo continued to do so.

The missionaries' scientific knowledge attracted upper-class Japanese, providing potential converts. Ieyasu made use of both Portuguese and Spanish missionaries to bolster foreign trade and to acquire knowledge of navigation and mining.

The arrival of a Dutch ship in 1600 established Japanese trade with Holland. This displeased Roman Catholic missionaries, because Holland was a Protestant country.

From 1612 heightened suspicion of Christianity by both Ieyasu and many local daimyo resulted in increased persecution of Christians. In 1614, Ieyasu issued a decree stating:

> Christians have come to Japan, not only sending their merchant vessels to exchange commodities, but also longing to disseminate an evil law and to overthrow right doctrine so that they may change the government of the country and obtain possession of the land. This is the germ of great disaster and must be crushed. These [missionaries] must be instantly swept out, so that not an inch of soil remains to them in Japan on which to plant their feet, and if they refuse to obey this command, they shall pay the penalty.

All daimyo were ordered to send missionaries in their domains to Nagasaki for deportation, destroy all churches and force Christians to give up their religion. On the deportation day six months later, three small ships were loaded with missionaries and Japanese Christians; one was sent to Manila, the others to the Portuguese colony of Macao. Some persons escaped offshore and secretly made their way back into Japan. Others avoided deportation by going into hiding.

Persecution and martryrdom by crucifixion, decapitation, and burning at the stake increased throughout Japan after Ieyasu's death, under his son, Hidetada, and his grandson, Iemitsu. Some Christians renounced their faith under torture by drowning, submersion in hot springs, and suspension head downward in pits of excrement.

But the vast majority, both peasants and daimyo, remained faithful unto death. The exact number of martyrs is not known, though the total certainly is in the thousands, and by some estimates in the hundreds of thousands.

In 1624 new orders issued in Iemitsu's name prohibited entry to all Spaniards, and commanded Spanish priests to leave. No Japanese Christian was allowed to go abroad, and trade with the Philippines was cut off. Foreign ships were ordered to register all persons on board, and both missionaries and those bringing them to Japan were burned at the stake. Rewards were offered for information on Christians, with amounts varying for missionaries, Japanese clergy, and lay believers. All remaining missionaries were forced into hiding.

Following a peasant revolt in 1637, the government made an all-out attempt to eradicate Christianity entirely. Remaining Christians, thoroughly intimidated, pretended to give up their faith. The government appointed officials to ferret out believers. One method used from 1658 was *efumi* (picture-trampling). Suspected Christians were ordered to trample upon a cross or a picture of Christ; those who shrank back were declared Christian. In 1669 *fumie* (copper tablets with a picture of Christ) were introduced. In the annual efumi ceremony in Nagasaki, all residents, including infants, were called upon to tread on the fumie.

Portuguese were now forbidden entry to Japan, and Dutch and Chinese ships were to be captured if Christian teachers were found on them. Dutch traders were confined to Dejima, a small island constructed in Nagasaki Bay. Christian books, printed in China and smuggled into Japan by Chinese merchants, were forbidden by the Shogun in 1687—even almanacs that only mentioned Christianity. Notices prohibiting the "evil sect of Christianity" were posted in every town throughout Japan. At last, it seemed that Christianity had been erased from Japan.

Opening the doors

In 1867, the 250-year reign of the Tokugawa clan collapsed when pressures within Japan combined with pressures from foreign powers to force Japan to end its long, self-imposed isolation.

The weakening of the Tokugawa government's centralized control, the emergence of a strong merchant class in Japanese society, and a growing movement among western Japanese daimyo to overthrow the Shogunate and re-install the emperor all contributed to Japan's readiness to open its doors to Western powers.

Increasing numbers of British, Russian and U.S. ships tried to enter Japanese ports in the second half of the nineteenth century. These attempts, coupled with news of the carving up of China by the

Western powers after the Opium War in 1842, made Japanese leaders respond to foreign demands to open Japan's doors to trade and relationships with other nations.

Commodore Matthew Perry arrived in Uraga, Japan, after initially landing in Okinawa, in 1853. He carried a letter from U.S. President Millard Fillmore asking that Japan treat kindly all Americans shipwrecked in Japan, open one or two ports and establish trade and diplomatic relationships with the U.S., and provide food and fuel to U.S. ships bound for China. Perry returned to Japan the following year to sign the first Japan-U.S. amity treaty. Treaties were made with Great Britain, Russia and the Netherlands by the end of 1855.

While few in Japan favored the total opening of the country, the government realized the need to modernize for its own self-defense and survival. For that, Japan had much to learn from other nations in the world.

Hidden Christians emerge

Although relationships with the U.S. were established by the Treaty of 1854 and relationships with European nations were established in following years, foreigners were not permitted to reside in Japan. In the nearby Ryukyu Islands, French missionaries awaited the opening of Japan. When Japan concluded a treaty with France, they entered the country as priest-interpreters under the consul-general of France. They soon constructed churches in Hakodate on Hokkaido, in Yokohama, and in Nagasaki to commemorate the canonization of the twenty-six martyrs crucified in 1597.

A month after the Nagasaki church's completion, Father Petitjean, a French priest, had an astounding encounter:

> On March 17, 1865, about half past twelve, some fifteen persons were standing at the church door. Urged no doubt by my guardian angel, I went up and opened the door. I had scarce time to say a *Pater* when three women between fifty and sixty years of age knelt down beside me and said in a low voice, placing their hands upon their hearts, "The hearts of all of us here do not differ from yours."
>
> "Indeed!" I exclaimed, "Whence do you come?"
>
> They named the village, adding, "All there have the same hearts as we."
>
> Blessed be Thou, O my God, for all the happiness which filled my soul! What a compensation for five years of barren ministry! Scarcely had our dear Japanese opened their hearts to us than they displayed an amount of trustfulness which contrasts strangely with the behavior of their pagan brethren. I

was obliged to answer all their questions and to talk to them of *O Deusu Sama, O Yasu Sama,* and *Santa Maria Sama,* by which names they designated God, Jesus Christ, and the Blessed Virgin. The view of the statue of the Madonna and Child recalled Christmas to them, which they said they had celebrated in the eleventh month. They asked me if we were not in the seventh day of the Time of Sadness (Lent); nor was Saint Joseph unknown to them; they call him *O Yasu Sama no Yofu* (the adoptive father of our Lord). In the midst of this volley of questions, footsteps were heard. Immediately all dispersed; but as soon as the newcomers were recognized, all returned laughing at their fright. "They are people of our village," they said, "They have the same hearts as we have." However, we had to separate for fear of awakening the suspicions of the officials, whose visit I feared.

From that day, believers who had been in hiding, now known as "hidden Christians," streamed to the church daily, leading missionaries to warn them lest Japanese authorities discover their existence. Missionaries visited the outlying islands and discovered thousands more hidden Christians: the total was estimated to be between twenty and fifty thousand. About half chose to re-unite with the Roman Catholic Church, the others continuing to maintain and pass on their faith as "separated ones." Missionaries discovered that the faith had been secretly transmitted for generations in each faith community by two leaders: one who could read and write presided at Sunday prayer services; the other served as the baptizer and was always training a successor.

As the emboldened hidden Christians emerged, many refused to participate in universally practiced Buddhist burial rites. This refusal was viewed as an affront, but was temporarily accepted by local officials. However, despite protests by European and American representatives and the overthrow of the shogun and the restoration of the emperor in 1868, anti-Christian edicts were reaffirmed, and thousands of Christians were arrested, tortured, and deported to remote areas of Japan.

Successive Catholic, Orthodox, and Protestant missionary efforts have had to contend with hundreds of years of anti-Christian propaganda and the fear and suspicion that stem from intense persecution. These have colored the thinking of Japanese people, preventing many from becoming Christians.

Japanese Religions

SHUKYO
religion

The three major religious traditions in Japan are Shinto, Confucianism, and Buddhism. In different periods of history, each has become the predominant religious influence. These traditions are interwoven throughout Japanese history to provide the basic framework of Japanese society. From them emerged the rites of passage conducted at each stage of the life cycle. They also dictate the forms for most personal and communal relationships in Japanese society today.

Traditional Japanese religious concepts differ from Western religious concepts growing out of the Judeo-Christian heritage. Western religious faith is based on belief in a transcendent deity, a concept of human sin that separates human beings from the deity, a saving act by the deity that overcomes sin to reconcile human beings and the deity, and the human response of ultimate commitment to the deity in gratitude for the saving act.

Features of Japanese religious traditions include:

1. Mutual interaction among religious traditions with minimal conflict and major mutual influence;
2. An intimate relationship between human beings and many *kami* (gods or spirits) found in nature, in the lives of certain human beings such as the emperor and shamans, and in the dead as revered family ancestors. Kami inspire feelings of awe, beauty, mystery and power;*
3. An emphasis on family, family lineage and ancestors above individual religious preference. The home serves as the center of daily religious practice, and temples and shrines as the places for annual and occasional religious ceremonies;

---

*Protestants used the same word, *Kami*, to denote God. While early Roman Catholic missionaries used the Latin word *Deus* for God, today both Catholics and Protestants use *Kami*, to which is added the title of respect, *-sama*, becoming *Kamisama*.

15

4. The concept of evil as human impurity that separates humans from one another and from kami, and the overcoming of this separation by rites of purification;
5. Annual festivals that serve as the major communal religious celebrations, including rice-planting and harvesting festivals, New Year's and summer festivals;
6. A concept of religion as an integral part of daily life, including economic and social spheres, not limited to special buildings and times apart;
7. The close relationship between religion and state, with religious authority usually being subservient to political power.

Shinto

Origins

The indigenous, ancient religious traditions of Japan were formalized and given the name *Shinto* (way of the deities) when other religions were introduced into Japan in the sixth century. Shinto has served both as the set of indigenous, loosely organized religious practices, creeds, and attitudes at the community level and as the official state religion of Japan during one period of history.

As wetland agriculture produced stable agricultural communities in Japan during the ancient Yayoi period (300 B.C.-300 A.D.), rice-growing became the basis of important Shinto rites still performed today.

During the Kofun archaeological period (300-710 A.D.), many small kingdoms were unified under the powerful Yamato clan, out of which emerged the imperial lineage. The two major national Shinto shrines at Ise and Izumo were established. Each local clan also had its own shrine or shrines.

To establish its authority and legitimacy, the ruling class compiled the *Kojiki* (712 A.D.) and the *Nihon-shoki* (720 A.D.), mythical narrations of Japan's origin and history, to which the imperial line traces its roots. The emperor serves as the chief Shinto priest in all court rituals, which include the annual rice-planting and harvesting ceremonies. From the tenth century, Shinto increasingly became a coherent religious system of myths, rituals, priests and shrines.

Toward the end of the Tokugawa shogunate (1603-1868), there emerged a nationalistic movement calling for return to the source of Japanese identity, imperial rule, and Shinto as the sole religion of Japan. This laid the foundations for the Meiji Restoration in 1868, by which the military shogunate was toppled from power and the emperor reinstated. Under Meiji imperial rule, Shinto was declared the state religion. Shinto shrines received support from the government. Shinto concepts were taught in schools throughout Japan up until the end of World War II (1945).

Shrine and ritual

Most Shinto ceremonies take place at a Shinto shrine. A shrine site is chosen for natural beauty or strategic location—in a grove of trees, for instance, or near the source of a river. The entrance to each shrine or sacred area is marked by a *torii* (simple gateway).

Commonly performed Shinto rituals almost always include symbolic offerings of food and rice wine. One of the rituals central to Shinto is the rite of purification, which includes purification from such unclean elements as disease and death, with offerings to restore relationships after wrongdoing. Purification ceremonies are also conducted for new buildings.

Confucianism

Origins

Kong Qui, known in English as Confucius, was a teacher-philosopher in China during the Zhou dynasty (1027-256 B.C.) Confucius developed a philosophical, ethical and political teaching that also contained religious elements. He believed that the ideal harmonious, hierarchial society could be achieved not through law but through the moral example of leaders, by the performance of proper rituals, and by individual behavior appropriate to a person's status in society. Confucius maintained that rulers should choose public officials not on the basis of birth but according to their moral and intellectual qualities.

Confucian thinking spread from China to Korea, where it exerted great influence. Two Korean scholars brought Confucian thought to Japan in 404 A.D. The new system was received with interest by Japanese leaders, who felt Confucian concepts of a harmonious political system could help them unify their country. While Confucian thinking was never adopted in its entirety by Japanese leaders, it was applied especially from the seventh to the ninth centuries and from 1603 to 1945. Even Japan's early historical chronicle, *Nihon shoki,* contains the Confucian view of state and emperor.

Confucian thinking influenced Japan most significantly, however, in the realm of education. From 608 A.D., government-appointed students were included in Japanese trade and diplomatic missions to China, and on their return home, they shared the knowledge they had acquired. A Confucian system of education, which included a central university and provincial schools to train Japanese men as government officials, was established by the government around 670

A.D. with the help of Korean immigrants; however, early Korean influence was soon surpassed by that from China. Religious ceremonies honoring Confucius and his disciples, conducted twice annually in all educational institutions from 701 A.D., became the primary Confucian religious ritual in Japan.

Four hundred students chosen from the families of court officials and Korean scholars were admitted to the central university to study Confucian classics, which stressed filial piety, that is, loyalty and devotion of child to parent. When students completed their studies, they took examinations for government service. Outside the capital, smaller provincial schools were modelled on the university. From twenty to fifty students were chosen from families of provincial officials, supplemented in some cases by sons of commoners.

In Japan the Confucian educational system was weakened by the selection of students by family background rather than for intellectual ability, by the emphasis on language study (Chinese was the language of Japanese bureaucracy), and by the emergence of Buddhist intellectual influence. By the end of the twelfth century, the Confucian educational system had collapsed.

In China, Confucianism underwent a revival during the Song (Sung) dynasty (970-1279). In the thirteenth century, this Neo-Confucianism came to Japan, where it emphasized spiritual and ethical concerns. Neo-Confucianism first took root in Japan among the Zen Buddhist community, which saw it as a useful complement to Zen religious teachings when relating to Japanese leaders. Out of this merging of religious systems came the *juso*, Buddhist-Confucian monks.

The virtue of loyalty

A fourteenth-century heroic tale elevated the Confucian virtue of a warrior's loyalty to his lord above the virtue of filial piety. This loyalty became a dominant theme of Japanese Confucianism, and was later adopted into the value system of the Japanese samurai (warrior) society.

When Japan entered a period of relative peace under the Tokugawa shogunate, Confucianism once again played a major role in government and education. Sons of warriors received training for government leadership at feudal domain schools or private schools. Some children of commoners were educated in basic literary skills in separate local schools. By 1868, 43 percent of boys and 10 percent of girls attended some form of schooling where they were taught Confucian concepts of loyalty and filial piety.

Tokugawa intellectual leaders wanted their society to be patterned on the Confucian ideal of maintaining social harmony through a hierarchical social system with four levels based on occupation: samurai, peasant, artisan, and merchant.

The Confucian virtue of samurai loyalty to lord, adapted to subject loyalty to emperor, was instrumental in bringing about the Meiji Restoration in 1868. This same concept of loyalty also contributed to nationalistic unity achieved through a synthesis of Confucianism, Shinto, and the imperial ideology, which remained in place until the end of World War II. A concrete expression of this synthesis was the Imperial Rescript on Education of 1890, which stressed the Shinto tradition of the imperial lineage and the Confucian concept of the subject's loyalty to the emperor. The Rescript was implemented not only in Japan but in Japan's Asian colonies of Taiwan, Korea, Manchuria, and China.

Only a few Japanese scholars pursue Confucian studies today. Confucian concepts continue to exert an important influence, however, in language, education, government, family, and society, extolling the virtues of loyalty, hierarchy and social harmony.

Buddhism

Origins

Siddhartha Gautama was born the first son of a king in a part of India that is now Nepal in the year 446 B.C. (some date his birth a century earlier). At age twenty-nine he renounced his luxurious life to search for the answers to the problem of human existence. Six years later he experienced enlightenment and achieved buddhahood (one who has awakened to the truth). Until his death he traveled through central India sharing his wisdom. Buddha concluded that humans are helpless in the face of life's suffering and that the root of all suffering is desire. He taught that denying self through spiritual discipline and practicing meditation could lead to understanding (enlightenment) and freedom from illusion and desire. His teaching also stressed compassion for all living creatures.

Buddhist missionaries went from India to China in the first and second centuries A.D. From China, Buddhism was introduced to Korea. In 552 A.D., a mission from a king of Korea carried Buddhist images, religious objects, and sutras (written precepts) to the Japanese emperor. The emperor welcomed the new religion, as did some court officials. Others declared that the Japanese gods would be displeased by the importation of a new religion. When those who supported Buddhism achieved power in the Nara period (710-794), Buddhism was made the state religion. Monasteries were established in each province of Japan and Buddhist studies begun. Thus, Japanese Buddhism first found favor with the ruling aristocrats and scholars.

Branches of Buddhism

Zen Buddhism originated in China in the seventh century, strongly influenced by Confucianism and Taoism, and was brought to Japan in 1191 A.D. Some branches of Zen appealed to the warriors and aristocrats, while others appealed more to the common people.

During the same period, the indigenous Nichiren and Pure Land Buddhist sects were established. They appealed to the common people by promising that the performance of certain simple rituals would ward off evil and suffering.

Christianity was initially used by military leader Oda Nobunaga to control the power of the militant Buddhist warrior monks in the late sixteenth century. In a similar way, after closing the country in 1639, the Tokugawa shogun used Buddhism to control the spread of Christianity by establishing the Buddhist parish system, under which all Japanese were required to receive a statement from their temple to show authorities that they were not a part of a religion that threatened the state. All funerals were conducted according to Buddhist rites, and Christians who refused these Buddhist rites were subject to punishment.

After the Meiji Restoration in 1868, when Shinto was established as the official state religion, Buddhism suffered a major setback.

Today Japanese Buddhism is divided into 13 sects. It maintains 80,000 temples, 150,000 priests, and several colleges. Buddhist influence on cultural art forms is seen in the tea ceremony, flower arrangement, and calligraphy, which still attract many students and continue to play an important cultural role in Japanese society.

Temples and rituals

Today most Buddhist rites are conducted at temples, except for some death-related services conducted in the home. Priests and monks conduct daily rites to deepen personal devotion through offerings and reciting sutras and mantras. Other rituals, conducted on behalf of the laity, seek the protection of Buddhas and heavenly beings for the country, groups, and individuals. In addition, priests also conduct funeral rites and memorial services on anniversaries of death for the deceased person's family and friends. Buddhism undertook ceremonies related to death when Shinto priests were reluctant to conduct them; Shinto views death as a source of ritual impurity.

Today annual Buddhist rites are conducted at New Year's, on the anniversary of the birth, death, and enligntenment of Buddha, during the spring and autumn equinoxes, and at the time of *obon*, the late summer festival when the souls of deceased family members are welcomed back for a visit with relatives.

New religions

In the nineteenth and twentieth centuries, a number of religious groups have been born; these are called *shinko shukyo* (newly arisen religions), often abbreviated *shin shukyo* (new religions). Many members of these groups avoid this title, describing themselves as lay movements that seek to recover and emphasize elements of traditional Japanese religions.

Beliefs and practices of Japanese popular folk religion, such as repeating the titles of sutras over and over and faith in shamans, are also incorporated into the new movements.

Social scientists suggest several reasons for the emergence of new religious traditions: the tendency of organized religion to become formalized and out of touch with people's lives, the shift from stable rural-agricultural community life to a mobile urban-industrial society with weakened ties to the Buddhist temple and Shinto shrine, and the gradual breakdown of a stratified feudal society.

In *The Rush Hour of the Gods: A Study of New Religious Movements in Japan* (Macmillan, 1967), H. Neill McFarland lists seven characteristics of the new religions: 1) a charismatic founder; 2) clear goals such as happiness, healing and prosperity; 3) strong sense of community; 4) highly centralized organization; 5) construction of mammoth headquarters; 6) mass activities such as pilgrimages and training programs; and 7) elements of various religious traditions expressed in novel ways combined with a sense of mystery.

Many of the earlier new religions, while attracting popular support, were persecuted by the government when they were seen as a threat to social harmony and the state.

Two of the fast-growing lay groups are Rissho Kosei-kai, known for effective organization of its membership into small counseling groups, and Soka Gakkai, out of which has emerged a major political party, Komeito (clean government party). Both groups have expanded overseas and engage in religious, cultural, and peace programs.

Religious customs today

Most Japanese participate in both Shinto and Buddhist traditions, and many also participate in some Christian traditions. Thus, the sum of adherents claimed by all religious bodies is higher than the total population of Japan.

Many Japanese choose a Christian or Shinto wedding ceremony, present their newborn infants at a Shinto shrine, attend a Christian church for a Christmas celebration, visit a Shinto shrine or Buddhist temple at New Year's to pray for good health or success in a school entrance examination, have a Buddhist funeral ceremony, and are buried in a Buddhist temple graveyard.

A traditional Japanese home includes both a Shinto *kamidana* (god shelf) in the kitchen, a place associated with life, and in the family room a Buddhist *butsudan* (ancestral altar), which contains the name tablets of deceased family members who are venerated there. Offerings of food and drink are placed on both the kamidana and the butsudan each day, assuming the home is large enough to accommodate both.

Shinto observances are associated with life, newness and productivity. Many companies have a Shinto shrine somewhere on their premises to ensure financial success. Buddhism is concerned with maintaining family awareness over time and even beyond death. Regular memorial services are held either at the family Buddhist temple or before the family butsudan, with decreasing frequency until the fiftieth year after the family member's death. Obon (festival of the dead), a late summer Buddhist festival, becomes a joyous occasion for welcoming deceased family members back for a brief visit. Many Japanese make an annual pilgrimage to their birthplace for this occasion, celebrating with special feasting, music and dance.

Protestant Beginnings

プ
ロ
テ
ス
タ
ン
ト

PUROTESUTANTO
Protestant

Protestants agreed with Roman Catholics that the Loochoo Islands (Ryukyu Islands, also known as Okinawa) might serve as the launching point for mission in Japan once that country opened its doors to the West, to Christianity, and to Christian missionaries. In 1845 British naval officers formed the Loochoo Naval Mission, which two years later dispatched its first missionary, Bernard J. Bettelheim, a converted Hungarian Jewish physician. Gifted linguistically but insensitive to the people of Okinawa, Bettelheim labored there for eight years. He compiled a language dictionary and translated portions of Scripture, but failed to gain the trust of the people or to establish an Okinawan church.

Missionaries in China maintained occasional contacts with Japan. They sent Bibles and religious tracts to Japan and contacted shipwrecked Japanese sailors in China, who gave them information about Japan and helped them study Japanese. They created interest about Japan among Western churches, which began to raise contributions mission work. The American Board of Commissioners for Foreign Missions received its first contribution of $27.87 "for missions in Japan" in 1828. After the treaty of amity between the USA and Japan was signed in 1854, missionaries from China visited Japan for brief periods, although they were not free to reside there.

Missionaries from USA via China

In 1859 the American Episcopal Church appointed two China missionaries, the Revs. John Liggins and C. M. Williams, to begin mission work in Japan. Liggins arrived in Nagasaki on May 2, 1859, two months before treaty provisions permitted foreigners to reside in Japan. On October 18 of the same year, J. C. Hepburn, M.D., and his wife, of the American Presbyterian Board, arrived in Japan. The Rev. Samuel R. Brown and D. B. Simmons, M.D., of the Reformed Church in America arrived the following month. Both Hepburn and Brown had previous missionary experience in China. Guido Verbeck, also of the Reformed church, was chosen for mission in Japan because his native language was Dutch; the Netherlands had a longtime presence in Japan.

Jonathan Goble, a sailor in Commodore Perry's expedition, had joined the U.S. Navy to get to Japan at a time when foreigners were not permitted to enter the country. After returning to the U.S. for study, Goble was sent to Japan with his wife in 1860 by the American Baptist Free Mission Society.

The American Board of Commissioners for Foreign Missions fund that began with the $27.87 offering had grown to $4,000 and was used to send the Rev. D. C. Greene to Japan in 1869 as the Board's first missionary there.

While still prevented from preaching Christianity and distributing Bibles, these early Protestant missionaries seized every opportunity to establish contacts with Japanese people, teaching English, dispensing medical treatment, and studying the language. They also prepared language texts for future missionaries and eventually compiled both a 40,000-word Japanese-English dictionary and a translation of the four Gospels.

In November 1864, the first recorded Protestant baptism took place: the candidate was described as a "Buddhist quack doctor selected by the Shogun's Council of State as a language teacher for Dr. Brown" by the Rev. J. H. Ballagh, a Reformed Church missionary, who performed the baptism.

The second and third baptisms took place in Nagasaki in May 1866. MURATA Wakasa, assigned by the Daimyo of Saga to patrol French and English ships in Nagasaki port in 1855, found a Dutch translation of the New Testament floating in the water. He sent a man to Shanghai to buy a Chinese translation of the New Testament, and with his brother and three other persons, began to study the New Testament. Over the next four years Murata regularly sent his servant on the two-day journey to Nagasaki to ask Verbeck about parts they could not understand. At last, in 1866, the two brothers requested Verbeck to baptize them, which he did in private to escape the wrath of Japanese authorities. In 1868 Verbeck also baptized a Buddhist, who was subsequently imprisoned for adopting his new faith.

As the government's suspicions gradually decreased, missionaries were invited to teach in government boys' schools. Nevertheless, edicts against Christianity remained in effect. Japanese were still made to register at their local Buddhist temples in order to receive burial. Both missionary and Japanese evangelists continued to experience occasional verbal and physical harassment.

The first mission school, opened in 1869 by Presbyterian missionaries, Christopher and Julia Carrothers, attracted both boys and girls, who were taught in separate classes. This school became Joshi Gakuin girls' school. Ferris Girls' School was opened in Yokohama in 1870 by a Reformed Church missionary, Mary Kidder.

A church is formed in Yokohama

Prayer meetings of missionaries and Japanese and English-speaking residents in Yokohama led to the organization of the first Japanese Christian church in that city in 1872. Nine young men, baptized on that occasion, and two men baptized previously were the founding members (they became known as the "Yokohama band"). As its first rule of government the church stated: "Our church is not partial to any sect, believing only in the name of Christ, in whom all are one, and believing that all who take the Bible as their guide, diligently studying it, are Christ's servants and our brothers." The Rev. J. H. Ballagh, Reformed Church missionary, served as the first pastor.

An ecumenical convention of missionaries, including Presbyterian, Reformed, and American Board personnel, and elders of the newly formed English-speaking churches in Tokyo and Yokohama, met in Yokohama in 1872. Their top priority was to produce a joint translation of the Bible. They set up an ecumenical committee of their denominational representatives plus representatives of the American Protestant Episcopal Mission, the English Church Mission, and the Greek Orthodox Church in Japan (founded by the Russian Missionary Society). The convention also declared the importance of educating a native clergy, publishing Christian literature, and maintaining Christian unity in Japan. So the groundwork for ecumenical witness was laid from the very beginning of Protestant Christian mission.

Rapid growth

In 1871, the Japanese government sent a commission to the U.S. to learn from American institutions and to press for revision of the unequal treaties with Western powers that Japan has signed in the 1850s. The commission faced opposition everywhere it went because Japan continued to outlaw and persecute Christianity. On its return to Japan in 1873, edict boards prohibiting Christianity were taken down. In 1889, the Meiji Constitution, which assured religious liberty to Japanese, was promulgated. These two events allowed missionaries greater freedom to evangelize. They also represented the government's effort to establish equal diplomatic relationships with Western nations.

American Methodist Episcopal, Canadian Methodist, and British Anglican Society for the Propagation of the Gospel missionaries arrived in 1873 and British Church Mission Society missionaries the following year.

In 1874 two Japanese ministers were repeatedly interrogated by officials for conducting a Christian funeral. Most graveyards were connected with Buddhist temples, and the laws did not allow Christians to be buried elsewhere.

Sunday was declared the official day of rest in 1876. In the same year a group of forty young Japanese men in a local government school in Kumamoto, Kyushu, became Christian. Taught English and Bible by a retired American military officer, Captain L.L. Janes, they made a solemn covenant to follow Christ and "enlighten the darkness of the Empire by preaching the Gospel, even at the sacrifice of their lives." Known as the "Kumamoto Band," the group experienced persecution from families and authorities but continued their preparation for Christian service and for outstanding Christian leadership at Niisima's school in Kyoto.

A similarly committed group of fifteen young men known as the "Sapporo Band" gathered around Colonel W. S. Clark, who came to Japan for one year to establish an agricultural school in the northern city of Sapporo, Hokkaido. Janes and Clark were among the large number of foreign experts employed by government or private concerns to assist in Japan's modernization.

In 1875 American Board missionary Dr. J.C. Berry visited prisons in different parts of Japan. His findings, submitted to the government in 1876, opened the door for a ministry to prisoners throughout Japan.

New churches were established in 1878 outside the ports of Yokohama, Nagasaki, and Hakodate, Hokkaido, originally the only cities open to foreign residents. In the same year Henry Faulds, M.D., of the United Presbyterian Church of Scotland, opened a school for students with visual handicaps in the hospital he operated in Tokyo. Faulds also worked to have portions of Scripture and other Christian literature printed in Braille.

An increase in the number of church members was accompanied by occasional outbursts of local opposition and ongoing opposition by the Ministry of Education. The Kyoto city government decreed that no Japanese should go to the houses of missionaries or any place where Christianity was preached. The Osaka Imperial High School ruled that two Christian teachers could neither preach nor teach Christianity.

According to missionary and Japanese colleagues reporting in 1882, the reasons educated Japanese gave for rejecting Christianity included: its supernatural elements; its doctrine of eternal life; its opposition to traditional ancestor worship; the supposed disadvantage Christianity posed to nationalism and sovereignty; and Christianity's conflict with modern science. Uneducated Japanese rejected

Christianity because of the fear of offending the government and friends; the strict observation of the Sabbath; the strictness of Christian morals; and the perception of Christianity as a demon's religion.

Churches grew rapidly from 1883 to 1888 as prayer services and revivals swept the country. Seminaries and schools were opened for both boys and girls in Tokyo, Yokohama, Kobe, and Osaka. In 1884, the Scripture Union began a program of daily Bible reading for persons throughout Japan. Even the leading opinion maker and educator, FUKUZAWA Yukichi, acknowledged the importance of the new religion and called on Japan to accept Christianity to ensure Japan's acceptance in the family of nations.

The appeal of Western ways

After 250 years of being tightly closed off from the rest of the world, the drive to "catch up" with Western nations led Japan to engage in an all-out campaign to adopt Western civilization and gain Western knowledge, especially in science and military science. Proficiency in English was one important tool but English teachers were few, so mission schools were crowded with persons seeking to master English. Christian school growth and prosperity peaked in 1888.

In 1885 three new mission groups arrived: the Presbyterian Church of the United States, The American Society of Friends, and the Evangelical Protestant Missionary Society. The first Southern Baptist missionaries arrived in 1889 to begin work in Kyushu. The first YMCA was established in Tokyo in 1880.

In this period of general acceptance, Christians addressed a variety of social needs. In 1886 a lecture tour by Mary C. Leavitt of the American Women's Christian Temperance Union stimulated the organization of temperance societies throughout Japan. The best-known was the nationwide Japan Woman's Christian Temperance Union, which addressed not only problems of alcohol and tobacco abuse but also the Japanese system of licensed prostitution.

Leprosariums were opened near Mt. Fuji in 1886 by a Roman Catholic priest; in Tokyo in 1894 by a Presbyterian missionary, Kate M. Youngman; and in 1895, in Kumamoto, Kyushu, by a British missionary, Hannah Riddell.

In 1887 a nursing school was opened in Kyoto by American Board missionary, J. C. Berry, M.D. In the same year a Japanese Christian medical student, ISHII Juji, gave up his studies to open a children's home in Okayama, renting an old Buddhist temple to accommodate the children in his care.

In 1887 a Japanese evangelist ministering to Japanese and Chinese immigrants in San Francisco visited Hawaii and organized mission work there among several hundred Japanese immigrants working on

sugar plantations.   He was assisted by the Japanese consul in
Hawaii, ANDO Taro, who was himself converted in 1888.   In 1894,
American Board missionaries in Japan, the Rev. and Mrs. O. H.
Gulick, moved to Hawaii to work with Japanese immigrants.

The *Fukuin Maru* (gospel ship) began a unique evangelistic ministry to island people in Japan's Inland Sea in 1899 as a project of
the American Baptist mission.   Captain Luke Bickel, a minister-
seaman, trained the ship's crew, worked with Japanese pastors,
preached, and produced Christian literature.   His son carried on the
ministry until 1927, when the Inland Sea became a training site for
the Japanese Navy.   The ministry was resumed by missionaries and
Japanese Christians in 1951.

Analysis of the period of the birth of Protestant mission and the
later period of rapid growth shows that the majority of persons who
gathered around the early missionaries, attended mission schools,
and committed their lives to Christ and later became church leaders
were members of the samurai class.   Trained to follow the lords to
whom they gave ultimate allegiance and disciplined in a strict
ethical code prescribed for their class, the samurai class lost its role
in society after the fall of the Tokugawa shogunate and the restoration of the Meiji emperor to the throne in 1868.   In 1889, the Rev.
D.C. Greene, the first ABCFM missionary, wrote that although
former samurai constituted less than 6 percent of the total population, they nevertheless made up over 30 percent of the church membership.   Thus, from its inception, Protestant Christianity in Japan
attracted urban, educated, and upper-middle class Japanese.   An
urgent question for the early Protestant Church was how to reach
rural Japanese and people in other strata of urban society.

Slowdown and resistance to Christianity

Just when some missionaries and Japanese Christians felt that
Japan was on its way to becoming a "Christian nation," church
growth and mission school attendance slowed.   Harassment and opposition from the general public, from Buddhism, and from the government increased in part because of a growing reaction against
Japan's wholesale acceptance of Western civilization.   Various political events distracted Japanese from Christianity; for example, the
1889 promulgation of the Meiji Constitution, which promised "Japanese subjects shall, within limits not prejudicial to peace and order,
and not anagonistic to their duties as subjects, enjoy freedom of
religious belief"; and the revision in 1894-5 of unequal treaties between Japan and the Western powers.

Other factors that reduced church growth and increased opposition were found within the church itself.   Some initial evangelistic

fervor waned. During this period of revived nationalism, some Japanese Christians tried to prove that they were not controlled by foreign interests and that the Japanese church was now able to exist independently of any such interest.

Some Christian schools yielded to government demands and removed all vestiges of Christianity from curricula and program in order to gain official recognition by the powerful Ministry of Education, which controlled accreditation of public and private schools.

"The Imperial Rescript on Education," issued in the emperor's name in 1890, was to exert great control not only over the course of education but also over Japanese Christians for the next fifty years. The Rescript enjoined all citizens to loyalty, filial piety, and sacrifice for the state to maintain the imperial throne. This document was read regularly at school ceremonies amid a reverent atmosphere. Students stood at attention and teachers stepped forward one by one to make a deep bow before the document, which bore the imperial signature. Any perceived lack of reverence was punished harshly.

UCHIMURA Kanzo, a young Christian teacher at a government high school in Tokyo, refused to bow during the ceremony, considering it an act of idolatry. He was dismissed from his teaching position for disloyalty. Uchimura, who was converted as a student and became a leader of the Sapporo Band, became an outstanding writer, social critic, moral prophet, and lecturer on Christianity and the Bible. He is the founder of *mukyokai* (non-church movement), which emphasized Christian freedom and the independence of Japanese Christianity from the West. Mukyokai is known for its quality Bible study fellowship groups and its lack of formal organization, fixed membership, clergy, and sacraments.

Japan's involvement in the Sino-Japanese War (1894-5) and in the Russo-Japanese War (1904-5) provided Christians the opportunity to prove their unquestionable loyalty to the nation. Young men served in branches of the military, while pastors and Christian groups were involved in ministries to Japanese troops and prisoners of war.

In contrast to other religions in Japan, Christianity's demand for ultimate allegiance and its strong international network raise suspicions that Japanese Christians are not willing to give their total loyalty to the emperor and state, especially in time of war. In times of resurgent nationalism, Japanese Christians have been tested by the question, "Who is greater, the emperor or Jesus Christ?"

In 1900, after four decades of Christian mission, Protestant churches in Japan numbered 416; church members, 43,273; missionaries, 500; Japanese clergy, 306; Christian schools, 133; and hospitals, 14. (Japan's total population was around 40 million.)

A United Church

GODO
united

KYOKAI
church

> As almost all Christian sects in this country have doctrines and theories which are not in harmony with the national policy of Japan or with the traditional thought of the people . . . they will have to be reformed to harmonize more perfectly with Japanese ideas in the future.
> —*Head of Japanese Government Religious Bureau*
> *(cited in* Christianity and Crisis, *February 10, 1941)*

The recognition by nineteenth-century missionaries that denominational differences were meaningless to the first Japanese converts and the strong sense of nationalism among the first Japanese Christians, who accepted Christ as a new spiritual foundation for nation-building, both contributed to ecumenical cooperation and the founding of a united Japanese church.

Movement toward unity accelerated, especially after Japanese Christians attended the 1910 World Missionary Conference in Edinburgh. The National Christian Council in Japan (NCCJ), founded in 1922, promoted church union from 1925, establishing a Church Union Committee in 1939 and formulating a United Church proposal in 1940.

Ultimately, however, the militaristic imperial government played the major role in actualizing church union. The National Mobilization Law of 1938 and the Religious Bodies Law of 1939 imposed strict controls on all religious organizations. The latter law was used to bring all branches of all religions except Shinto, the state "super-religion" (declared non-religious by the government), under a single integrated organization to facilitate totalitarian control.

Japanese authorities threatened, harassed, and arrested ministers and laypersons under the harsh Public Order Preservation Law. In order to survive, Protestant denominations hastened to sever ties with overseas parent mission boards and, under government pressure to act quickly, formed one Protestant church, the United Church of Christ in Japan (called *Kyodan*). The union took place in 1941 without sufficient preparation or theological consensus concerning church order and a confession of faith. All Roman Catholics were organized into a similar body.

Wartime pressures bring unity and divisions

The Religious Organizations Law of 1939 reflected the Imperial Constitution and the Imperial Rescript on Education, which declared that Japan was ruled by a "god-incarnate" of Shinto pedigree in a "line of emperors unbroken for ages eternal." Christian churches were allowed to confess their faith only if they showed loyalty to this emperor. Even so, the Japanese government was suspicious of Christians and oppressed them in various ways.

All 120 pastors of the former Holiness Church, now a part of the united church, were arrested in 1942 on charges of "disseminating statements which reject the national structure," grounds for imprisonment under the Public Order Preservation Law. Specific charges were related to the Holiness emphasis on the Second Coming of Christ, incompatible with the emperor's divinity. Seven of those arrested died in prison or as a result of imprisonment. All 270 former Holiness churches were closed and their members scattered. These events shocked Kyodan leaders, but in their attempt to protect the church, they forsook their Holiness sisters and brothers (see page 36).

Even before the Kyodan was formed, many church leaders accepted state Shinto as a "super-religion" and revered the emperor. Mounting pressure led other Christians to worship at Shinto shrines. Some church leaders even urged Christians in Korea and Taiwan, now Japanese colonies, to accept shrine worship, which brought much suffering to Christians in those countries. Church leaders also cooperated with wartime mobilization policy, even dispatching missionaries to China, the Philippines, and Indonesia as part of the military pacification program. The Kyodan, attempting to rationalize Japanese atrocities, sent a letter to Asian churches which interpreted Japan's military expansion as historical progress and God's will.

Social pressure was exerted against both churches and individual Christians because of prejudice against Christianity as an "evil religion," a carryover from Japan's isolationist era (1639-1854). Christianity was allowed to exist so long as it proved useful for Japan's modernization, and Christians made significant contributions in the fields of individual ethics, education, social work, and medicine. But when militarism and ultranationalism became dominant, Christianity was branded a "foreign" or "enemy" religion. Wartime propaganda of this sort led ordinary Japanese citizens to join authorities in denouncing Christians as "non-citizens." Many Japanese Christians, being in a tiny minority, followed national policy to avoid police threats and the hostility of fellow Japanese.

Japanese Christians' concern for self-survival prompted them to swear allegiance to the emperor, to deny the authority of the Word, and to overlook the misery and suffering of people both in Japan and in other Asian countries that were victims of Japanese aggression.

Two types of Protestant thinking prevailed in this period. Some Christians clearly separated gospel truth and worldly affairs, regarding faith as primary and acts of concern for the world as secondary. Even when state power forced churches throughout Japan, Taiwan, and Korea to engage in Shinto shrine worship, these believers still considered themselves true Christians because they had faith in the crucified and resurrected Christ.

Other Christians, understanding the gospel and the world as one, addressed concerns of the world out of Christian conscience. Their inability to assess the realities of the world led them to accept the logic of the ruling power as pressures mounted. The result was wartime "Japanese Christianity," an erroneous harmonizing of the Christian God with Shinto gods.

The postwar era

Wartime defeat, bringing the end of militarism, the collapse of the absolutism of the emperor system, and the introduction of democracy, albeit via the U.S. occupation, offered an unparalleled opportunity to change Japan's value system and way of life. The new Constitution established "peace, human rights, and democracy" as the fundamental values of the nation. In this setting the church could make a new beginning, too.

The Kyodan General Assembly statement in 1946 touched only lightly on the church's wartime responsibility. Its main emphasis appealed for a "Christ-centered movement for new nation-building." Church leaders regarded their wartime conduct as that of victims forced to cooperate with war policies and did not really question how their cooperation victimized others.

Christians, struggling to survive and to replace destroyed church buildings, received assistance from occupation authorities and North American churches. With the freedom to evangelize, churches soon initiated evangelism programs. Kyodan leaders neglected to look back and to express repentance for their wartime complicity. Postwar missionaries avoided the problem of war responsibility, perhaps out of compassion for their Japanese colleagues and their zeal to produce evangelistic results.

The Kyodan faced its next crisis when more than half of the former denominations withdrew to resume their previous denominational status or to form new groups because of differences concerning the sacraments and ministry or a desire to reclaim denominational creeds or confessions, as in the case of Lutheran, Anglican, and Reformed bodies.   Non-credal groups like the Salvation Army and "pure gospel" groups seceded when the Kyodan began preparing its own Confession of Faith.   Coooperating overseas mission board partners often supported withdrawal actions.   The Korean Christian Church in Japan (KCCJ) withdrew because of language differences and the desire to avoid union with the oppressor.

The three largest former denominational groups—Presbyterian, Methodist and Congregational—recognized the significance of union, despite its flawed formation, and chose to remain in the Kyodan.   Eight North American denominations with close historical ties to these groups also saw significance in the union and organized the Interboard Committee for Christian Work in Japan (IBC) to support the Kyodan.   Most former Presbyterian, Methodist, Congregational, Disciples, and Alliance churches and some Baptist, Reformed, Lutheran, and Holiness churches remained in the Kyodan.

In 1951 another wave of withdrawal occurred when a number of former Presbyterian churches left the Kyodan to form the *Nippon Kirisuto Kyokai* (Church of Christ in Japan), which is unrelated to any overseas mission board.   The alleged reason was the Kyodan's ambivalent attitude concerning a confession of faith.   This prompted Kyodan leaders to complete the Confession of Faith hurriedly.   Adopted by the 1954 Kyodan General Assembly, the confession contained only the Apostles' Creed and a foreword stating the basics of Protestant faith.   It was sufficiently comprehensive to include various denominational views but made no reference to church-state issues or the problem of the Kyodan's formation.

Postwar evangelism

The early postwar years, coinciding with the Allied occupation (1945-52), were a "boom" period for Christianity as people came to church in search of spiritual support.   Nationwide evangelism programs and rural, industrial, women's, and youth evangelism programs were launched.   Some evangelism programs were self-supporting, avoiding reliance on overseas aid.

Evangelism became more difficult when the religious boom ended and people were swept up in rapid urbanization and secularization.   As traditional Japanese cultural and religious values were reasserted, evangelistic efforts succeeded mainly in the urban areas of Japan.

Significant efforts in rural and industrial mission were under way by the late 1940s and early 1950s. Rural preaching points, painstakingly established, at first focused primarily on gaining converts but later worked alongside community farmers, disabled persons and other discriminated-against persons in rural society. Rural evangelists also supported movements for organic farming and farmer-consumer cooperation.

Industrial mission also initially centered on bringing laborers into the church but soon broadened as industrial mission staff began to live in community with laborers, sharing their burdens and working for social justice. Industrial mission also focussed on the plight of urban day-laborers, poorly paid women workers, and culturally and ethnically discriminated-against laborers.

The change in terms used to describe industrial mission in the postwar years indicates the change in the church's thinking: from "Occupational Evangelism" in the 1950s to "Urban Industrial Mission" in the 1960s to "Urban Rural Mission" in the 1970s, recognizing how closely urban and rural areas are related in the process of industrialization. More traditional evangelistic methods were applied in *danchi dendo* (evangelism in the sprawling new middle-class urban housing developments).

Social action

The U.S. occupation began with the disarming of Japan, but when the Cold War intensified in the 1950s with the Korean War, the U.S. reversed its policy, making Japan its most strategic Pacific base. So Japan took its first steps back toward rearmament. Many citizen movements were aroused to actively support Japan's new "Peace Constitution," to build a peaceful nation, and to oppose nuclear arms and miltary bases on Japanese soil. In the 1960s, the Kyodan issued statements calling for preservation of the Constitution, protesting U.S. nuclear submarines' port calls in Japan, designating the first Sunday in August as "Peace Sunday," and supporting actions for peace in Vietnam.

Another focus of Christian social action has been opposition to the nationalization of Yasukuni Shrine (see page 57) and the resurgence of the emperor-system ideology. Christians have responded to this reactionary trend by organizing and participating in signature campaigns, teach-ins, lobbying, hunger strikes, and demonstrations in cooperation with Buddhist and new religious groups, citizens' groups, and labor unions.

Christians also oppose the 1966 proclamation of February 11 as National Foundation Day, a day commemorating the first emperor's victory over his enemies and the founding of a new nation, according to an imperial cult myth. Instead, Christians declare this day as the Day for Protecting Freedom of Religious Belief.

Japanese Christians now recognize that they were not only victims of war but also victimizers and aggressors who caused their Asian neighbors immense suffering. The Kyodan "Confession of Responsibility during World War II," issued in 1967, seeks the mercy of God and the forgiveness of Asian neighbors for mistakes committed in the name of the Kyodan at the time of its formation and during the war years. The Confession produced debate within the church, with some people arguing: "It's not necessary"; "The church shouldn't get into politics"; "The wartime church kept the faith, though making some mistakes"; and "The Kyodan protected the local churches that way."

The Confession opened the way for the Kyodan to establish new relationships with sister churches in Taiwan and the Republic of Korea, two countries that suffered greatly under Japan's militarist expansion. Mission covenants with the Presbyterian Church of Korea, the Presbyterian Church of the Republic of Korea, and the Korean Methodist Church were ratified in 1967. A mission covenant with the Presbyterian Church in Taiwan was established in 1963 and reconfirmed in 1985.

Just as the people of the Ryukyu Islands, commonly known as Okinawa, have been discriminated against by Japanese society, so Okinawa Christians have been treated as less then equal by Christians on the main islands of Japan. When Japan regained full independence and sovereignty with the signing of the Japan-U.S. Peace Treaty in 1951, Okinawa was put under U.S. trusteeship. With this political separation from Japan, Okinawa churches, until then a part of the Kyodan, were cut off, and they formed their own United Church of Christ of Okinawa. The union between the Japan Kyodan and the Okinawa Kyodan occurred in 1969, after the Japan Kyodan acknowledged that it had ignored the fate of Christians in Okinawa, who were left to suffer the agony of domination by U.S. military bases. Debate continues in the Kyodan over whether the union was a true union of equals or the absorption by a larger body of a smaller body, which was forced to accept both the name and the Confession of Faith of the larger body (see page 85).

Another major conflict within the Kyodan, and indeed within the larger Christian community, arose over the decision to join in ecumenical sponsorship of a Christian pavilion at the 1970 world exposition in Osaka, EXPO '70. Supporters argued that Christians are called to mission in all situations, including witness to Christ who is present in EXPO '70. Opponents declared EXPO '70 to be a government and big-business demonstration of Japan's technological and financial power, and a symbol of economic expansion into Asian countries. They maintained that the church's role should be to stand with those persons in Japan and throughout Asia who are victimized by Japan's economic prosperity.

An historic service of repentance and apology to 64 former Holiness pastors and their family members took place at the Kyodan General Asembly in 1986. The Kyodan moderator confessed that when the Holiness pastors were imprisoned during World War II, the Kyodan neither refuted the charges against them nor offered any support or defense of them.

Today the Kyodan is seeking to live responsibly before God and neighbor, acknowledging that this kind of faithfulness involves an ongoing conversion process. This is the foundation of the Kyodan's hope for tomorrow.

ONE SUNDAY MORNING

"If I were a missionary, I'd share only the joy of salvation in Christ, and would receive the suffering of the other." Moved by these words of a Japanese pastor at our 1990 missionary conference, I traveled a few weeks later to Shizuoka City, near Mt. Fuji, to visit the church he serves.

It was raining hard when I arrived at Shizuoka Kusabuka Church at 8:30 am that April Sunday morning. I put my umbrella in the crowded rack and changed into slippers, placing my shoes in the large shoe box that filled an entire wall of the foyer. I signed the registry book and was shown into a small room at the back of the sanctuary where church school teachers were checking last-minute details for the morning program. At 8:40, the teachers moved into the sanctuary where children from pre-school through junior-high-school age were waiting. One junior-high student presided during opening worship, and another played the organ. Their worship included songs from the children's hymnal, prayers, Scripture reading, a sermon by one of the teachers, and an offering. Then everyone moved to classes for each age group. Because of lack of space in the church building, three rooms in the adjoining parsonage, including the kitchen, were used for classes. Church school lasted an hour.

As soon as the children left the sanctuary, preparations for the morning service of worship began there. A man installed hearing aid devices in a front pew. A woman placed the bulletins and offering envelopes in members' mail boxes at the back of the sanctuary. Another checked to see if the cassette tape lending library was in order. Sermons are taped each Sunday for people to borrow.

Worshipers entered the sanctuary one by one or in small groups, carrying their own Bibles and hymnbooks, and quietly sat down. The worship service began precisely at 10:00 a.m. with an organ prelude. By the time the first hymn had been sung, the entire sanctuary was filled, and the ushers and persons who came late had to sit in a small room at the back. In a small room down the hall about ten small children were being cared for by their mothers. There were 128 persons in attendance, fewer than usual because of the rain, the minister said.

After the service, a number of special groups met—the choir that sings for special evangelistic gatherings each May and December, a high school students' group, the executive committee of the women's group, church school teachers, and a special study group of adults.

The church membership is 156; many belong to three-generation Christian families. Prayer is emphasized here; almost fifty attend the two prayer meetings held each Wednesday morning and evening. "Before people join the church, I strongly urge them to attend these prayer meetings," says the pastor, "because I think it's important for them to know how to pray."

TSUJI Nobumichi and his wife, Tetsuko, became pastors of Shizuoka Kusabuka Church in 1954.* He described his Christian experience and the church to me:

"I come from a Holiness Church background. Both my father and grandfather were ministers in Holiness churches. All Holiness churches suffered oppression by the Japanese government during World War II, and were ultimately forced to disband in 1943. Ministers were arrested for proclaiming that when Christ comes again, the emperor will be subordinate to Christ. My father was sentenced to two years in prison, and died during this imprisonment.

"The church members abandoned my family in the midst of this crisis. This helped me realize how important it is for churches to have a solid foundation in Christian faith. A community of believers that is firmly rooted in the preaching and hearing of God's word and participation in the sacraments is fully able to confront any form of political power.

"When my wife and I came in 1954, we sought to build a church in which no Christians would leave or be abandoned by the church. At that time, church membership was about one hundred, with an

---

*See page 93.

average Sunday morning attendance of about twenty.   Evening services and prayer meetinqs were seldom held because of lack of interest. I was concerned about how the church could be revitalized. I recalled John Calvin's words that preaching and hearing God's word with openness and participation in the sacraments are the basis of the Christian church. I began to work to bring this about.

"Our church's theme this year is 'Fellowship in and Advance of the Gospel: Serving the Lord Enthusiastically.' The church's three major goals are: passing on the faith from parents to children (in which the church school plays an important role); spreading the Good News to all members of the family, including in-laws; and confronting issues in the community clearly and aiming to serve as needed.

"In addition to regular Sunday morning and evening worship services, church school for children, and weekly prayer meetings, the youth, women's and men's groups all have active Bible study programs. Other church-sponsored programs include the Bethel Bible Study series, a class in sign language, and special groups for persons over seventy and for mothers of young children.

"The administrative council of the church is the real source of strength in working toward the church's goals. They are a great support to me personally, especially at this time when I am serving as Moderator of the Kyodan."

Most churches in Japan are very small, and thouqh having a long history, struggle each day to make a meaningful witness in their communities. Churches like Shizuoka Kusabuka Church offer a ray of hope in this struggle.

—*Margaret Warren*

Part Two

The Group Society: Inside the Group

DAI-NI
Part Two

SHUDAN
SHAKAI
*group
society*

NAI
inside

第二　集団社会　内

The Family

KAZOKU
family, household

In the traditional extended family where three or four generations lived together, marriages were arranged by parents in the interest of the family rather than according to individual desires and needs. Although some changes began to take place in the nineteenth century with Japan's opening to the world, Confucian ideals of loyalty still prevailed. Continuation of the family name was more important than individual character. Eldest sons received preferential treatment. Daughters were often treated as less than slaves, leaving the parental home to devote their lives to serving their husbands' families. Women were not even granted a place in heaven, according to tradition.

The Family Register system, established by the Meiji government a hundred years ago, requires that every family member's name be listed under the name of the male head of the family. At marriage a woman's name is transferred from her family's register to her husband's; otherwise, children born to the couple would be considered illegitimate and would receive drastically reduced shares of family inheritance. Family Registers have often been used to investigate a person's family background at the time of employment or marriage. Legal restrictions now make such information less accessible.

Another traditional concept, propagated by the government especially since the Meiji era, is that the emperor is the father of the Japanese people. Since by law the emperor must be male, little possibility of change in male-dominated Japanese society is likely in the near future.

Since 1945 Japanese families have undergone dramatic transformation. Large, extended families living in close-knit neighborhoods have given way to urban nuclear families with only one or two children. Some modern families, stripped of traditional supports, are struggling and too often failing to adjust to change.

Traditionally Japanese people have taken great pride in their children and given priority to their care and education. But many parents have lost confidence in their child-rearing abilities. Family specialists declare that hard-working fathers' absence from family life is a key problem .

Especially since the oil crisis in the 1970s, companies have encouraged male employees to concentrate fully on their work. Evenings and even weekends are spent with business associates. Men often leave home early in the morning and return home only to sleep, often after midnight. Corporate transfers force some men to live away from their families because the family is reluctant to give up the family home or make the children change schools, especially at the crucial junior high and senior high school levels.

The gradual but perceptible weakening of the man's role in the family deprives children of their fathers and wives of their husbands. While the divorce rate remains low it is growing, especially among older couples.

The aging of society

Coping with the growth of its elderly population is a major problem facing Japanese society today. In 1989, 11.6 percent of the population was 65 years old or older. By the year 2000 it is expected to climb to 16.3 percent, and by 2020, it is expected to reach and then stay at 23.6 percent.

Two major concerns for an aging Japanese society are medical care and housing. Adequate medical care must also include concern for emotional and physical needs. The increase of nuclear family units means that extended family members and neighbors often can no longer look after the needs of elderly persons. Families living in small urban apartments often have no space for aging parents, and if a wife works outside the home, no one is present to provide daily care to elderly family members. Today about 63 percent of all persons over age 65 live with children. In urban areas the younger generation often lives on the second floor of the family home, independent of aging parents who live on the first floor. Many young families cannot afford their own homes and each generation often feels more secure living near the other.

Housing for elderly persons, such as retirement complexes and nursing homes, is inadequate. Most of the "desirable" housing is private; both entrance fees and monthly expenses are high. Public low-rent housing and nursing homes exist in many areas, but people often have to wait up to a year to enter. Public nursing homes provide only basic care; usually eight to ten people share one room. The caregivers are also elderly persons with no job skills, who work because of economic need.

High-cost housing

About sixty percent of all Japanese own their own homes. Homes cost an average of ¥50 million (U.S. $357,143) today, forcing families to make large house payments all their lives. Wives often reenter the work force to contribute toward house payments and children's educational expenses. But once women have quit work to marry, it is hard for them to find full-time jobs. Thus more and more Japanese are giving up the dream of owning their own homes.

Japanese people are skillful at utilizing household space. The floors of most rooms are *tatami* (thick woven straw mats), and *futon* (thick cotton-filled mats) are laid out at night to sleep on. Many homes have a *kotatsu*, a low table with an electric heater attached to the underside over which a heavy quilt is draped in winter to hold in the heat. The family gathers there for meals, watching TV, and family conversation.

Recently some young couples have begun to value family time more than devotion to job and acquiring wealth. Husband and wife share housework and do volunteer work in the community, participating in peace, anti-nuclear, and environmental movements. Some couples buy and renovate old farmhouses and engage in organic farming. Others join together to organize their own schools and communes.

Children: cherished and pressured

Although many prewar families had five or six children, today the average number of children is one or two, which means that each child receives more of the parents' time. Babies sleep beside their mothers at night and often are strapped on their mothers' backs during the day, thus spending almost all their pre-school years in close physical contact with their mothers.

After school each day children and youth are involved in various lessons, school clubs, and after-school tutoring classes. Any remaining free time is spent watching TV, playing TV video games with friends at home, or engaging in sports outside. High school students sometimes have part-time jobs. They cannot obtain a drivers license until they become eighteen. Dating is not encouraged until after high school, although many young people spend free time as couples or in groups with friends.

While domestic violence directed against children has increased slightly, parental over-protection and extreme pressure for educational achievement are far greater problems for children. Most children continue to live at home until marriage, which maintains the strong parent-child bond of dependency until adulthood.

The School

GAKKO
school

HOKAMA Eiji

"Those who captured us told us to sing" (Psalm 137:3).

I was asked to sing a certain song to make the National Athletic Games, held in Okinawa in October 1987, a success. It is the same song that my parents sang forty-four years ago with more fervor than people in any other part of Japan to show that they were "real" Japanese,* but as an Okinawan born after World War II, this song is the last song I want to sing. No matter what, I cannot sing it.

When the band at my junior high school was invited to perform at the National Athletic Games, as music teacher I accepted the invitation on two conditions: 1) that my band not be made to play *Kimigayo,* the ancient court song in praise of the emperor used as the national anthem during World War II and still considered the unofficial national anthem by many today; and 2) that we not have to participate in ceremonies involving the *hinomaru*, the rising sun flag, which served as the Japanese flag during World War II and which is in use unofficially again today. The games officials accepted these conditions.

The band received ¥90,000,000 (U.S. $640,000) for new instruments, new uniforms, and the use of two huge buses, all of which made me very uncomfortable. As promised, on the day of the rehearsal a tape recording of *Kimigayo* was played over the loudspeaker, so the band did not have to play it.

Two weeks before the games, however, two games officials came to my school bringing the musical score for *Kimigayo*. They asked the school principal to convince me to conduct it at the games. The principal called me to his office, handed me the score, and asked,"What are you going to do?"

---

*See pages 82-86.

"I've been thinking seriously about *Kimigayo* and hinomaru for the past three years," I replied. "I am not about to change my mind now. I have always cooperated with you in every way I could, but I cannot on this one matter." After the principal reported my decision to the officials, he was summoned several times to discuss the matter.

Our school band's first scheduled appearance was the ceremony when the lighted torch was carried in. On that day the students donned their new band uniforms. Just as we were about to leave for the ceremony, word came that we would not be performing that day. The confused looks on my students' faces made me angry for, just as I had feared, my students were going to be made to suffer because of my conviction. When I realized that it was going to be a battle with no holds barred, I wavered momentarily.

Before the last rehearsal for the ceremony, the principal and dean once again called me in. "If you refuse to perform, our school will be the only one not performing. You will be the only band director not directing." Newspaper reporters appeared at my school, asking to talk with the principal, with me, and with the students. So the issue appeared in the newspapers.

A games official telephoned one of the student band members at home saying, "You know that if the band refuses to perform *Kimigayo*, you may not get to participate in the games. Even though your band teacher refuses to conduct, couldn't you students get together and practice in secret so that you can perform?" From that time on, the school officials took great care to see that I did not have any opportunities to be alone with my band members.

At a meeting of games officials and school administration, I was asked if I would step down from the podium at the games ceremony during the playing of *Kimigayo*, handing the baton to a university music teacher who would conduct the band for that one number. The school officials decided to present this matter to the band members for their approval. After this proposal was made, there was a long silence during which the students stared at me. They finally replied by asking for time to discuss the matter among themselves before making their decision.

Before returning home that night I found a chance to talk with the band members, explaining the reasons for my position and asking them to go home and talk calmly with their parents before giving their answer to the principal the next day.

When I got home that night the school principal called and asked me to come back to school for a final conference. He himself had been called to another conference with the games officials that evening. He requested that I not talk with the students any more, saying that he would receive their reply the next morning. He also informed me that the teachers' union had abandoned its long-held opposition to *Kimigayo* and hinomaru and that I now stood alone.

The next morning, he met with the band members to hear their reply. At first there was silence; then, one by one, the student voiced their opinions:

"I don't want to perform."

"I've thought about it seriously and read what was written in the newspapers. I don't want to play."

"From the very beginning I wasn't interested in participating in the National Athletic Games."

"Why are all the adults trying so hard to force us to participate when we don't really want to?"

When all the students refused, the principal had no other choice but to communicate their decision to the games officials.

These are the kinds of pressure that we in Okinawa faced during the National Athletic Games. The same pressures exist today throughout Japan, with anyone who stands out risking excommunication from the group for opposing hinomaru, *Kimigayo*, the emperor system, the military build-up, or any other of the government's attempts at political control. This is a problem for Okinawans, for all Japanese, for all human beings, and a problem related to our Christian faith, I believe.

Hokama Eiji teaches music at a public junior high school in Okinawa. He is an active member of the Tairagawa Preaching Point (Kyodan) and the Okinawa District Social Concerns Committee.

A short history of education in Japan

Education for Japanese children was introduced in the mid-fifteenth century. At that time, a small number of boys whose parents were especially interested in their education went to "temple schools" where they were taught reading, writing and arithmetic; handwriting and use of the abacus were emphasized. This model of education continued for the next four hundred years. Though girls were prohibited from entering school during most of this time, stories are told of girls who wanted to attend school so badly that they dressed as boys.

In 1872 the Meiji government launched a national system of compulsory education, establishing elementary schools throughout Japan. Although education was available to all children, many children living in discriminated-against buraku* areas were treated as less than human; family poverty forced some of these and other children to work.

Although girls were permitted to attend school, many didn't because it was generally felt that girls didn't need education; their assigned role was to help at home. Those girls who did go to school studied separately from the boys and were taught a different curriculum.

During this period, missionaries from North America established a number of schools for girls. Though the graduates of these schools represent only a small percentage of all Japanese women, Christian schools have from their beginning strongly influenced the education of girls and women in Japan.

After World War II, under the guidance of the American Occupation, a new law prohibited children under sixteen from working on the premise that all children are entitled to an education. (However, it is only recently that those living in discriminated-against buraku areas, children of Korean residents, and children with handicapping conditions have attended public schools freely.)

Japanese schools

A Japanese child *must* go to school between the ages of six and fifteen, during the elementary and junior high school years. However, children typically begin their formal schooling at three or four, in private nursery schools and kindergartens, and 94 percent complete high school.

The school year begins April 1 and ends March 31 the following year, with about 240 school days per year. Classes are usually held for half a day on Saturdays. Some private schools are moving to a five-day week, but the length of the school week is still a live issue.

The school calendar has many special days, organized around such projects as science fairs and class trips. All elementary students go on day trips, but by the fifth and sixth grades excursions include at least one overnight stay. For most children these trips are their first opportunities to travel without a parent and beyond their own part of Japan. Weeks are spent preparing for the sights to be seen and the expectations for their behavior.

Schools are plain yet pleasant places. Typically they are constructed in L- or U-shaped formations partially enclosing a schoolyard, where morning assembly, recess games, and sports classes are

---

*See pages 69-74.

held.   Schools may also have a garden, where the children grow vegetables and flowers, and a bicycle-parking area.

Inside the two- or three-story building are long corridors with classrooms along one side, windows along the other.   Numerous displays show the children's work, often appropriate to the season. Though classroom furnishings are not fancy, the rooms are light and lively; walls are covered with children's art and along the many windows are plants and projects created by students.

The younger the children, the less fixed are the furnishings, for teachers like to move the desks into various patterns, depending on the task at hand.   In elementary school, girls and boys sit together, but by junior high the sexes tend to be separated.

All public elementary schools provide hot lunches subsidized by the government, as do some junior high schools.   Students in other schools bring their own box lunches.

Traditionally, students clean their school every day.   Usually each class is divided into several small groups, with rotating assignments to clean classrooms and other school areas.   At the end of the semester, all students work together to clean the entire school and grounds.

Junior and senior high schools place strong emphasis on home-room activities to teach the importance of cooperation in group learning and activities.   Homeroom teachers assume a large role in guiding their students; some even become surrogate parents.

The number of students per class varies widely depending on school location.   The nationwide average is 31.5 for elementary and 38.1 for junior high schools, with a maximum class size of 45.   The classroom atmosphere is very lively, even noisy.   Classrooms belong to the students; teachers have desks in a large central teachers' room.

Japanese students are almost always promoted with their age group; rarely are they advanced because of ability or held back by "failure."   Participation in the group and its shared experiences are considered very important.   The government Ministry of Education in Tokyo sets basic educational guidelines for curriculum, aiming to provide a high level of education for everyone in the country; the result is Japan's nearly 100 percent literacy rate.   But because the curriculum lacks flexibility, a large number of students has dropped out: some refuse to attend school, others attend but distance them-selves emotionally from school.

Ninety-four percent of junior high school graduates go on to the senior high level (1988).   In 1988, 28 percent of senior high school students were enrolled in private schools, as were about 77 percent of university and college students.   This large percentage of private schools indicates that the government does not provide an adequate number of places for levels above the junior high school.

There are no tuition fees in public elementary and junior high schools. Tuition is paid by students in private schools and in public high schools and post-secondary institutions. While public education is less expensive than private, access to it is more limited and difficult. Scholarship aid, in the form of loans, is available in both public and private schools.

The purposes of education

Japanese feel that the nation's primary and most reliable resource is a well-educated and hardworking population. Children's education, therefore, receives top priority. Social consensus has restricted births to an average of less than two per family. Families focus attention on the future of these valued children. Moral education emphasizes diligence, endurance, deciding to do the hard thing, wholehearted dedication, and cooperation.

Schools and parents also have a special concern for the child's physical development. To be a good child is to be strong; strength is achieved by working as hard as one can. Physical education includes morning exercises for the entire school and more specialized classes in sports (many schools have swimming pools). The purpose is not to develop athletes but to learn to challenge oneself and develop unity with others.

The Japanese educational system emphasizes group life. Cohesion of the group is more important than active competition in the classroom. Teachers generally spend time working with slow learners rather than dividing classes to meet the needs of students with many levels of ability.

Juku ("cram schools")

From an early age, children participate in extracurricular lessons of many kinds. Many elementary-age children go to non-academic private institutions after school or on Sundays to learn skills in calligraphy, abacus, art, music, and sports, while junior and senior high students tend to go to academic or preparatory juku, which stress math, English, and Japanese language study.

Juku prepare students to take entrance exams into the next level of schooling. Because high schools are not part of the compulsory educational system, young people must take exams to enter even public high school. High schools are judged "better" or "worse" largely on the number of their graduates that enter the most prestigious universities. Because the name of one's university is very important in securing a job, the competition is intense.

The juku tend to place secondary students under great pressure because they occupy so much time. Students go to school in the daytime, attend juku in the evening, and often study late into the night. Often parents admonish them to study and improve their grades. Some students react to this pressure by flying into rages and striking parents or teachers; the frequency of this violence in the home/school is a continuing concern.

Education for internationalization

Today there is much talk about education for internationalization and a search for what real internationalization means. Some interesting programs are emerging.

A number of schools have established sister-school relationships with institutions in other countries, conducting exchanges of students, faculty, and information. A few colleges and universities from North America have established branches in Japan, and some Japanese educational institutions have established branch schools on all levels in North America and Europe.

The government sponsors a program that brings young people from many different countries to Japan to teach English conversation in public schools. Though the number of these teachers is relatively few, at least some students are exposed to persons of different races and backgrounds. Many schools are taking their students on school trips to other Asian countries to observe firsthand the life of the people and experience their cultures.

Another program is for students who have lived a number of years in another country because of their fathers' work. During 1987, approximately ten thousand elementary and secondary school children returned home after a long stay abroad. These students find it very hard to adjust to the regimented atmosphere of Japanese schools after experiencing more flexible education overseas. Several schools for such students have opened, but more are needed. Some private schools, especially Christian schools, are openly welcoming these returning students into their regular programs.

Japanese education has been highly praised by some and strongly criticized by others. Parents, teachers, and youth in many places are uniting to appeal for education that truly centers on children and their individual needs. Although the number of persons involved is still small, their efforts do indicate a desire for change and for development of initiative and creativity.

The Company

KAISHA
company

A Japanese company that manufactures cassette tape decks at its plant in Kyongi province, Korea, shut down production abruptly on October 18, 1989, dismissing 450 Korean workers, 400 of whom were women. The company claimed it faced bankruptcy. The company union, one of three organized in Japanese-owned companies in Korea during the Korean workers struggle in 1987, declared that the company sought to destroy the union. Faced with loss both of family support and of future employment through blacklisting, union members held daily protests outside the company gate demanding negotiations with the company, all to no avail.

Representatives of Korean women workers in three companies came to Japan in December 1989 to make their demands to the Japanese parent companies for negotiations conducted according to the collective bargaining system, reinstatement of the dismissed workers, reopening of the factory, and immediate release of the union president still held by the police.

With the support of the National Christian Council of Japan, the Asian Women Worker's Center (Tokyo), the companies' Japanese workers' unions, and the Japanese mass media, the four Korean women laborers engaged in rallies, demonstrations, hunger strikes, and appeals to the Japanese government and Diet members. Under this pressure, the companies finally agreed to negotiations with the workers, which resulted in one company issuing an apology for its unethical closing of the factory and paying the union ¥56,000,000 (U.S. $386,207) in workers' compensation.

Resources and rebuilding

Japan is made up of four main islands and many smaller ones. Because the islands are largely forested and mountainous, only about twenty percent of the total area is inhabitable. From ancient

50

times, Japan's agricultural base has been the production of rice. Having few natural resources, it has had to rely on importing raw materials both for its own use and for producing exportable goods. Thus, modern factories are established along the sea coast, enabling the import of raw materials and the export of finished products on the same ships.

At the end of World War II, Japan's economy was in disarray. The new Peace Constitution did away with military expenditures, and all resources were devoted to restoring the economy. Postwar industries were forced to borrow from banks and other lending institutions, but as the economy developed, profits rose and companies became able to operate on their own capital. Japanese citizens' high rate of savings, 16 to 18 percent of income, provided the capital necessary for investment.

Today Japan has the highest per capita Gross National Product in the world and is the world's largest creditor nation. Every year exports far exceed imports. Japan ranks among the world's top nations in ability to mass-produce high-quality electronic equipment, machinery, and automobiles for export. Japan's strength on the world market has been achieved by strong domestic competition and consumer demand for high-quality products and dependable after-sales service.

Company organization

Most Japanese companies are comprised of executives, workers, and shareholders. At their general meeting, shareholders choose executives from the ranks of workers who have served the company for many years. These executives then establish company policy based on a long-range plan. They actively invest funds in developing new techniques, equipment, and facilities needed to carry out the plan. They also carefully consider the long-term needs of workers and are especially interested in their workers' development. They attempt to know workers individually, helping them to find positions where they can best use their skills. While this pattern is efficient, workers increasingly consider it also paternalistic.

When the economy takes a downturn, executives do their best to transfer workers to other divisions of the company to avoid lay-offs. Since the early 1970s, the unemployment rate has remained under 3 percent. Salaries are based on employee age and the skills of the work group rather than on individual performance.

Japan's national welfare system is underdeveloped because many companies provide rent and pension subsidies to employees, as well as the use of recreation and leisure-time facilities. Companies seek to promote good relationships among workers with an eye to achieving greater productivity.

In general, employees in larger companies remain with the company until they retire, and even after retirement many continue to work for a related company. Young people today choose a company on the basis of its reputation, benefits, salary, and working conditions rather than by specific job descriptions. Salary and training are largely determined by whether a person agrees to remain with a company until retirement.

Workers at all levels are encouraged to take initiative in submitting suggestions to improve efficiency. Decisions are not always handed down from the top but are often influenced by the workers themselves.

Labor unions are usually organized within companies rather than by occupational categories, and workers assert their rights on the basis of "what's good for the company is good for us," that is, prosperous employer-employee co-existence or "collective security." In late 1989 a new nationwide labor movement was inaugurated when 78 unions formed the *Shin Rengo* (Japan Trade Union Confederation.) Membership totals about 8 million workers, 5.5 in the private and 2.3 in the public sector. The opening convention called for gaining living standards equal to those in Western Europe and the U.S.

Because stock shares in Japanese companies usually cost about ¥50 (U.S. 28 cents) per share, shareholders cannot expect to reap huge profits on dividends. However, the value of stock often increases sharply. In most cases, only major shareholders participate in company management. Shareholders' ownership of shares in several corporations helps provide stability in the market and security for national long-range planning.

Industry-government relationship

With shortages of both capital and resources, government and industry were forced to work together to develop a postwar industrial policy. This policy placed high priority on developing industries that would activate the economy: electric power, steel, coal, and shipbuilding. Close cooperation between industry and government has been a factor in Japan's industrial growth. It has also meant that large corporations exercise great influence on government policy.

The improved economy has brought increased salaries, an appeal for shorter working hours, longer vacation time, and improved retirement benefits as well as for improved housing and public services. Young people today are beginning to choose their companies based on the kind of work they want to do rather than a company's reputation. Some people are changing companies mid-career, causing the lifetime-employment system with its age-based salary increments to break down. (At best, this system applied to Japanese male regular employees of large corporations, about thirty percent of employed workers in Japan.) In other words, a worker's technological skill is becoming more important than company loyalty.

Challenges to Japanese companies

One result of economic development centered around large corporations is the gradual disappearance of the small- and medium-sized businesses that have supported this development. As competition becomes more intense, newer and better products are developed, and small businesses that formerly mass-produced one or two product parts for large companies now find it difficult to meet production deadlines and still make a profit.

One means of increasing profits is to build factories overseas where labor costs are lower. Not only does this practice hurt small Japanese companies and piecework contractors who employ homemakers but it also increases hostility toward Japan. Although wage scales and benefits paid by Japanese companies overseas, especially in third-world countries, may be somewhat above the local standard, prohibitions or limits on unions, sub-standard working conditions, and pressures on workers (especially women) to be passive and obedient contribute to gross exploitation of workers. Thus, Japanese companies overseas face many problems.

A partial "solution" to small-company problems is the hiring of part-time women workers, who are easy to lay off when no longer needed. While many "part-time" workers work full time, they do not receive full employee benefits.

In companies still operating on a patriarchal system, especially those closely related to the government, workers' freedom of thought and belief are still threatened and controlled. Some companies control their workers' votes in elections. However, as women and young male workers begin to express their opinions, such control will undoubtedly become more difficult.

Today very few women participate in Japanese companies at executive levels. There is evidence, however, that Japanese companies are beginning to change. Workers moving from company to company are breaking down the patriarchal system. Companies will no longer provide welfare assistance, which will force the government to assume this responsibility.

Japanese companies are called upon today to become truly international: sensitive to the needs and customs of people in other countries and caring both for human life and for the environment.

Nation-State and Emperor

KOKKA
nation-state

国
家

TENNO-SEI
emperor system

天
皇
制

NAKAYA Yasuko

I couldn't believe my ears that day in January 1968 when one of my husband's Self-Defense Forces (SDF)* superiors informed me that Takafumi had died in a traffic accident while on duty. I rushed to his unit headquarters where his body had been taken to confirm the horrible reality with my own eyes. Assuming that I would be able to take his body home with me for the wake, as is Japanese custom, I was crushed when the SDF official told me I would have to leave the body there, that I would be able to stay with my husband's body for only a few hours, and that all the preparations for the funeral were to be made by the SDF.

I felt so alone that night as I returned home. The SDF had literally taken my husband from me. I was left without even the comfort of a Christian funeral in my home church where I would have been surrounded and upheld by my minister and Christian friends. Following the SDF funeral I was presented the urn containing my husband's ashes, which I placed in the church crypt.

Four years later, in 1972, SDF officers visited my house on several occasions to ask for my husband's personal documents. Inquiring why they needed these records, I was informed that they planned to enshrine Takafumi as a military martyr in the Gokoku (defense of the country) Shrine. I told them that as a Christian I would never permit such a thing. Later, when I received an invitation to the SDF enshrinement ceremony on June 1, 1972, I again issued a protest. I was informed only afterward that the enshrinement ceremony had taken place, and that shrine memorial services would be held annually on the anniversary of his death to venerate my husband. I was shocked when they told me that my

*See pages 120-121, 127.

husband had been deified.   As a Christian I naturally oppose treating the war dead as gods, and I could not allow my husband to become an object of worship at a Shinto shrine.

With the strong support of my minister and church, I decided to go to court in January 1973 to demand that my husband's enshrinement be retracted.   The decisions both at the district court level in March 1979 and at the high court level in June 1982 recognized my claim regarding the violation of my personal religious right to choose the way to remember my husband, but neither court recognized my appeal for annulment of the enshrinement.

On June 1, 1988, the Japanese Supreme Court overturned the two lower court decisions, dismissing my suit and ending my fifteen-year court struggle to repeal the enshrinement of my husband in a Shinto shrine.

Japan talks about internationalism, but continues to promote national chauvinism.   True internationalism comes from recognizing freedom for the hearts and minds of others.

Responding to the Supreme Court Decision, OHSHIMA Koichi, chairperson of the NCCJ Special Committee on the Yasukuni Shrine Problem, stated on June 6, 1988, "We cannot overlook the denial of the individual's right of religious freedom.   Attention must be drawn to the fact that this series of rulings has political significance in terms of granting active support for Japan's present inclination toward militarization.   We must also point out that making the principle of the separation of religion and state deliberately ambiguous is to court the danger of a revival of Japanese militarism, which will only pose a new menace to the people of Asia and the Pacific."

Breaking the "chrysanthemum taboo"

The death of Emperor Hirohito (posthumous name, Emperor Showa*) in January 1989 provided a unique opportunity for Japanese people, Christian and non-Christian alike, as well as for people in other Asian countries and throughout the world, to break "the chrysanthemum taboo" and to both reflect on the emperor's sixty-year reign and examine the role of the emperor system itself.   In Western countries based on Judeo-Christian principles, people find it difficult to grasp the position that the emperor system occupies in both Japanese history and Japan's social organization today.   Examining the following four issues may help to clarify the dilemma facing all Japanese, especially Christians who seek to be faithful today.

_____

*A late emperor takes the name of his era. See page v.

The role of the emperor

"The Emperor shall be the symbol of the State and of the unity of the people, deriving his position from the will of the people with whom resides sovereign power. The Imperial Throne shall be dynastic and succeeded to in accordance with the Imperial House Law passed by the Diet . . . . The Emperor shall perform only such acts in matters of state as are provided for in this Constitution and he shall not have powers related to government."

The Constitution of Japan, Chapter I, Articles 1,2 & 4
(Promulgated November 3, 1946; effective from May 3, 1947)

"To grasp the significance of the emperor system of Japan, we need to go back about 120 years. The Meiji Restoration in 1868, which followed more than two hundred years of national seclusion, shook the whole society. European culture now flooded the Japanese islands. The government thought it urgent to create a national unity by a strong centralization of power, supplemented by prestige. The 16-year-old Mutsuhito (Emperor Meiji) fulfilled this role of 'manifest destiny.' . . . The wealth and power which 260 daimyo had possessed were now concentrated in the emperor and the loyalty once directed to each local lord was turned to the single person at the top of the state. Thus the modern 'absolute' emperor system came into being.

"So the Meiji government carried out a number of policies under a powerful military influence. The first was to inaugurate Shinto as the national religion . . . . The emperor became the high priest of the whole nation and the supreme commander of the imperial army and navy. The Imperial Constitution stipulated that the emperor was divine and inviolable.

"The men who headed the Meiji Government had more in mind, however, than just the deifying of the emperor to unify the nation. They wanted to make use of the emperor to carry out their intention to expand the Empire of Japan, which subsequently would lead to the invasion of many Asian countries and severe suffering by the people of Japan as well. This system continued until Japan's defeat in 1945.

"It is almost a miracle that any form of emperor system survived the war. Of course, Japanese authorities made a desperate effort to maintain the system. The Allied Powers also wanted to use the emperor system to achieve the Occupation's objectives.

"The pattern of the emperor system was preserved in postwar times. The emperor became a symbol of Japan and of the unity of the Japanese people. 'Symbol' is interpreted to mean that the emperor has no political power.

"The new Constitution (1947) was founded on the denial of the Imperial Constitution (1889). The Shinto Directive in 1945 banned the concept of the divine emperor, the divine islands of Japan, and the divine origin of the nation. State Shinto was thus disbanded and state-sponsored worship at shrines prohibited. The new Constitution guaranteed freedom of religion and the principle of separation of religion and state. . . .

"However, postwar history testifies to the restoration of prewar ideologies and systems in new ways. Examples of this trend include:

o A bill to restore National Foundation Day was passed by the Diet in 1966 (see page 34).

o A bill to nationalize Yasukuni Shrine* was presented to the Diet in 1969 and failed five times in six years. In 1975, the bill disappeared and public worship at Yasukuni Shrine by the prime minister began. Ten years later, in 1985, Prime Minister Nakasone visited the shrine as prime minister, not as a private individual. This formal worship has been temporarily suspended, however, because of protests from other Asian countries, especially China.

o A recent incident involving a struggle against enshrining a deceased officer of the Self-Defense Forces (SDF) is described at the beginning of this chapter.

o A growing atmosphere of miltarism and ultra-right influence include the official use of imperial era name for the reign of succeeding emperors to date all official documents, and the promotion of displaying the rising sun flag and singing *Kimigayo* (song of praise to the emperor) as the national anthem.

"Because of this trend to return to former ways, which we feel to be in absolute contradiction to the present Constitution, we strive to do everything we can to enable our country to keep on the correct path, so that peace and human dignity for all persons everywhere may be realized."

> *Young Women's Christian Association of Japan*
> *November 24, 1988*

---

*Yasukuni Shrine, founded by Imperial command in 1869, defines its purpose as "the worship of the divine spirits who gave their lives in defense of the Empire of Japan." It indicates, further that it "is peculiar to Japan inasmuch as the unknown warriors of Europe have not been apotheosized," that is, elevated to the rank of gods.

"It is an undeniable fact that after the Meiji Restoration, the emperors of Japan, in concert with state Shinto, became the spiritual pillar of Japan's imperialism and through this formed the central motivating force for Japan's brutal invasion of other Asian nations.

"Because of this, our [Korean] homeland came under the political domination of Japan and for thirty-six years of colonial rule the people of Korea experienced immense suffering beyond all imagination. As so-called children of the emperor, the use of our names and our language was prohibited . . . . At the same time, Christians who refused to worship the emperor at Shinto shrines were imprisoned, tortured, and murdered.

"After World War II, the emperor was allowed to remain as the central symbol of the Japanese nation and ruled from the top within the mythical mirage of Japan's hegemony . . . .

"What kind of future do we face under a system in which the horrors of the past are hidden and only a beautified facade image of the emperor is promulgated among the people of Japan? All the cries for life coming from Koreans in Japan are considered outside the pale of the emperor system and as such disturb the peace of a myth-laden facade of homogeneity under the emperor of Japan . . . .

"We are deeply concerned with these problems and we appeal to church members not to be deceived by the massive amounts of mythical reportage that will come to be paraded across the warped stages of history, but rather to seek out the genuine truth of our Lord.

Youth Association, Korean Christian Church in Japan
October 1988 (*from* Japan Christian Activity News, *no. 660*)

"The man named Hirohito and called Emperor died on January 7 [1989]. Throughout Japan, there is great commotion over this man and his son, Akihito, who succeeds him. Even infants are saying, "His Majesty the Emperor," and learning the terms of worship used for Hirohito and Akihito. On January 9, the ceremonial binding of a master-servant contract was held between Akihito and adults representing all levels of government. Thus, the extent to which persons in Japan are steeped in the discriminatory idea that some human beings are inherently superior to others is obvious.

"The buraku discrimination* we seek to eliminate comes precisely from this kind of discrimination based on birth. It is not only that Hirohito is a war criminal. He ruled from the top, as the supreme discriminator in the vertical pattern of human relations created by

*See page 69-74.

the emperor system. I ask all of our readers to understand the death of the emperor from the standpoint of the *buraku* discrimination which exists in Japan. The *buraku* liberation movement is a struggle against the discriminatory Japanese society which thinks of the emperor as supreme."

from Crowned with Thorns, *no. 15, February 1, 1989*
Newsletter, Kyodan Buraku Liberation Center

"After I began working on issues related to women, I began to see how much authority the emperor system has, how bound the people are by it, how they lay down even their lives for it, believing that it is an honor to do so. As I myself have become a mother and see how the women's peace movement has flourished since the war, because mothers who give birth to and raise children feel the importance of protecting life, I'm then forced to ask the question of how mothers during the war were so readily willing to send their own sons into that war.

"In looking at the relationship between women and the emperor system, I think there are two facets. The first is that . . . it is a national institution. The emperor system has indeed been used since the Meiji Restoration as a very effective means of shaping Japan into a coherent nation. I think it correct to say that this national system is based on the family. In this family system, there is always a 'head' of the family who is as a general rule the eldest son . . . . What this means is that each family has its own little emperor, and the emperor rules these little emperors. You might say that within the emperor system, the emperor sub-contracts the control of the women and children to the head of the family.

"The other facet deals with the relations between the emperor and the citizens in another way, describing the 'heart' of the emperor as that of a 'mother.' During the war, as the emperor system was strengthened, the Japanese mother concept was also widely talked about and built into a very honorable concept. [Japanese women who bore ten children 'for the emperor' were given medals.] Unlike mothers in Great Britain or the United States, the Japanese mother would sacrifice her own life, if necessary, for her child. This self-sacrifice was greatly admired and praised. In this way, women were made to feel good about being mothers and, at the same time, the emperor was described as having this same mother's heart, meaning that the emperor would sacrifice himself completely out of this love for his people. The people thus were made to feel a deep gratitude and indebtedness to the emperor.

"One reason why the emperor system is wrong is that as it becomes stronger, the forces for integrating the people are also intensified, bringing about the potential for a system of complete national unity.

"The time when national unity is most necessary is in the time of war. When the danger of war is felt, the nation moves to pull its people together, to 'homogenize' them. What is necessary to bring about this national unity is not the military police, but rather the molding of the peoples' self-awareness that they are indeed 'the Japanese people.' And what makes the Japanese unique, what do only they hold in common? It is, of course, that only in Japan can one find this marvelous emperor.

"As I relate to this phenomenon, I realize that I, too, must re-examine and correct the foundations of my own lifestyle, so that I will not be led into that same trap."

KANO Michiyo, of Women's Life Today group
YWCA, February 1987

Imperial accession rites

The $70-million enthronement and the accompanying *Daijosai**
(Great Food-Offering Ceremonies) in November 1990 to mark Emperor Akihito's formal accession to the throne raise delicate questions. The Daijosai are explicitly religious (Shinto) in nature. Are these imperial family, public, or state ceremonies? Do they violate the Japanese Constitutional guarantee of separation of religion and state? Also in question is whether the ceremonies should be funded by the Imperial Household Agency or by Japanese tax-payers, many of whom do not support and some who actively oppose the emperor system.

In December 1989, the government designated the enthronement ceremony, to be attended by 2,600 Japanese and foreign dignitaries, as a state function, and the Daijosai, to be attended by 1,200 Japanese representatives, as an Imperial household function of a public character.

On April 12, 1990, President YUGE Toru of Ferris Women's University, a Christian school in Yokohama, together with the presidents of three other Christian universities, issued a public statement declaring that the two enthronement ceremonies violated the separation of religion and state and symbolize a return to imperial divine sovereignty. All four presidents received threatening phone calls and letters after they issued the appeal calling for free discussion of the issue. On April 22, two shots were fired into Yuge's home. Police

---

*A private, mystical ceremony in which the new emperor is said to feast with and spend the night in communion with the sun goddess.

investigators conclude that the violence was the work of a right-wing group seeking to suppress opposition to the emperor system.

Hinomaru and **Kimigayo**

Students, teachers, parents, concerned citizens, and Christians are joining their voices in protest over the Japanese Ministry of Education's attempt to designate the hinomaru as the national flag and the *Kimigayo* as the national anthem by issuing a directive in March 1989 to schools throughout Japan requiring their use at all school entrance and graduation ceremonies. Both the flag and the anthem, as symbols of imperial Japanese aggression throughout Asia during World War II, disappeared from sight temporarily, reappearing in 1950 when the Education Minister called for the revival of the "national" flag and anthem to encourage patriotism. Today all government buildings and meetings once again display the hinomaru, and *Kimigayo* is played at government-sponsored events, even though the two have no legal basis. Concerned citizens and Christians declare the reintroduction to be just another sign of Japan's lack of repentance over past military aggression against Asian neighbors and a move toward re-militarization. Some students, teachers, and parents protested the government directive during 1990 graduation and entrance ceremonies by boycotting the ceremonies, removing the flag, or refusing to stand or sing when the anthem was performed.

War responsibility

"With many Asian people, we feel compelled to express our dismay that the present leadership of the Japanese government is oblivious to the unjust historical relationship between Japan and the rest of Asia.

"Many injustices were committed in the name of *Tenno* (emperor). After some reflection and dialogue we have reached a general consensus that what actually mattered was not so much Tenno as a person but the modern Tenno system, which was provided and abused as an ideological basis for Japanese imperialism.

"We want to believe that the leaders of the Japanese government and society are resolved that such mistakes should never happen again. But recent experience causes us to be alarmed about the re-emergence of an unrepentant spirit of the Tenno system. This involves textbook issues, the Yasukuni shrine, alien registration and fingerprinting issues, the government-sponsored Shinto rite at Tenno's enthronement and funeral, and the escalated arming of the so-called defense force. . . .

"We affirm our solidarity with the Christian communities in Japan and hope their sincere concern will be heard and implemented in terms of policy change by the Japanese authorities."

PARK Sang Jung, former general secretary
Christian Conference of Asia, February 22, 1988

"The National Christian Council in Japan sends supplications to the brothers and sisters in Christ through an evaluation of the meaning of 'the emperor's reign' as manifested from the Meiji era to the present. This is done in the spirit of confessing our sins committed against neighboring countries in Asia and the Pacific and through a clarification of war responsibility in relation to our sisters and brothers in the Lord.

"On the basis of our faith, the churches, Christian organizations, and individual Christians of Japan must inform themselves as to the problems of the emperor system and examine its manifestations in daily life. One of the greatest mistakes of the past, committed by the churches in Japan, was generated by ignoring the abiding problems created and sustained by the emperor system.

"Instead of military invasion into other countries as in past years, Japan reaped huge profits through the Korean and Vietnam Wars. From this base, Japan once again began and continues a highly exploitative economic invasion of other countries. The basis of this present brand of structural international discrimination and oppression is the emperor system, which remains taboo [untouchable] in Japan and therefore free from any criticism within Japanese society. This means that any criticisms of Japanese national policies in this regard become targets of violence and repression.

"Supported by the Gospel, we must confront boldly and overcome the taboo which hides the emperor system from criticism. Today the freedoms given by God and the human rights of all peoples in Japanese society must be guaranteed, and we pray for the coming of a new era in which we commit ourselves to the welfare of humankind and to peace in the world. Particularly, we pray for the Lord's justice and peace among the peoples of Asia and the Pacific, and we will make every effort to bring about the true meaning of reconciliation. May the Creator of history and our Lord guide us by his leading hand so that we can bring about the transformation of Japanese history."

TAKEUCHI Kentaro, bishop, Anglican Church of Japan,
moderator, National Christian Council in Japan
MAEJIMA Munetoshi, general secretary, NCCJ
September 1, 1988

Part Three

The Group Society: Outside the Group

DAI-SAN
Part Three

SHUDAN
SHAKAI
*group
society*

SOTO
outside

第三　集団社会　外

Ainu

*Ainu design from International Indigenous
People's Conference Report*

CHIKAPPU Mieko

In 1969, the book *Ainu Minzoku* (Ainu People) was published to commemorate the Centennial of the Pioneer Development of Hokkaido, the northern island of Japan. Both the emperor and the prime minister attended the centennial ceremony to congratulate themselves on one century of "development," which for us Ainu has been a century of invasion.

The book was supposedly published to "study" the Ainu, regarding them as a "dying race." Photos in the book, taken and printed without our consent, included my picture, which had been taken for a movie on Ainu people by a well known "specialist" on Ainu culture. A photo of the back of an Ainu man naked from the waist up that appears in the book was used to show how hairy Ainu are, a feature often pointed out by Japanese to humiliate us.

I protested the use of these photos, which displayed us like specimens without our consent. Claiming that our consent was not necessary because the photos were used for scientific research, neither the specialist, one of the book's authors, nor the book's publisher offered any apology for the exploitation. To end this continual systematic discrimination against Ainu people, I sued the authors and publishing company for violation of portrait rights and defamation.

Much of our traditional clothing decorated with the traditional Ainu embroidery handed down from our grandmothers, our ornaments, and our tools no longer belong to us. Ainu "specialists" have collected them as precious specimens for study, believing that Ainu are destined to die out under Japan's policy of assimilation. For token payments of money or *sake* (rice wine) to Ainu, the specialists became famous through publication of their "research." Today many of our Ainu treasures are stored in museums and universities throughout Japan, enclosed in glass cases out of our reach.

"Ainu specialists" have also excavated our graves throughout Hokkaido, confiscating both ancient and recently buried Ainu bones and entire corpses and storing them in the research center of Hokkaido University Medical Department. The professor responsible for this collection stated, "I excavate graves because I love my country. I do it to prove that Ainu are also Japanese." In 1982, after the professor's death, Hokkaido University finally agreed to return the bones of one thousand Ainu to family members, and unclaimed bones were stored in a vault on university property. The university has promised to revere the deceased Ainu by holding an annual memorial ceremony. Nevertheless, the tomb is officially labeled the "Specimen Preservation Vault," and the remaining bones can still be used for research.

Through its educational system and the words of its leaders, the Japanese government declares Japan to be a racially homogeneous nation. But it is impossible to arbitrarily deny the existence of our people by stressing assimilation and ignoring reality. We Ainu people, the original inhabitants of Japan, have barely survived the atrocious oppression of the majority Japanese. Today we exist as a small minority threatened with total assimilation into the majority society. My daughter asks me, "I'm Ainu, so why do I speak Japanese?"

In September 1988, the Tokyo District Court settlement ruled that the book's authors and publisher issue me a public apology and pay me one million yen (U.S. $7,700) as a "reconciliation fee" toward my legal fees. This partial victory was the first step toward recognition of the legal rights of Ainu in Japan. There is still a long journey ahead.

Ainu displacement and discrimination

History records that the Japanese assault on Japan's aboriginal people began in the seventh century with the establishment of a centralized emperor system. The territory of the *Ezo* ("those savages who do not obey Imperial Court orders") included the northern part of Honshu, the Kurile Islands, Sakhalin, and Hokkaido. The last three lay outside Japanese jurisdiction at the time.

These peoples were gradually pushed northward to Hokkaido, and soon this island, *Ainu Moshiri* ("land of the Ainu people" in Ainu language) was also invaded. The Japanese government established a penal colony there, and when the land was found to be fertile, first Japanese ex-convicts and polical refugees and later merchants settled there. A Japanese government outpost, established in the late sixteenth century, cooperated with the merchants in systematically exploiting the Ainu, forcing the men to engage in hard labor away from their families, causing the elderly and children to starve and the women to endure rape. This inhuman treatment, together with the diseases and alcohol received from Japanese, decimated the Ainu population. Famous revolts against the Japanese invaders in 1457, 1669, and 1789 pitted Ainu bows against Japanese firearms, until ultimately the Ainu resistance was crushed.

Although the Japanese government originally recognized Hokkaido as belonging to the Ainu, after the Meiji Restoration it unilaterally declared Ainu land "unoccupied," dispatching troops in 1874 to "protect" the frontier and the new Japanese immigrants. Deprived of their traditional occupations of hunting, fishing, and cutting timber, every Ainu family received forty acres of barren land to farm. Ainu were also forced to declare themselves "former natives" in their official family registers, to give up their own language and culture, and to adapt to agricultural life.

According to a 1986 Hokkaido government survey, the Ainu population numbers 24,381, although accuracy is difficult because of intermarriage with majority Japanese and migration to other parts of Japan. About 70 percent of all Ainu live in two communities in southern Hokkaido. In Hokkaido, 78 percent of Ainu junior high school graduates continue on to high school, compared to 94 percent of non-Ainu graduates. In the same way, only 8 percent of Ainu high school graduates enter college, compared to 27 percent of non-Ainu graduates. The number of Ainu households receiving government assistance is three times that of non-Ainu households in the same area.

Ainu believe that all nature is sacred, and is to be respected, nurtured, and passed on to future generations. Ainu law punishes those who irreversibly destroy the environment.

Today, Ainu groups are engaged in the stuggle to restore and transmit Ainu language and culture, to replace the discriminatory "Hokkaido Former Natives Protection Law" of 1899 with an alternative law, and to eliminate all forms of discrimination against Ainu people.

A mission prototype

John Batchelor, a 24-year-old British Anglican seminary student, arrived in Hakodate, Hokkaido, in 1877. He was strongly influenced by Walter Dening of the Anglican Church Missionary Society (CMS), who had been sent to Hokkaido to evangelize the Ainu but who focused his energies on the Japanese instead. Batchelor's first encounter with an Ainu made a deep impression on him, and he soon became aware that the Japanese did not regard Ainu as human beings.

Batchelor studied both the Japanese and the Ainu languages, and in 1879 was appointed as CMS lay missionary to the Ainu. There was some interest in the Ainu in Great Britain, and in 1865 a British Consulate official robbed some Ainu graves. This act resulted in an international incident forcing England to apologize and to pay reparations.

Batchelor lived briefly in Ainu villages. In 1885 he baptized his first Ainu convert. Batchelor soon incurred the wrath of the Japanese, however, for speaking Ainu language in defiance of the government assimilation policy prohibiting its use. As one who preached abstinence, seeing the devastation that alcohol wreaked on the Ainu community, Batchelor was not popular with Japanese businessmen who made money selling alcohol to Ainu. He was even accused of being a British spy, though these charged were dropped in 1885. Batchelor was ordained to the Anglican priesthood in 1895 in Tokyo.

Batchelor published an Ainu-Japanese-English dictionary in 1889. He also translated the Bible into Ainu language using the Roman alphabet, there being no written Ainu language. The translation was published by the Japan Bible Society in 1897.

In 1899 the discriminatory "Hokkaido Former Natives Protection Law" was passed. (It remains in effect today.) The government's Hokkaido Agency established twenty-one elementary schools for Ainu children between 1901 and 1909, but in keeping with the government assimilation policy of educating all people to be imperial subjects, the Ainu language was not taught in the schools. In 1937, all the schools were closed and the students assimilated into the Japanese educational system. In keeping with government policy, in 1900 Batchelor recommended that the language of instruction in all Anglican mission schools in Hokkaido be Japanese. Of the total membership of the Anglican church in Hokkaido in 1903 (2,595), almost half were Ainu, a tribute to Batchelor's evangelistic labors.

In 1903, Japan held the Fifth Domestic Industrial Exposition in Osaka. Like all Japanese expositions, this event was closely linked with the emperor system. The Anthropological Pavilion reflected Japan and European colonial policy in Asia. On display were Ainu, Koreans, Taiwanese mountain tribe people, Kiri tribal people of India, people of Java and two women from Okinawa. An Okinawa newspaper protested this "display of human specimens," which resulted in the closing of the pavilion. Batchelor was responsible for introducing both the Ainu who appeared in the Osaka pavilion and those who appeared on display at the 1904 St. Louis Exposition.

Batchelor was regarded as an Ainu authority, and he wrote and lectured widely.   Between 1901 and 1936, he met and received awards from the emperors Meiji, Taisho, and Showa.   As Ainu church participation dropped sharply, Batchelor organized and was a leader in various government programs to "educate, civilize, enlighten, care for, and protect" the Ainu.

He left Japan in 1940 on the eve of World War II, and died in England before the end of the war.   Although Batchelor's original intent was to live with, evangelize, and serve the Ainu people, when he became known for his knowledge of Ainu language and culture he unwittingly became a tool of the Japanese government and the emperor system in oppressing and discriminating against the very people he came to serve.   He thus serves as a model in examining the role that missionaries, the church, Christian schools, and Christian social work are called to fulfill, and their stand in Japanese society today: as those who stand with the oppressed or as those who stand on the side of the powers that oppress.

Ainu discrimination and Christian mission today

The number of Ainu Christians is small, but individual Christians, churches, and ecumenical bodies throughout Japan, especially those in Hokkaido, are committing themselves as an integral part of mission to stand in solidarity with Ainu in their struggle to recover their basic human rights, to gain government recognition as a distinct people, and to preserve Ainu culture.   Specific programs to that end include: 1) opposing government exploitation of Ainu through its promotion of tourism; 2) contributing toward Chikappu Mieko's court costs; 3) standing with two Ainu whose land is being expropriated as a dam site; 4) protesting government construction of nuclear waste and nuclear power plants on Ainu land; 5) incorporating the issue of Ainu discrimination into church Christian education curriculum; 6) introducing both the beauty of Ainu culture and the existing discrimination against Ainu to Christian and non-Christian Japanese; 7) establishing educational scholarships for Ainu children; 8) participating in the movement to implement a nondiscriminatory Ainu Law; and, 9) providing continuing opportunities for exchange between Ainu and other discriminated-against minorities within Japan and in other countries.

AMAGI Augustine, Anglican bishop of the Diocese of Hokkaido, sees the crucial issue to be Ainu people's aboriginal rights, including rights to the land and underground resources of the whole island of Hokkaido; the right to keep and develop the traditional Ainu culture and lifestyle; and the right of political self-determination.

Persons from Discriminated- Against Buraku

Emblem of the National Leveler's Society, first grass-roots' buraku liberation movement. Original is blood-red crown of thorns on black background, to which a white star, symbolizing hope, was later added.

buraku: Although the original meaning is "small village or group of houses," buraku also refers to an area or person subject to discrimination.

IGARASHI Terumi

I was first told of my buraku origins when I was seven years old, not by my parents but by a non-buraku child. At school other children taunted me with "You're dirty!" "You smell!" "Don't come near me!" They tied my hands behind my back, put worms and snakes on me, and threw rocks at me when I tried to run away from their cruelty. They refused to play with me or even to hold my hand unless the teacher ordered them to do so. Even then, they only took hold of my little finger begrudgingly, hastening to wash their hands immediately afterward.

The discriminated-against buraku in which I lived did not receive the same gas and water improvements as the surrounding neighborhoods. Our unpaved streets were so narrow that fire engines could not enter. Fifteen to 20 people lined up to use each common toilet in our neighborhood. We had only one public bath for over 1,100 residents. Two or three familes often crowded together in a house of only 430 square feet in floor space.

Children dropped out of school because they were embarassed to admit to their teachers they did not have money for school fees. Instead, they told their teachers each day that they had forgotten their school money. The teachers labeled the children liars, reinforcing the existing discrimination.

Many adults in discriminated-against buraku were unemployed. The only jobs available to them were those considered "unclean" by

Japanese society, such as meat processing, janitorial work, and shoe and sandal-making.   The salaries they received were 60 percent of the national average.   Women in discriminated-against buraku labored under a double burden of discrimination.

When I was sixteen, after completing my compulsory junior-high-school education, I entered the work force.   There was no need for further education for a girl, according to the thinking of the people in my buraku.   Enduring discrimination for generations taught them that education did not guarantee a good job or living wage to persons of the discriminated-against buraku.   My parents sat me down to a lecture on the necessity of hiding my buraku origins, warning me that I must never fall in love with a person from outside the buraku.

I took a job with a company where I continued to experience discrimination.   My supervisors declared that I was poorly educated and had no ability.   Although we were the same Japanese, my co-workers talked behind my back, saying, "Her blood is different!" "She eats different food!" "She's violent!" "'They' have eye disease!" Unable to handle such treatment, I moved from job to job.   I blamed my misery on my mother.   When in anger I shouted at her, "Why did you give birth to me?" she was unable to explain buraku discrimination to me.   Only later did I realize that in hating my mother, I, too, was perpetuating buraku discrimination.

Like many other residents of the discriminated-against buraku, I tried to hide my origins, doing my best to avoid being followed on my way to and from work each day.

At age thirty, when I felt the emotional burden had become more than I could bear, I married a man who did not come from a discriminated-against buraku.   He encouraged me to stop trying to hide who I really was.

Limited-term legislation has resulted in improvements in the physical conditions in buraku areas, but despite the constitutional guarantee of equality of all persons and education campaigns to eliminate discrimination, my two children today face many of the same taunts that I did as a child.   Discrimination in education, employment, and marriage continues to exist within Japanese society and within the consciousness of individual Japanese people today.   Large companies and families often conduct investigations of prospective employees or marriage partners with the help of secretly published directories and personal computer records of buraku areas.

Many men from discriminated-against buraku who have received neither education nor vocational training can live only by working at manual labor.   Women work as waitresses, although some who are illiterate cannot write customers' orders or checks.   For such persons, merely buying a train or subway ticket from a machine and reading the name of the destination station becomes a demeaning, daily ordeal. Mothers are unable to keep records of infant feedings or doctors' instructions for infant care.

I became a member of the staff of the Kyodan Buraku Liberation Center shortly after it was established in 1981 to address the issue of buraku discrimination within the church. I was encouraged by IMAI Kazuichi, the center's first director, who assured me that deep anger at a lifetime of humiliating discrimination was the prime qualification for the job.

As a child, in my home as in most buraku homes, my parents worked long hours just to keep food on the family table, often working on piecework at home until late at night. This left little energy for family members' communication at the end of the day. Children usually dropped out of school at an early age to earn money for the family, and were thus deprived of education in self-expression and interpersonal relationship skills. Life was lived, therefore, with a minimum of conversation and expression of one's true feelings. Thus, my parents were unable to share with me their pain and anger. Today I am the only child in my family to make public my buraku origins. My sister reports that after I appeared in a documentary film on public TV recently, the attitude of her work colleagues changed drastically toward her, but that eventually this resulted in frank dialogue on buraku discrimination.

I myself was not able to bring myself to tell my story in public until four years ago. Though it is still painful to do so because it forces me to recall many incidents that I would rather forget, as a Buraku Liberation Center staff member I frequently share my life story with churches and other groups to focus Japanese Christian eyes on buraku discrimination in church and society. We work as a center to liberate the hearts and minds of Christians who continue to discriminate and to gain support for the vital task of buraku liberation, which is being carried out by persons of the discriminated-against buraku themselves.

Buraku discrimination and the church

The origins of deep-rooted discrimination by 98 percent of Japanese citizens against 2 percent of their Japanese sisters and brothers are not clear. What is clear is that the discrimination was systematized during the Tokugawa Shogunate (1603-1868), which divided all Japanese people into four occupation-related social strata: 1) samurai; 2) farmer; 3) artisan; 4) merchant. Persons not included within this rigidly defined system of social control were the emperor at the top and the "non-persons," relegated to the bottom of the social pyramid.   To the latter were assigned specific occupations including those considered "unclean" according to Shinto and Buddhist concepts of personal pollution: the slaughter of animals, the tanning of animal hides and manufacture of leather products, and the burial of the dead.

Many of these discriminated-against persons were made to live on the poorest land on the river banks and outskirts of town, areas not even included on the maps of that day.   When social control seemed endangered, new regulations were handed down, dictating against intermarriage with persons of other social strata and prescribing curfews, dress, and the limits of social intercourse.

This rigid social stratification became thoroughly entrenched in Japanese consciousness over the centuries.   Despite sporadic legislative attempts to eliminate discrimination, educational programs to alter the mindset of the discriminator, and policies for improving living conditions and opportunities of persons living in the discriminated-against buraku, such insidious discrimination continues to pervade Japanese society in many forms today.

In 1871, three years after the Meiji Restoration opened Japan's doors to the rest of the world, the Emancipation Edict removed the Tokugawa divisions of social caste.   With the emperor at the summit, society was now divided into royalty (the emperor's extended family), nobility, former samurai, and commoners.   Those included in the commoners group—former artisans, merchants, and farmers— used a derogatory term, "new commoners," to differentiate the former outcastes from themselves, thus perpetuating the age-old discrimination directed against one group of Japanese.   The Emancipation Edict removed the tax-free status and the guarantee of certain occupations from persons of the discriminated-against buraku, placing new burdens on them.   This elimination of social caste also meant persons formerly occupying the upper strata now directed their anger against persons who had formerly occupied a place even below the lowest rung of society.

Struggle for liberation

The first grassroots buraku liberation movement, *Zenkoku Suihei-sha* (National Leveler's Society), organized in 1922, took as its emblem a blood-red crown of thorns set against a black background. Later a white star, symbolizing hope, was added.   The nationwide movement gained momentum, actively denouncing all acts of discrimination, until 1942.   Then government pressure on all citizens' movements to disband and unify under the state, along with internal ideological differences, caused the organization to disband.

In 1946 the movement reorganized as the *Buraku Kaiho Zenkoku Iinkai* (National Committee for Buraku Liberation), which was reorganized in 1955 as the *Buraku Kaiho Domei* (Buraku Liberation League). Its efforts were largely responsible for the Social Integration Policy Law, passed in 1969. In 1987, the law was extended another five years for specific programs already under way. After 1992, the government indicated, there would be no further specific programs for discriminated-against buraku or their residents. The law included government programs to end discrimination in employment and education and to improve living conditions in discriminated-against buraku areas. Today concerned persons continue to press for the enactment of a "Fundamental Law for Buraku Liberation," to be effective until discrimination is eliminated.

The Japanese family register system is a major factor in perpetuating the discrimination. Every Japanese is registered at the time of birth in a family's permanent register at the local city hall, making it possible to trace any individual's birthplace or permanent address. This is one way that prospective employers and families of marriage partners can trace whether a candidate is from a discriminated-against background. Although restrictions adopted in recent years close family registers at city halls, access to residence or voters' lists is still possible. From these a person's registered address can be determined.

Facing discrimination within the church

Until recently, few individual Christians or congregations have been involved in the buraku liberation struggle. But in 1975 the Buraku Liberation League challenged the Kyodan on its discriminatory position toward the discriminated-against buraku and toward church members from discriminated-against buraku. Then the whole church was forced to take up this issue.

Presentation of a long list of discriminatory terms appearing in Kyodan publications and the ensuing dialogue led the Kyodan to establish a Special Committee on Buraku Liberation Issues in 1975 and the Kyodan Buraku Liberation Center in Osaka in 1981. Today the Center sees its primary purpose as working to eliminate discrimination within the structures, teachings, and the lives of persons in the church. The NCCJ also formed a committee on buraku discrimination issues in 1976. In 1981, *Doshuren*, a national asssembly of about seventy religious organizations, including Christian, Shinto and Buddhist bodies, was founded to address discrimination within religious communities and teachings.

One form of discrimination within Buddhism was the practice of bestowing posthumous names upon persons. Priests bestowed clearly discriminatory names on persons of the discriminated-against buraku.

Within the Christian church, even so renowned a Christian as evangelist, writer, and social worker KAGAWA Toyohiko (1888-1960) was discovered to have held and expressed in his writings clearly discriminatory attitudes toward the Japanese sisters and brothers with whom he lived and worked in the pockets of poverty in Kobe. Since 1986, the Kyodan has called on all local congregations to make a thorough study of Kagawa's discriminatory attitude in his writings as a way of coming to terms with the discrimination existing in every person and, indeed, in the church itself, in order to work toward the complete elimination of such discrimination.

The Kyodan Buraku Liberation Center also seeks to provide opportunities for persons from discriminated-against buraku to build networks both with other discriminated-against groups in Japan and in other countries to establish solidarity for the common task of overcoming discrimination.

Symbolic of society's treatment of persons from the discriminated-against buraku is the murder of a high school girl in 1963. ISHIKAWA Kazuo, a young man from a discriminated-against buraku, was arrested, tried on the basis of trumped-up evidence, convicted, and given a death sentence which was only later commuted to life imprisonment. Christians join other concerned persons in demanding a full review of the case and calling for all evidence to be made public, in light of the clearly discriminatory attitudes shown in the investigation and trials.

Korean Residents

Symbol used in the anti-fingerprint movement. Message in Japanese says "Abolish the Alien Registration Certificate Fingerprint System."

CHOI Sun Ae

I'm really not a political person. I'm a musician, and I would much prefer to study and play and teach my students rather than protesting against the Alien Registration Law or appearing in court. But my father taught us (my brother and sister and me) a strong sense of Korean identity and pride in our ethnic roots.

Actually, my involvement in the struggles of the Koreans in Japan is not some kind of planned activity. I was born in Osaka and lived most of my life in Kokura City (that's in Kyushu). I don't remember any really awful experiences as a child as a result of my Korean ancestry. In primary school I used a Christian name, Lois, and boys would torment me because of that.

In junior and senior high school I attended a Baptist school for girls. Here there was no tormenting. The only problem I had was with the teachers and administrators over my name. Once a vice-principal asked me how to pronounce my name. I said *Choi*, but the vice-principal said, "*Sai* (the Japanese pronunciation) is all right, isn't it?" In class, teachers sometimes would avoid my name completely. For example, in math class when everyone in the class would be asked to answer questions, the teacher would just skip me. I also had a hard time getting friends to pronounce my name. But I didn't consider these major problems and I was elected president of the student activity program at my school.

I will have to confess that I did have something of an identity problem. I tried to be a Japanese. In looks, I think I could pass for a Japanese. Sometimes when I saw a Korean on a bus, I would avoid that person. In this struggle with my identity, I thought the best thing was just to be a good person no matter what my roots were.

75

While I was at university, I discovered that my younger sister was struggling with her own identity. She said she didn't want to be fingerprinted. Actually I had given up the struggle for myself by then, but I saw in her the person I used to be.

At university I had a roommate. One day in secrecy she told me she was from a discriminated-against buraku area. Hearing her experience was shocking to me. I wasn't surprised at discrimination directed against Koreans. I just tried not to pay attention to it. I tried to think good thoughts. But my roommate's situation was different. Her parents had told her not to marry an "ordinary" Japanese. They told her never to reveal her identity because it would cause problems.

I got really angry hearing her situation. I felt some responsibility for the discrimination she was forced to endure. I felt that if I didn't do something, such prejudice and discrimination would only be repeated. My roommate said she envied me. "You are Korean. You have a country. I cannot talk about my situation. I cannot really struggle."

These are the main reasons I refused to allow my fingerprint to be taken. As a Korean, in this way I could do something for my sister and my friend. People will continue to suffer if we don't do something about it. My sister wanted to refuse giving her fingerprint. I wanted to help her. It was about time for my Alien Registration Certificate renewal. I had felt hurt when I was fingerprinted for the first time at age sixteen, but I got used to it. Now I felt that we had to start changing things somehow. Even some little thing would help. Refusing to be fingerprinted was one thing we could do.

CHOI Sun Ae is a music teacher at several schools in the Tokyo area. She formerly taught at Kinjo University in Nagoya. She holds a bachelor's and master's degree from Aichi Prefecture Fine Arts University and a master's degree from the University of Indiana, USA.

Because Choi went to the United States in order to continue her music study without first obtaining a re-entry permit, she was given only a six-month visa upon her return to Japan. Even though born and brought up in Japan, she lost her appeal for a permanent visa in the lower court, and is now appealing this decision in Japan's Supreme Court. On June 15,1990, Choi was at last granted a re-entry permit in response to her request to leave Japan to attend an international music competition in Italy. Although approval came too late for her to attend, Choi declared, "A small amount of hope has emerged. This must have been a big decision for the government."

How Koreans were brought to Japan

Korea is Japan's close neighbor and a significant major ethnic forebear of the Japanese. Korea has played a vital role as the main conduit of Asian mainland culture to Japan and is gradually being recognized for its own unique contribution to Japanese culture. For example, several of Japan's oldest shrines feature major religious objects of Korean origin, and the imperial family itself has some Korean ancestors in its distant past.

Japanese warlord TOYOTOMI Hideyoshi also used Korea as the corridor for his invasion of China in the sixteenth century. Japan invaded Korea once again at the beginning of the Sino-Japanese War (1894-5). Japan's official annexation of Korea in 1910 resulted in a methodical attempt to erase Korean cultural identity, forcing all Korean citizens to adopt Japanese names, language, and citizenship.

Following the Great Kanto (Tokyo-Yokohama) earthquake in 1923, Korean residents in Japan were accused of starting the resulting fires and poisoning wells. Japanese vigilante groups, some official, hunted down and killed 6,661 Koreans, over half the Korean population of Tokyo at that time.

During the 1930s, the collapse of Korea's rural economy and Japan's military buildup brought 670,000 Koreans to Japan to work in defense factories and mines. Over 365,000 Korean men were drafted by the Japanese military. Later, eight to ten thousand Korean women were conscripted and dispatched to World War II battlefields to serve the sexual desires of Japanese military personnel.

At the end of World War II, many of the two million Koreans then living in Japan returned to Korea. However, over 550,000, aware of the chaos in post-colonial Korean society and having employment and citizenship in Japan, chose to remain there.

Both the Japanese government and the Supreme Command for the Allied Powers (SCAP) demanded that all Korean residents be assimilated into Japanese society. Sensing the Japanese resentment over this policy, SCAP urged that stronger measures be taken to control Koreans in Japan. To this end, the alien registration system was established in 1947, Korean schools were closed, and an election law was passed limiting voting to Japanese citizens.

The 1952 San Francisco Peace Treaty officially ended World War II, but it did not resolve the problems of Koreans in Japan. Rather, they were stripped of Japanese citizenship, leaving them stateless. Japan's 1952 Alien Registration Law was revised in 1988 after considerable struggle, changing the system to a first-time-only fingerprinting of all foreign residents, usually at age sixteen.

The experience of discrimination

OH Soo Hae, KCCJ Education Department secretary, and Japan commissioner on the WCC Programme to Combat Racism, shares her personal insights as a Korean in Japan:

> The Japanese government does not want to recognize the existence of minorities in Japan. Former Prime Minister Nakasone denied the existence of Koreans in Japan when he said that there are no minorities. The ideology of the purity and uniqueness of the Japanese race was pushed as something close to perfection from the Meiji era onwards—a system of rule and control with a nationalism centered on the emperor system. To prove their theory, they had to stamp upon or ostracize any foreign element. Under such a regime, of course, the existence of Ainu, Okinawans and Koreans could never be acknowledged or allowed, and persons of the discriminated-against buraku were ignored as nothing more than an invisible element.
>
> "If you don't like our laws, get out and go home; if you are going to stay, be quiet, obey, and naturalize as Japanese." This is the message from Japanese police and Ministry of Justice authorities to the large community of foreign residents in Japan.
>
> Our experience can be summed up in two terms: prejudice and systematic discrimination. The problem of personal names illustrates this. Discrimination within the hearts and minds of the Japanese forces Koreans not to use their given Korean names. When Korean residents look for employment they need to hide their Korean identity by using Japanese names. Korean students are unwilling to use Korean names because they are afraid of losing friends if their Korean identity is known.
>
> Another serious problem in relation to assimilation is that of ethnic education. The Japanese government does not provide any ethnic education for the children of Korean residents enrolled in public schools. Although 70 percent of the pupils in my daughter's school in Osaka are Korean, the school has neither a single Korean teacher nor any kind of ethnic curriculum.
>
> Discrimination also exists in legal procedures. Although the Alien Registration Law was changed, these changes involve centralizing in Tokyo the control of all foreign residents by the use of computers. Even one-time, forced fingerprinting of sixteen-year-old Koreans has a harmful effect; that is an age when injury to personal identity and loss of social relations are most serious. The Alien Registration System represents the continuation of social alienation and racial harassment and clearly

indicates a lack of any basic change in the repressive, anti-alien mindset of Japanese power cliques.

For Koreans in Japan, 1991, the time of the revision of the present Japan-Korea treaty, is a major milestone when the future of their childrens' children will be decided. Will the aggressive alienation and ethnocide continue, or will Japanese and Koreans discover a new future together in a reconciliation that is redemptive and restorative for all?

The experience of the 1960s, when power cliques in Japan and Korea gave Korean residents in Japan no hearing but bartered away our lives arbitrarily, must not be repeated. The treaty must be reviewed with full, free opportunity given to Koreans in Japan to fulfill their mission in Japan among both Japanese and Koreans.

Today, the basic demands of Korean residents in Japan include: permanent residence for third-generation Korean residents; elimination of the alien registration system; an end to deportation for committing serious crimes; the end of the re-entry system; the right to work as municipal employees, particularly as teachers; provision of ethnic education in Japanese schools; and laws ending employment discrimination.

The Korean Christian Church in Japan

In 1907, three years before Japan annexed Korea, the Korean YMCA established a Tokyo branch to serve Korean students studying in Japan. Two years later, the congregation meeting in this Tokyo YMCA received its first pastor from the Presbyterian Church in Korea. From 1915 the Korean Methodist Church cooperated with the Presbyterian Church in sending missionaries for three-year periods to engage in ministry with Koreans in Japan. Evangelistic efforts began among the Koreans in Japan brought to serve as cheap labor in Tokyo, Yokohama, Kobe, Osaka, Kyushu, and Hokkaido. Twenty-one places of worship were established and 922 members were added to the new church rolls. The small Christian communities throughout Japan provided much-needed refuge and comfort for Koreans trying to survive in a hostile alien land.

From 1927, the Presbyterian Church in Canada joined the churches in Korea in supporting the mission program among the increasing numbers of Koreans in Japan. This continuing sister-church relationship includes the exchange of personnel.

The Korean Christian Church in Japan (KCCJ), founded in 1927 and formally adopting its constitution in 1934, brought together churches scattered throughout Japan to form one autonomous denomination. By 1939 the KCCJ had grown to number 59 churches, 23 pastors, and 3,825 members.

The wartime policy of nation unity that followed Japan's invasion of China in 1937 pressured the still officially unrecognized Korean church as it did Japanese churches. Additional pressures were based on discrimination against Koreans. To ensure its survival, the Korean church was forced to merge with one of these churches, the Japanese Christian Church, in 1940. Merger terms included obedience to that denomination's creed; exclusive use of the Japanese language in worship, although newcomers to Japan understood only Korean; and reexamination of Korean clergy to qualify for Japanese church ministerial qualification standards.

When the United Church of Christ in Japan was formed in 1941, the Korean Church in Japan became a part of that united Protestant body. This merger forced Korean Christians in Japan to worship at Shinto shrines during World War II.

Because the KCCJ was deemed a stronghold of Korean opposition to Japanese policy, and also because Christianity itself was viewed as an enemy religion, many Korean pastors and laypersons in Japan were unjustly arrested and forced to spend the war years in prison.

In November 1945, a minority of the Korean Christians left the Kyodan to establish the present Korean Christian Church in Japan as a confessional church with its own articles of faith and constitution. Several of the pastors who remained in Japan and some three hundred church members cooperated to rebuild damaged churches and erect new ones. Early postwar evangelism was focused on greater Tokyo, Kyoto-Osaka-Kobe, and the southwestern part of Japan.

The KCCJ is a member of the NCCJ and the Christian Conference of Asia and an associate member of the World Council of Churches. This ecumenical participation provides opportunities for growth and cooperation in mission with minorities in Asia and other parts of the world.

A ministry of upholding human rights

Because it focused so strongly on its own reconstruction in the early postwar years, the KCCJ has been forced to reflect on whether it has truly borne the afflictions and pain of Korean sisters and brothers living in Japan. Thus, as a part of its ministry, it has dedicated itself to work for the achievement of human rights for all Korean residents in Japan who suffer discrimination by Japanese society. It supports the all-out struggle against the alien registration system, which applies to all foreign residents in Japan but is basically directed toward Korean residents.

The struggle of PARK Chong Seok against unfair employment practices by Hitachi Corporation in the 1970s, his court battle and ensuing victory opened up new possibilities for the church. Working to achieve justice through bringing such issues of minority discrimination to the attention of Japanese society and the world has become a vital mission concern.

Today the 72 KCCJ churches and mission points, 60 pastors and workers, and 3,793 church members engage in ministry with the one million Korean residents in Japan. On its 70th anniversary in 1978, the KCCJ restated its mission:

We believe the special mission God has revealed to us here in this country is a ministry of reconciliation and unity, which are of the essence of the gospel. We are participating in the great reconciling and unifying work of removing the historical division between the Korean people of the North and South,* and the Koreans and Japanese, and of bringing them together by the cross of Christ. We declare to all people that we must fulfill this ministry of reconciliation.

Here openly in the midst of our divided brothers and sisters in Japan we confess Jesus Christ and his cross which we carry as we proclaim the gospel which makes what is separated one.

The Covenant of Cooperation established in 1984 between the KCCJ and the Kyodan serves as a concrete symbol of that reconciliation: two estranged peoples and churches united through the grace of God in Christ. On this occasion, the Kyodan pledged itself to seek to right the wrong of Japan's past oppression of Asian neighbors as well as present economic exploitation and discrimination against Korean residents in such systems as the fingerprinting of aliens.

Today the KCCJ continues to minister to the Korean community through twelve social service and action institutions, which include programs for senior citizens, community centers, pre-schools serving both Korean and Japanese children, and language and culture programs to assist Korean residents in reclaiming their cultural identity.

---

*The division between north and south in Korea carries over to Korean residents in Japan; for example, two separate citizens' organizations exist, the South Korean Residents' Organization and the North Korean Residents' League.

Okinawa

Lion-dog is a traditional Okinawa symbol.

YOSHIDA Teiko

I remember well the period of turmoil when Okinawa was returned to Japan (1972) and removed from the United States occupation status. Some people desperately wanted Okinawa to be returned to Japan and others hoped for an independent Okinawa. As a junior-high-school student, I felt that Okinawa should be independent, but that it would be very difficult because Okinawa is made up of small islands.

Okinawa's reversion to Japan was accomplished, but Okinawa is still occupied by, and is a colony of, both the United States and Japan.

The people of Okinawa had great expectations for reversion, strongly desiring to be free from the United States and other foreign control. They suffered under the American occupation, while Americans were not subject to any of the legal restraints placed upon Okinawans. People hoped that after reversion their land would be returned to them for agricultural use.

When the Ocean Marine Exposition was held in Okinawa in 1975, people expected that their lives would be enriched. Some borrowed money to build hotels and open shops, but big business came from the Japanese mainland and built large luxury hotels, restaurants, and shopping malls in collaboration with airlines and travel agencies. Many Okinawan people went bankrupt and are still burdened with huge debts.

Expectations were also dashed by the rapid appreciation of the yen against the dollar. During occupation, Okinawa was forced to use U.S. dollars, but when we changed to Japanese currency after reversion, our meager holdings depreciated rapidly.

Before reversion we needed passports to travel to mainland Japan. When I visited the mainland three years after reversion, people asked me if I could speak Japanese. Hearing such questions and realizing that the lifestyle of mainland Japanese was made possible at the sacrifice of many Okinawans, I was filled with sadness.

Okinawa's unique culture developed during the seventh and eighth centuries. In the fifteenth century the island chain became a trading crossroads for China and Korea. The Satsuma clan in southern Japan invaded the Ryukyu Kingdom (Okinawa) in the sixteenth century, easily conquering the peaceful kingdom, a trading nation that had never engaged in warmaking. Satsuma domination continued until 1879, when the islands became a prefecture of Japan.

The new Meiji government instituted an assimilation policy, belittling Okinawan language, customs, and culture, and imposing Japanese language and culture on our people. During World War II the Okinawan people were forced to cooperate with the Japanese military. Toward the end of the war, Okinawa became a stone to be thrown away, as the mainland Japanese military sought to protect the emperor and Japan proper from the U.S. invasion. Okinawan people were sacrificed when they became an obstruction to military strategy.

After reversion the people's expectations for a peaceful Okinawa were completely ignored by the intrusion of the Japanese Self-Defense Forces. Now, not only were there U.S. military bases on our islands but Japanese military bases as well.

Despite all of this, as a child I myself did not experience discrimination. I went to church from an early age, for my mother was a Christian. I was taught that being a Christian means to endure difficulties and to love one's enemies. If I became a victim of discrimination I was simply to endure it, so I was shocked to hear the words of a college student from the mainland who said that his parents told him he should not marry a woman from Okinawa, although he was going to college there. I wondered why people on the mainland felt a need to treat us that way.

I soon realized that there are realities inherent in discrimination and prejudice which the individual cannot overcome. I became afraid of people, intimidated even though I had done nothing wrong. I began to belittle the beauty of Okinawa, negating Okinawan culture and tradition. I imagined that my friends, my family, and even I myself were somehow inferior.

When I came to Tokyo to enter theological seminary, my Okinawa accent was corrected, which was a way of negating my cultural heritage. Other Okinawans advised me not to talk too much about Okinawa, or people would know where I came from. Why can't I talk about my culture and the magnificent grandeur of nature in Okinawa?

The issues of Okinawa are not problems related to Japan alone. They include issues related to the great suffering brought about by U.S. militarism. Because there are still many U.S. bases in Okinawa, my parents, family, and friends face the possibility of war and the threat of nuclear weapons each day.

TAKAZATO Suzuyo

"War" is the term often used as the opposite of "peace." From women's standpoint, "violence" is a more appropriate term.

As a women's counselor I have seen many women who suffer pain of body and mind from long years in U.S. military-related prostitution. We can consider the long-term existence of U.S. military bases as a form of national violence. Okinawa has come to be called an island of bases. A military base in not simply the stationing of missiles and the storage of nuclear weapons; a base is a society that aims for victory by war and control by violence and in which the military always takes precedence. In such a society men are isolated from ordinary life for indoctrination purposes. The violent character of their militaristic society threatens the surrounding area and pollutes the social environment.

In order for the local community to escape that violence, a breakwater is needed to receive it. In Okinawa, women are that breakwater. It is said that during the Vietnam War, one in forty Okinawa women were prostituted to American military personnel.

Today we can see national violence of both the United States and Japan at work in Okinawa. Again women are forced to serve as a breakwater to save Okinawan society from military violence.

Military-base issues as well as peace and anti-nuclear movements must be reexamined from the perspective of women and children, those persons in a weak position in society. Live artillery exercises conducted by U.S. marines across public highways are strongly opposed by citizen groups. Yet, adjacent to the base entrance where the protests take place, Filipino women work unnoticed under terrible conditions, serving as sexual vessels for men from the base. A local bar owner says, "The people of the town can sleep in peace because the Filipinas are here as a breakwater."

We must insure that the peace we seek for ourselves does not mean oppression for other people. We want to be done with that peace which means peace for one person but violence for another.

TAKAZATO Suzuyo is a former women's counselor, a member of the Naha City Council, and a Nishihara Church (Kyodan) member.

Christian mission in the Ryukyu Archipelago (Okinawa)

In 1891, the American Baptist Church, using funds from Scotland, dispatched a Japanese minister to establish the Okinawa Preaching Point, the first Protestant church in Okinawa. Other churches were soon established by the Japan Methodist Church, Japan Episcopal Church, Japan Presbyterian Church, Okinawa Congregational Church, Japan Holiness Church, and the Salvation Army.

At the time of the formation of the Kyodan in June 1941, the five existing denominations in Okinawa—Japan Baptist Church, Japan Methodist Church, Japan Presbyterian Church, Japan Holiness Church, and the Salvation Army—became part of Kyushu District of the Kyodan. Four years later in 1945, Okinawa churches were destroyed in the bloody Battle of Okinawa.

Separated from the church in Japan by a political treaty, the newly independent Okinawa Christian Federation was established in 1946, reorganized into the Okinawa Christian Church in 1950, and into the United Church of Christ of Okinawa (Okinawa Kyodan) in 1957. After the war, as in Japan, some churches withdrew from the United Church in Okinawa to reestablish their denominational ties. At the time of union between the Okinawa Kyodan and the Japan Kyodan in 1969, the independent Okinawa Kyodan was reduced to the Okinawa District of the Japan Kyodan. Nevertheless, in many ways Okinawa District today maintains its self-identity as a church.

When considering mission outreach, Okinawa churches recognize the significant role that the indigenous Okinawan religion still occupies in society today. Inquirers often come to Christianity after they have consulted *yuta*, women religious counselors with strong mystical power, to understand and solve personal and family problems.

A long-standing issue for the Christian community in Okinawa is its position regarding the military bases in Okinawa. In the immediate postwar years, many churches and Christians cooperated closely with U.S. military bases, chapels, and chaplains. Today most churches see their role as speaking out against the systematized discrimination and violence perpetrated by U.S. and Japanese militarization in Okinawa and as standing with and ministering to the suffering of the victims of that violence.

The founding statement of the ecumenical Okinawa Christian Heiwa (Peace) Center, established in 1984, expresses the vision of many Christians in Okinawa today:

Okinawa is the bearer of a sacred heritage. In previous centuries it gained reknown as the "Country Without Weapons," and its people played a significant role in Asian cultural exchange.

In this century, however, Okinawa was turned into a place of war, death, and destruction. Furthermore, as the so-called "keystone" of Japanese/American policy, the role of a military base which threatens the lives and peace of our neighbors has been thrust on Okinawa.

Thus, the conditions under which we live on Okinawa are a problem with far-reaching consequences not only for us but for all citizens of Asia and the Pacific region. However reluctantly, we are forced to face these consequences.

During the period of Japan's military aggression in the Asia Pacific region, Okinawa, as a part of Japan, was inadvertently on the side of the aggressor. At the same time, under postwar Japanese and American policy, Okinawa has become a victim.

The stance of Okinawa Christian churches takes on grave meaning in this context. We are called upon to become "Bridges of Peace" in the spirit of our Okinawan forebears, so that the peoples of Asia and the Pacific region can live together as true neighbors. We believe that we have been called upon to fulfill this role as Christians to whom the "Gospel of Peace" is entrusted . . . .

We join in solidarity with the peoples of Asia and the Pacific region to solve our common problems without resorting to the use of military, economic, or any other power.

Women

JOSEI
woman

DOI Takako

I haven't particularly taken up women's issues in my career.   But whenever I take up welfare, rights, or local problems, the people who feel most left out are women.   So even if I didn't especially talk about women's issues, women feel these problems the most.

(quoted in The New York Times, *May 8, 1989)*

Doi Takako is a lawyer, scholar of the constitution, and the first woman to head a political party in Japan.

OHSHIMA Shizuko

Throughout Japan's long history, women like Kiyoe have been forced to endure sexual harassment, have not vocalized their feelings, or even if they did, they were not fully heard. That tradition is now being denounced by Asian women in Japan. If their voices are drowned out or go unheard, our work at HELP has no meaning, for I believe that there is a definite link between sexual harassment and prostitution. Both when Japan was a poor country and when it became rich, its basic attitude toward women in a powerless position has remained the same. Until Japan as a nation comes to terms with the long history of this problem, Japan will not come of age internationally.

(Quoted in Japan Through the Eyes
of Women Migrant Workers)

Ohshima Shizuko is founder and former director of HELP Asian Women's Shelter, established by the Japan Woman's Christian Temperance Union.

Women as traditional outsiders

In one sense the traditional role of wife and mother assigned to Japanese women has given them a place "inside the group," that is, in the primary social group, the family.   Nevertheless, women's almost total exclusion from participation at any other level of society has, in a very real sense, placed Japanese women "outside the group" as ones who experience discrimination and whose options for participation in society are limited.   During the feudal period, samurai wives in particular became non-productive units of society, unlike female members of cooperative agricultural units in rural Japan.   Japan's modernization reinforced a strict division of sexual roles with no possibility for social participation for the vast number of Japanese women.   Exceptions were daughters of poverty-stricken families. Some were contracted out to work away from home under harsh conditions in textile factories. Those from even poorer homes were sold by desperate families into licensed prostitution within Japan or in other Asian countries.

Sweeping changes enacted by Japan's postwar Constitution in 1947 granted Japanese women legal equality (Article 14); universal suffrage (Article 15); equal marriage and property rights (Article 24); equal education (Article 26); and equal access to election to the national Diet (Article 44).   The Labor Standards Law of the same year prohibits wage discrimination.   Under the revision of the Nationality Law in 1984, a child's nationality is no longer determined by the nationality of the father but may follow that of the mother. Despite these protections, in almost every sphere of society Japanese women continue to experience sexual discrimination.

The emergence of the nuclear family in the postwar years has reinforced strict role division, with the woman's role continuing to be the homemaker and caregiver to children, husband, and, in many cases, elderly parents as Japan's society ages rapidly.   Japanese company demands on employees, which include long working hours, short vacations, and total loyalty, all help maintain the traditional male-female role division. Husbands' improved employee benefits and overall increased affluence lure many wives into the comfortable security of depending on husbands' earnings. Women's role now includes that of family consumer, the target of advertising media campaigns.

Education and employment: not yet equal

Educational opportunities are open to women today. Although many women students opt for coeducational institutions, many parents prefer women's schools. They believe that their daughters will be safer, retain their femininity, and have better employment opportunities as graduate of women's junior colleges than as graduates of four-year-coeducational institutions. In 1990, 37 percent of all undergraduate college students are women. Over 50 percent of women college students study in two-year junior colleges. Seventeen percent of four-year colleges are women's schools.

Society assumes that women, despite receiving an equal education, will only work for several years after graduation before quitting their jobs when they are married or their first child is born. Employers benefit from hiring short-term, low-level employees rather than maintaining increasingly costly employee benefits for long-term employees.

Re-hiring women on a part-time basis with no benefits after their children are in school also makes good fiscal sense to employers. Women part-time workers who have no built-in security are a convenient, expendable cushion against fluctuations in the economy. This includes women who contract to do piecework at home, though in recent years, piecework has been largely taken out of the hands of Japanese women and relegated to women in other Asian countries, where lower pay scales increase company profits.

Increasing numbers of women are flouting social mores by choosing not to drop out of the work force even after marrying and bearing childen, but they face many barriers. Although Article 23 of the Law for Equal Employment Opportunities for Men and Women, passed in 1986, requires employers to establish a maternity leave system for women workers, only twenty percent of business enterprises have adopted the temporary maternity leave system. The lack of adequate public, company, and private child-care facilities also poses problems for women who work out of necessity or choice. Long commuting times coupled with long working hours and regular overtime place heavy physical and emotional demands on working women, on whom the major burden of childrearing continues to rest. Few employers are experimenting with flex-time or half-time employment for couples who wish to share evenly in childrearing. With all these obstacles, then, only highly motivated and physically robust women can hold up under the double burden of home and job, because the new nuclear family pattern does not include other extended-family women to share household duties and child care, and only a few younger Japanese men are attempting to share these tasks.

The issue of sexual harassment is starting to receive serious attention from the media and the general public. But this problem is viewed in the narrow sense of treatment that women endure from male colleagues on the job, not treatment women experience throughout society. Concerned lawyers cite the need for a counseling service and revisions of the 1986 Law for Equal Employment Opportunitites to include measures against sexual harassment on the job. An even more basic issue is the mindset of most men and some women that women are basically inferior to men and should therefore occupy an inferior position both in the workplace and throughout society. The traditional concept of the male-female relationship—as either son-mother or man-sexual partner, with no room for men and women to relate as equal colleagues—hinders effective work relationships. Some men state that women's full-time participation in the work force is such a recent phenomenon that men have not yet learned how to relate seriously as colleagues.

A base for participating in power

The involvements of Japanese women who are not employed outside the home have traditionally been limited to improving their skills in such traditional art forms as flower arrangement and tea ceremony. Today increasing opportunities include lessons in tennis, golf, swimming, aerobics, and involvement in the community and the larger society through volunteer work and a variety of grass-roots movements.

One of the earliest of these is the nationwide homemakers' consumer movement, which has successfully challenged the government and big business on pollution and product price-fixing. A nationwide consumer's cooperative, which attempts to change methods of consumption by promoting self-managed, less wasteful lifestyles, was founded in 1965 when a Tokyo homemaker organized two hundred women to buy milk in quantity to reduce the price. This cooperative, involving 170,000 family units and an annual turnover of $287 million, refuses to handle products detrimental to health and environment.

Women's voluntary participation in community activities forms the backbone of many grassroots movements seeking to address such issues as children's education, peace, environment, and aging. Women's participation also becomes the family's window to the community, as heavy company demands for time and for loyalty to company interests keep male breadwinners' community participation minimal. Involvement in local community citizens' movements has given women organizational and leadership skills as well as a base of support from which to wage campaigns in local city council and prefecture assembly elections in order to address issues of concern.

The year 1989 was a landmark for women's political participation through the election process. Ruling party officials' acceptance of personal bribes from business enterprises, their attempts to cover illicit sexual involvements with hush money, and an unpopular new 3 percent consumer-goods tax combined to topple elected officials from the prime minister down. Reformist women candidates gained enough voter support to sweep into office in unprecedented numbers at all electoral levels throughout the country. At the national level 22 women were elected to the House of Councillors, the Upper House of the Diet, increasing the total number of women Councillors to 33, or 13 percent of the 252 Upper House seats. In the February 1990 national elections, a record 12 women were elected to the House of Representatives, the Lower House, an increase of five seats out of 512. Of the total 764 members of the Diet, 47 are now women.

Women's issues emerge in society

The feminist movement as it exists in the West has not gained the support of most Japanese women. In the 1970s rather extreme tactics by a small group of young Japanese women protesting women's discriminatory treatment in the workplace gained media attention and earned the movement the epithet "Women's Lib," still used today. Nevertheless, nationwide women's organizations such as the Woman's Christian Temperance Union have long worked for the elimination of sexual discrimination and exploitation and for the achievement of women's equal and full participation in society.

The 1975 U.N. International Women's Year (IWY) and the Convention to Eliminate All Forms of Discrimination Against Women* strengthened the women's movement. The Headquarters for Planning and Promotion of Policies for Women was set up within the Prime Minister's Office. In addition, the IWY Liaison Council, representing 41 nationwide women's organizations and chapters of women's unions, was established as a networking body in 1975.

Abortion is not a new issue to Japanese women. *Seito* (Blue Stocking), the literary feminist group that published a journal by the same name from 1911, listed among its concerns: arranged marriage system, geisha and the mistress system, lack of employment opportunities and accompanying poverty of women, desire for independence from family and men, and abortion. Abortion has traditionally been practiced as a primary means of birth control. Postwar economic ruin rather than concern for women's rights legalized abortion through the Eugenic Protection Law passed in 1948 and revised in 1949 and 1952. The law permits abortion under certain conditions, including when "for physical or economic reasons, continuation of the pregnancy or delivery would serious damage the

---

*Signed by Japan in 1980 with the promise to amend existing laws to correspond with the convention.

health of the mother." The law also made provision for nationwide contraception counseling offices. In 1955, out of every ten women practicing birth control, seven used abortion and three contraception. By 1965 the seven to three ratio had been reversed.

It is estimated that one million legal and one million illegal abortions occur every year, mainly as a result of contraceptive failure. After the condom, abortion has been the major form of birth control. Japan's powerful medical association has successfully blocked widespread use of the Pill as a method of birth control, making it inaccessible to most Japanese women.

Until quite recently, the public school system has had no program of sex education. This, coupled with a communication gap between generations, means that most youth pick up information on sex from friends and from sexually explicit media. The profusion of comic books, read by all ages of Japanese, portrays sex not as a part of a loving, intimate relationship but as a violent demonstration of power and control of the male over the female. The sex education program recently introduced into junior and senior high-school curricula focuses on anatomy and physiology rather than on attitudes and relationships. The church has not seen sex education as falling within the realm of Christian education.

While tradition has approved only marriage and motherhood as the life pattern for women, a small but growing number of women are making a conscious choice to remain single and, in some cases, to bear children. The divorce rate is rising, but the options available to a divorced woman are limited and there is no comprehensive system of continuing alimony and child-support. Thus many women have no recourse but to endure silently even the most difficult marriages, with the socially sanctioned physical and emotional abuse that exists in them.

Women in the church

From the advent of Christian mission in Japan, women have been drawn to Christianity because of the universality of the message of God's love in Jesus Christ that overcomes all barriers and by Jesus' treatment of women. Large numbers of women have also participated in the church because of the attention that early missionaries gave to Japanese women and girls by establishing women's mission schools and other programs directed to unmet needs of women and children.

Yet as a part of society the church reflects societal attitudes. Most Japanese churches are organized in a vertical pattern, with a male minister at the apex, adult male members in leadership positions at the middle level, and women of the church as the bulk of the pewsitters and servers of tea. In most congregations, the women's organization is the prime fundraiser and supporter of the total church program. Most denominations have regional and national women's organizations, and ecumenically, the NCCJ women's committee actively addressses women's concerns both nationally and internationally.

A recent survey of the Kyodan leadership indicates women represent 15 percent of the total membership of the national executive council, although 75 percent of all Kyodan members are women. The executive committees of the 16 regional districts include 16 women members, down 4 from the previous two-year period. Statistics for women's participation in other denominations would no doubt be similar.

Women ministers have a long, proud history in Japan. The ordination of the first woman clergy among the denominations that became part of the Kyodan took place in 1933. Early missionaries encouraged women graduates of mission schools who dedicated their lives to Christian work. These "Bible women," serving in a variety of roles, prepared the church to accept ordained women clergy. Today, among the 2,072 active ordained and licensed Kyodan clergy, 301 or 15 per cent are women. It is important to note, however, that the majority pastor small churches or serve as associate pastors of churches, often where their husbands are the pastors.

Today all NCCJ member churches except the Anglican Church of Japan recognize the ordination of women. In 1990, that church approved forming a Committee to Promote Women's Ordination.

Within the past five years women pastors have begun holding annual nationwide conferences for study and fellowship, and have joined together to publish collections of their sermons.

Laywomen are beginning to study theology and women's role in the church in local, regional, national, and ecumenical settings. They are re-reading the Bible from a woman's viewpoint and evaluating and re-writing the ritual traditionally used in wedding ceremonies, in light of the sexist bias of the present ritual.

In November 1988, the 25th Kyodan General Assembly approved the establishment of a Special Committee on Gender Discrimination. The committee seeks to establish similar committees at the district level to work toward women's increased participation in leadership positions in the church; assist theological seminaries to deal with gender discrimination issues; and address the issue of women pastors' assignments.

Persons with Disabilities

Drawing by KIMURA Hiroko of Okinawa, who over-comes her handicapping condition of cerebral palsy by holding pencil or paintbrush with toes of her left foot*

MIZUNO Genzo

Father and Mother

I have cerebral palsy; because of me
My mother and my father
Suffered much anguish and doubt.

"Have our ancestors cursed us?
Does the house face in the wrong direction?
Did we give our son an unlucky name?"

When I believed in Christ
The doubts of my father and mother were dispelled
Because they too believed.

On January 2, 1937, a second son was born to the Mizuno family in the small town of Sakaki, Nagano Prefecture. His father named him Genzo, hoping he would grow up as strong and healthy as this popular hero of Japanese history.

Until he was ten, Genzo fulfilled his father's hopes, but that year he became ill when an epidemic of dysentery swept the town, leaving him totally paralyzed, even his voice. He could see, he could hear and he could blink his eyes. Although the doctor initially thought Mizuno had lost his ability to think, his family soon discovered his very lively brain was merely imprisoned inside his helpless body. His mother put the fifty Japanese symbols on the wall and

---

*Ms. Kimura has established hostels, in Yamaguchi Prefecture and on Ie Island, Okinawa, where handicapped and non-handicapped persons can gather to share life and common concerns.

94

pointed to them in turn. When she reached the symbol he needed to communicate his thought, he blinked his eyes. Four volumes of poetry were completed through this laborious process.

For four years the Mizuno home's atmosphere was dark and filled with pain. Superstition and the Buddhist belief in the effect of evil deeds in a previous existence caused his parents to question themselves and neighbors to condemn them. Mizuno lived in a tiny back room with no windows and most townspeople thought he had died.

A local pastor, hearing about Mizuno, went to call on the family. He left a Bible and with it a ray of hope. Mizuno and his mother read the Bible and listened to the Lutheran Hour radio broadcasts together. With his mother writing the answers he dictated, Mizuno completed a Bible correspondence course.

Mizuno found new life in Christ, as did his parents. The biblical story of the man visually handicapped since birth, in which Jesus' disciples ask the question, "Why did this happen?" (John 9:2), helped the Mizuno family in their despair.

Jesus' answer, "It was not that this man sinned, or his parents, but that the works of God might be made manifest in him," seem to be embodied in the Mizuno family. The devotion and help of his mother and sister-in-law made it possible for the world to be enriched by Mizuno's poems of faith during the remaining years of his life and even after his death.

Out of hiding into awareness

Mizuno's poem reflects the traditional view of Japanese society regarding persons with handicapping conditions. Feelings of shame have led families to hide these persons from public view, denying them access to education, employment, and participation in society.

Legislation passed in 1948 made special compulsory education available for students with visual and hearing disabilities. A similar 1973 law, effective in 1979, made compulsory education available to all students with physical and mental disabilities.

Today students with handicapping conditions severe enough to prevent them from participating in ordinary elementary and junior high school classes are provided education in separate classrooms within the same school or at separate schools. These are usually grouped according to the type of disability, such as visual, hearing, speech disorder, other physical disabilities, and mental retardation. As much as possible, students in special classes are incorporated into the total school program, joining other students for sports and cultural activities. In 1986, 95,858 students with disabilities studied in 918 schools; teachers are provided for each two or three students.

The U.N.'s designation of 1981 as the International Year of Disabled Persons, with events held in Japan and overseas to commemorate the year, stimulated public awareness of the rights and potential of the 3.5 million persons in Japan with handicapping conditions.

Christians pioneered also in providing care and opportunities for persons with handicapping conditions. Local and national governments followed their lead in establishing programs to address these needs, often relying on the expertise of Christian social workers to advise and staff government facilities.

Today Japan is attempting to remove barriers to full participation in society. "Not being able to see, or not being able to walk is not what is difficult. Not being able to work in society and play with others is what hurts the most," testifies a sight-impaired member of the Diet, complaining about the common perception that all seeing-impaired Japanese work as masseurs and acupuncture specialists.

The Labor Ministry, committed to ensuring that every person has equal employment opportunities, has achieved passage of a law encouraging companies to hire a prescribed quota of persons with handicapping conditions. Funds accumulated from the financial penalties levied against companies failing to do so are used to make workplaces accessible to all persons.

Access to public transportation continues to be a major barrier to social participation for Japanese with handicapping conditions. Despite Japan's highly developed public transportation system, persons with mobility limitations are severely hindered by steep steps and narrow doorways on buses, trains, and subways; long flights of stairs leading to train and subway platforms; and pedestrian overpasses. In urban areas, musical traffic lights, Braille ticket vending machines, and sidewalks featuring slightly raised pathways are first steps in making independent travel possible for persons with visual disabilities.

The church's response

Although the church has often pioneered in social work, individual churches have been slow to make their facilities physically accessible to persons with handicapping conditions. Because both their available land and financial resources are limited, many small churches have steep flights of steps that can pose automatic barriers to participation in worship and church activities.

When surveys revealed that a rather large number of clergy have handicapping conditions, the Kyodan held the first consultation with handicapped pastors in 1984 to discuss their special needs. As a result, the church pledged to appoint and enable increased participation of handicapped pastors on standing committees.

The question of persons with mental-retardation handicaps receiving baptism was dealt with in the same year, prompting the decision that any person who can make some form of confession of faith may receive baptism.* When such a confession is impossible, the sacrament may still be administered, based on the faith of the church.

In June 1986, a new church was established and a special ministry to persons with handicapping conditions begun in Tokyo by the Rev. AOKI Masaru, himself visually impaired. After becoming a medical doctor and subsequently losing his vision, Aoki was comforted by a story of Jesus' healing a visually handicapped man. He became Christian and entered the ministry. Throughout his 25-year ministry, assisted by his wife, Michiyo, he has worked to enable persons with handicapping conditions to participate in society. The purpose of Aoki's new ministry is to deepen the understanding of church and society regarding persons with handicapping conditions. An ecumenical support group enables Aoki's ministry of addressing congregations, schools, and other groups, and organizing conferences on this theme.

Churches and social work institutions have fostered the volunteer movement to enable persons with disabilties to participate in the community. These groups have also addressed the issue of language sensitivity to avoid use of discriminatory terms.

---

*In the Kyodan and many other denominations, baptism is administered to adults. Parents may choose to have their infants dedicated during a service of worship.

Asian Neighbors

Sketch of Asian woman worker in Japan,
by KISHITA Akiko, member of
Nishi Chiba Church (Kyodan)

Japan's Asian neighbors: Can we come in?

Japan's increasing wealth, the contrasting poverty of some of its Asian neighbors, and Japan's continuing unwillingness to accept "unskilled" migrant labor from other countries, as is clearly stated in the harshly implemented Japanese immigration law, have created a new challenge for both government and caring persons in Japanese society.

The 1980s saw a rapid influx of Asian youth making a desperate attempt to improve their own lives and support their families back home. Four groups of people coming in numbers significant enough to raise public concern are women entertainers, men laborers, farm brides, and "economic refugees." Japanese "war orphans" returning from China and Japanese immigrants returning from South America form another group of people knocking at Japan's door.

Asian women entertainers

Increasing affluence and continuing social tolerance of short-term, extra-marital sexual liaisons are factors that contributed to large numbers of Japanese men visiting neighboring countries on well-organized prostitution tours in the 1970s. Continued protests by women's, Christian, and citizens' groups in the destination countries and in Japan, as well as the shame experienced by the Japanese prime minister who faced demonstrations during a tour of Southeast Asian countries in 1980 curtailed these tours somewhat.

Stage two of Asian women's sexual exploitation occurred as young women from neighboring countries began to be imported to Japan in the early 1980s to work as hostesses, entertainers, and in the prostitution part of Japan's mammoth entertainment-sex industry. Some women are recruited by legal agencies in their home countries, brought to Japan on legal six-month entertainer visas, and placed in clubs throughout Japan to dance, sing, and relate to

Japanese men. They receive monthly salaries ranging from $350 to $1,000 minus travel and other expenses.

A much larger number of women, estimated at between 100,000 and 200,000, work illegally in bars, clubs, hot-spring resorts, and hotel-brothels throughout Japan, entering the country on two-week tourist visas that prohibit work. Most of these women are brought to Japan by *yakuza* (Japan's crime syndicates), which view the women as sources of profit and subject them to inhuman living and working conditions, exploiting them sexually and denying them their basic human rights. The women's illegal status and lack of written contracts and guarantors makes it virtually impossible for them to protest their treatment. When they are arrested or voluntarily surrender to immigration authorities, they undergo harsh investigation and subsequent deportation at their own personal expense. Recruiters and employers have not been subject to penalty, although the newly revised immigration law, approved by the Diet in December 1989 for implementation in June 1990, levies stiff fines and prison terms against both illegal workers and those persons recruiting and employing them.

The Japan Woman's Christian Temperance Union (JWCTU), sensitized by a century of addressing the sexual exploitation of Japanese women, was one early voice protesting this exploitation of Asian women migrant workers. In 1986 House in Emergency of Love and Peace (HELP) Asian Women's Shelter was opened as the JWCTU centennial project. HELP's ministry has grown from a shelter and telephone counseling ministry to include legal aid, public consciousness-raising, and advocacy for change in government attitudes and laws to protect the human rights of Asian women migrant workers. Individual Christians and churches throughout Japan and overseas support HELP as one way to stand in solidarity with their Asian sisters.

Asian men laborers

In 1988, while 81,407 foreign workers were admitted to Japan to engage in such "skilled" jobs as English teacher, entertainer, and cook, 17,157 "unskilled" foreign workers were charged with violating immigration laws and deported. The numbers of those charged with violating immigration laws rose by one-quarter in the first half of 1989.

Of those persons charged with working illegally, 24 percent were Pakistani, 23 percent were Filipino, 18 percent were Bangladeshi, and 14 percent south Korean. The figures for Pakistani and Bangladeshi signify men who come to work at unskilled jobs, such as construction laborers or small factory workers. Illegal workers from the

Philippines and Korea are more evenly divided between women working in the entertainment-sex industry and men working as unskilled laborers.

While Asian women migrant workers suffer extreme sexual exploitation, Asian men migrant laborers endure other forms of human rights violations. Using their life savings or borrowing heavily from friends and family to pay recruiters' commissions, they often discover the promised jobs do not really exist when they arrive in Japan. Men migrant workers are put to work to fill job openings that Japanese laborers refuse to perform, involving long hours, minimal safety precautions and benefits, and sub-standard wages. Often brought to Japan on tourist visas by yakuza labor networks to work illegally, the men workers have no legal recourse for appeal in case of accidents, illness, or non-payment of wages. Thus, like their women counterparts, when found they are rounded up, investigated, and quickly deported.

Although the number of Asian women migrant workers far outnumbered men workers in the early 1980s, the number of male migrant workers has increased sharply in the past few years. The government has responded by increasing its efforts to keep out unskilled foreign labor, upholding the present immigration law, and imposing tighter control through a revised law.

Concerned citizens, including Japanese day laborers, students, and Christians, joined together in 1987 to form Kalabaw kai (Kotobuki* Association in Solidarity with Asian Migrant Workers), which seeks to support the laborers in securing their basic human rights. WATANABE Hidetoshi, Kyodan pastor and Kalabaw kai representative, describes the plight of male migrant workers:

> Why are migrant workers so eager to come to work in Japan? The reason is clear. It is only natural when one day's wage in Japan is equal to one month's in the Philippines.
>
> Why this huge income gap? The reason is also quite clear. All the riches of the migrant worker's country have been brought to Japan. While people in the Philippines, a country of abundant natural resources, are starving, we in Japan—a country poor in natural resources—indulge in gluttony, even throwing away food. Lumber, fish, mineral products, bananas, and coconuts are brought to Japan at a profit; and in return, U.S. and Japanese products, from automobiles and electric appliances to toothpaste, are being sold to Filipinos, again at a profit.
>
> It is only natural that the flow of human beings follows the flow of riches. As "developed" countries have prospered through

*Area between Tokyo and Yokohama.

robbing third-world countries, in return they now have to deal with the problem of "immigrants" appearing on their shores.

If the situation is allowed to continue, wretchedness and injustice will increase, and the resentment of Japan's Asian neighbors will continue to grow, punishing our children as the next generation.

We must guarantee legal status and equal wages for equal work to migrant workers already in Japan. All of the things that Korean residents in Japan have fought for and continue to seek are also necessary for the migrant workers who come as "new immigrants." Securing these rights for them is a responsibility to be shared by all of us who live together in this Japanese archipelago.

Asian brides of Japanese farmers

A recent form of profit through sexual exploitation is the importation of women from other Asian countries as brides of Japanese men unable to find wives in their own country. Because of the economic plight of Japanese agriculture, the demands placed on a young wife in a rural extended family, the isolation from conveniences and from social opportunities, few Japanese women are willing to marry farmers today. Rural men are thus easy prey for private and civic marriage arrangement agencies. Their services include the prospective bridegroom's travel to the prospective bride's country to choose a partner; the engagement and wedding ceremony, a gift to the bride's family, the honeymoon and trip back to Japan—all for a flat fee totalling as much as ¥3,000,000. (U.S. $21,429). Bridal qualifications include unblemished youth, good health, a family situation that will not require financial support, no previous knowledge of Japanese language or experience in Japan (to guarantee she has not worked as an entertainer in Japan), and enough education to make her useful but not "difficult."

In many cases a group tour of men from one rural community visit an Asian country where group marriages are arranged. Some marriages last, despite differences in language, culture, and concepts of marriage. A November 10, 1989, article in the *Mainichi Daily News* reports on unsuccessful marriages:

> A town in Akita Prefecture is to close an international marriage agency following the failure of four marriages between Japanese farmers and Filipina brides, the town mayor announced.
>
> Masuda, a town in a depopulated rural area of the northern prefecture, officially started to promote international marriages

between Japanese farmers and Filipinas when it established an agency called the "Akita International Friendship Association" in April 1987. The mayor reported that the agency succeeded with the cooperation of Cavite City in the Philippines. The marriages ended in divorce owing to the brides' difficulties with their new Japanese families, and the women have since returned to the Philippines.

The go-between service also failed to secure the financial support of the local assembly, which rejected the mayor's request for funds to finance the agency. The assembly said local authorities should avoid involvement in residents' personal affairs.

Japanese Christian women have joined other concerned people in protesting this wholesale buying of strong young women from families in poverty-stricken Asian countries to supply farm labor, to bear offspring, and to care for aging parents in the rural communities of Japan.

"Economic refugees"

Japan has maintained a rather consistent closed-door immigration policy toward political refugees. When Indochinese boat people sought asylum in other countries in the 1970s, the Japanese government was hesitant to accept them until forced by international public opinion to accept 10,000 refugees. Government and privately established facilities, including Catholic church centers, provided language study and vocational training to prepare refugees for new lives in Japan or the country of their final destination.

A new wave of refugees reached Japanese shores when 22 boatloads carrying 2,704 refugees arrived between May and October 1989. Identifying themselves as Vietnamese, the refugees described their goal as "a better life." Further questioning revealed that the majority were not from Vietnam but had boarded the Vietnamese ships when the ships docked in China and picked up new passengers, all of whom had paid out large sums of money to an agent for passage and travel documents. Determining that the refugees' goal in coming to Japan was to seek work and insure "a better life," not for political asylum, the Japanese government announced its policy of distinguishing between "political" and "economic" refugees. Those persons deemed economic refugees would be deported. Stricter screening procedures determined that 1,600 of the 2,700 persons were Chinese "economic refugees," and they were deported and returned to their country.

Asian women migrant workers come as entertainers; Asian men

come as laborers; Asian brides of Japanese farmers come as wives; and the Asian refugee boat people are classified as "economic refugees." The common factor in their coming to Japan is economic poverty, both personal and national, which drives them abroad. It is only natural that they choose nearby, prosperous Japan as the solution to their desperate plight. But Japan, having long been a "*sakoku*" (closed country), finds it difficult to feel responsible for persons beyond its borders and thus has maintained a rigid official policy of refusing entry to all "non-skilled" workers, while increasing somewhat the number of specialists and exchange students granted entry.

Japan's overseas children: Can we come home?

Japanese war orphans in China

Another group of people seeking entry to Japan, considered somewhere between foreign migrant workers and "real" Japanese, are the thousands of children of Japanese military and civilians who were left in China in the mass confusion at the end of the war. Reared, and in some cases adopted, by Chinese families, these "war orphans," now middle-aged members of Chinese society, have come to Japan in government-sponsored groups since 1981 to search for their long-separated families. Many are unable to find their relatives; some who realize their dream of being reunited with family find the adjustment to Japanese society, language, and culture too difficult, and return to China.

"U-turn immigrants"

A second group of Japanese seeking to come home are the "U-turn immigrants," those persons who went to South America during Japan's lean pre- or post-war years in search of employment and a new life. Today second- and third-generation Japanese immigrants, faced with economic and political instability in the countries to which they or their families emigrated, are returning to Japan in search of work to support their families in South America. They are demanding that they receive the same treatment and benefits as other Japanese, rather than being categorized as foreign migrant workers.

A bitter reality is that while Japanese emigrants were received by other countries in the past, today Japan closes its doors to needy immigrants. Christians and other concerned citizens are calling on Japan to realize that real "internationalization," a much-touted term in Japan today, is not founded on a one-sided concern for only one nation's interests.

Outside the Group, American Style

The wood carving referred to in "My World War II."

NOGAMI Yukiye

My World War II

My daughter ran breathlessly into the house, a library book under her arm. Bubbling with excitement she turned to a photo of an exquisite carved wood bas-relief. "Look! It's Grandpa's (TANAKA Iwazo) work—and the art work of other Japanese-Americans, too!" I stared at the photo of the carving, patterned after traditional Chinese scrolls, that my father had painstakingly created while in the re-location camp in the early 1940s.

Memories of the war years welled up inside me. I remembered being in church on December 7, 1941. Most Japanese-American communities had both a Buddhist temple and a Christian church, but our Yamato Colony* had no temple, only a Methodist church, probably because some of the early immigrants in our neighbor-hood had attended Christian schools in Japan.

That Sunday a German-American man came to our church to re-assure us Japanese-Americans that we had nothing to worry about. Our relief was short-lived, however, for almost immediately we were placed under a curfew by the government, and our movements were limited to a five-mile radius from our homes. Rumors of Nisei (second-generation Japanese-American) sabotage and the efforts of economic pressure groups to drive all Japanese-Americans out

---

*A community in California. The name was chosen because 1) Yamato is an ancient name for Japan; 2) Yams (sweet potatoes) were grown there and the near by town was Atwater; and 3) the community's founders in 1910 wanted a name that would not further exacerbate the current anti-Japanese feelings.

of California paved the way for the relocation process. By March 1942 our family was informed that we must leave our farm. It was sold and our personal belongings were stored in a government ware-house. In May we were sent to Merced Assembly Center where we spent the hot summer in tar-papered buildings with crude latrines that offered little privacy. Our daily fare consisted of pork-and-beans and jello. How I missed rice and fresh fruit and vegetables!

In September our family was sent to Amache Relocation Camp in southeastern Colorado. The drawn window shades of the old railway cars in which we rode prevented us from knowing where we were going. Our train stopped often for oncoming trains, making our journey seem to last forever.

Construction of Amache Relocation Camp was not yet complete when we arrived. Home for our family of 6 was a 20 by 24-foot room featuring a brick floor laid on top of the dirt, one small window, and a pot-bellied stove. Dry desert winds blew sand through cracks in the walls. In winter how we wished that the latrines were not located in a separate building with the laundry room and showers. The mess halls could not accommodate everyone at the same time, so we ate in shifts. Adequate food for infants and young children was unavailable most of the time. As concern for health grew, a hospital was finally constructed, but medical supples were meager and personnel few.

All camp labor was performed by internees, with each department headed by a Caucasian. Our wage scale, $19 a month maximum, seemed pitifully small. As the war continued, many men and boys in camp worked for local farmers whose farmhands had been drafted, helping harvest sugar beets and melon. Later I realized that much of the produce would never have been harvested had it not been for internee labor.

Communication with the outside world was infrequent. We didn't write to friends because our mail was censored. Church groups were supportive, although we gradually realized that many church people did not even know about our internment. How happy we were when boxes of books arrived from the Quakers, who eventually even set up a scholarship program for college-age internees. Their support continued both throughout our internment and after we were released from camp, when they helped with our relocation. They comforted people attacked and abused by fellow Americans who called us "Japs," believing somehow that we were the enemy. Some of my best friends in California called us names and favored the relocation camps. As American citizens we Nisei could not understand why our loyalty to the United States was questioned just because of our physical appearance.

After a year in camp, when my loyalty was cleared, I was offered a position with the U.S. Civil Service in Washington, D.C. I remember walking into the office to which I was assigned and discovering FBI reports and rolls from dictaphone cylinders on interned Japanese-Americans on file there. There was nothing incriminating, only inconsequential information such as "This person was seen walking past the Japanese Embassy on such-and-such a day." Later I heard that such flimsy evidence was sometimes used against us internees.

After work, I volunteered at a USO which served the 442nd combat team replacements coming through Washington, D.C. So many 442nd Nisei appeared every Saturday night that the regular USO couldn't accommodate them, and an additional one was built. Later I had mixed feelings when I heard that Nisei composing the 442nd Combat Infantry Regiment were awarded the highest proportion of purple hearts of any outfit in the U.S. Army. I was deeply proud of my heritage, of the people of Yamato Colony who had turned California's San Joaquin Valley into a garden spot, and the men who had fought so bravely for their country. Yet I was also wounded and deeply angered by America's callous treatment of Japanese-Americans. When my parents and my brothers who returned from the war went back to California from Amache Relocation Camp to reclaim their stored possessions, they found nothing left, nothing at all. I vowed, "Never again. Never again will I be a part of letting this kind of thing happen!"

Executive Order 9066, signed into effect by President Franklin Delano Roosevelt on February 19, 1942, two-and-a-half months after Japan's bombing of Pearl Harbor, uprooted 110,000 Americans of Japanese ancestry from their homes on the West Coast, deported some, and put others in internment camps in remote parts of the country between 1942 and 1946. Lives of Canadians of Japanese ancestry were similarly disrupted by detention and deportation between December 1941 and March 1949. These acts were the culmination of discrimination against Asian-Americans, which had begun early in the twentieth century.

Petitions for redress of grievances including loss of income, land and other personal property, defamation of character, charges of sabotage, and questioning of personal loyalty to country have resulted in the United States government agreeing to pay $20,000 per person and the Canadian government $21,000 per person as compensation for suffering inflicted during World War II.

Part Four

Japan's Role in the World Today

DAI-YON
Part Four

第
四

SEKAI
world

世
界

NIOKERU
in

に
お
け
る

NIHON
Japan

日
本

Trade

BOEKI
trade

Friction occurs when you rub things together. The closer the two countries become, the more friction will be felt. Things have gotten worse because Japan has become independent . . . . Now is the time for the second Meiji Restoration, the time to open the country.

MORITA Akio, chairman, Sony Corporation

The current Japanese-American bickering over a trade imbalance is serving no good purpose . . . . There is a wide range of American and other goods of foreign brands such as Del Monte and McCormick on Japanese shop shelves . . . . Del Monte tomato juice, although sold under an American brand name, may have been made from tomatoes produced in Japan or Taiwan and is distributed by a Japan-based corporation. "Seven Eleven" is no longer an American chain store but is a Japanese corporation run by Japanese.

It is no longer appropriate to identify commodities and their producers by nationalities. It would be ridiculous to discuss whether the Honda in Ohio is Japanese or American and whether Japan IBM is Japanese or American . . . . Statistics show that foreign corporations control 12 percent of Japan's GNP, and that American firms are by far at the top of the list. U.S.-affiliated corporations' activities are, however, not necessarily reflected in the U.S. government's trade statistics, because some of them manufacture their goods in Japan, Korea, Indonesia, or Taiwan and sell them on the Japanese market.

In this economic world today, corporations, consumers, and investment know no national boundaries. It would be anachronistic to measure international economy by country-by-country statistics alone. There is no sense in carrying on government-level negotiations on trade problems on the basis of such statistics, which do not reflect the economic realities.

OHMAE Kenichi, Management consultant and economic critic*
(Quoted in Mainichi Daily News, *May 6, 1990)*

From beneficiary to partner

Economic relations are Japan's No. 1 problem in international relations today. Why are mutual understanding and cooperation between Japan and its trade partners so difficult to achieve? Why are tensions especially high between Japan and its longtime trade and mutual-security partner, the U.S.?

Japan and the U.S. are industrialized nations operating within the first-world capitalist-democratic bloc as major economic powers. Does this mean that they have common goals and operate by similar principles to achieve these goals and move ahead together? Not necessarily, for the two countries' perceptions and methods differ.

As the acknowledged leader of the Western bloc in the postwar era, the U.S. operated under a policy that sought to rebuild its own economy and the economies of the war-devastated countries of Europe through the Marshall Plan. It also extended generous support to Japan in order to rebuild that war-torn country. U.S. postwar policy served to assure a market for American exports, and to that end, it was successful. At times, this policy involved short-term sacrifices and setbacks in U.S. economic prosperity in order to achieve long-range global economic stability.

Most Japanese, especially those who experienced suffering in World War II, quickly acknowledge their indebtedness to the U.S. for the enormous outpouring of care they received immediately after the cessation of hostilities. The U.S. set Japan back on its feet and set those feet on the path leading to recovery and prosperity. Japan was able to concentrate on rebuilding its economy thanks to its new Peace Constitution and to the Japan-U.S. Security Treaty, both products of the U.S. occupation. These documents forbade Japan to re-arm and provided it protection under the U.S. defense umbrella.

Thanks to the generous assistance of the U.S., the Japanese government's drive to achieve economic stability, and the cooperation of well-educated, industrious citizens, Japan achieved a remarkable recovery of its economy and its self-confidence. As a result, the Japan-U.S. economic relationship has shifted dramatically from bene-

---

*OHMAE is author of *Beyond National Borders* (Homewood, Ill.: Dow Jones Irwin, 1987; paperback edition by Kodansha International Ltd., 1988).

ficiary and benefactor to equal economic partnership in which each competes with and undergirds the other. Their economies, the two largest in the world, together account for 40 percent of the world's GNP.

Different approaches to economic policy

In order to continue operating as economic partners, governments and citizens in the two countries must understand the basic economic guidelines by which each country operates. Each needs to be aware of the other country's efforts to improve the health of the economic alliance and to avoid blaming the other for its own economic ills. Growing isolationist and protectionist sentiments in the U.S. and rising neonationalist sentiments in Japan feed on each other. These interests, served by increasing economic friction, have not encouraged objective reporting of actual improvements resulting from accommodations made by each side.

Recently, some U.S. analysts have claimed that Japan is unable to change its international trade practices. In reality, Japan's trade surplus decreased by 1 percent between 1985 and 1989. Japan's imports increased 40 percent annually between 1986 and 1989, bringing the per capita import level up to that of the U.S. Most barriers blocking imports or foreign companies' entry into Japan have also been removed since 1980. A key factor in this new opening of Japan has been the increasingly independent stance taken by major Japanese companies regarding government control of the economy.

The Structural Impediment Initiative (SII) talks between Japan and the U.S, opening in 1989, have provided opportunities to make adjustments necessary to correct the economic imbalance between the two countries. Because the tendency in these bilateral talks is for the U.S. to attempt to maintain control over Japan and for Japan to make concessions only to pacify the U.S., more important to the global economy is Japanese and U.S. participation in the multilateral General Agreement on Tariff and Trade (GATT).

To understand Japan it is important to realize that, unlike most other world powers, Japan does not have a clearly defined foreign policy that governs its international relations. Following the debacle that resulted from its grandiose attempt to achieve international leadership through military aggression, Japan determined that any future world role it might play would be economic, not military or political.

Japan's well-worked out economic policy determines its international relations and national security. This economic policy has been carried out successfully because of the alliance between government and corporate business and the cooperation of Japanese citizens. This three-way partnership has made available to the government the financial resources essential for competing effectively on the world market. Citizens' savings, averaging one-fifth of monthly income, are available for government investment or stimulation of the economy. The savings rate has dropped, from 23 percent in 1978 to 18 percent in 1988, because the population is aging and pension and welfare benefits have increased.

Pragmatism, principles, and protectionism

The one government economic program that has not been immediately successful is Japan's recent proposal to encourage consumer spending, including increased purchasing of imported items, as a way to stimulate the economy and reduce the huge trade surplus. Astronomically high land prices make it impossible for many Japanese to own their own homes today. Costs of affordable housing and high retail prices limit purchasing power. Japanese are eagerly taking advantage of overseas travel and shopping, reasonable in comparison with prices at home.

Superficial Westernization in Japan leads other countries to perceive it as a first-world nation that operates on Western democratic principles. Not only is this perception not true; it is also the grounds for misunderstanding and tensions in trade relationships. The U.S. and other Western nations operate on the basis of certain "universal" principles, even though they do not always adhere to them. In contrast, Japan operates on the principle of pragmatism, that is, "what works." This approach makes it difficult for Japanese to understand how the U.S. can have a clear foreign policy and yet lack an integrated economic policy. It also makes it difficult for Japan to grasp why Americans tolerate shoddy workmanship, focus on short-term profits, allow unlimited consumer credit spending, and fail to address the problem of a poorly educated workforce.

Another operative Japanese principle has been vertical, lifetime loyalty to the immediate superior or group. This group loyalty extends to the company or the nation and protects powerful economic constituencies that make major political contributions. For example, loyalty to the rice and citrus growers' associations has blocked food imports in these categories. Loyalty to the construction industry, which has a system of closed bidding, has made it difficult for non-Japanese companies to enter the construction market. Loyalty to the health professions and pharmaceutical industry has prevented liberalization of health care.

Japanese pragmatism has led not only to protection of the domestic market but also to expansion overseas. More favorable business conditions in other Asian countries and in North America—lower land prices and operating costs and less costly labor forces—have encouraged Japanese corporations to set up companies according to their own model in those countries as well as to purchase already existing companies.

An increase in the number of Japanese companies and the amount of Japanese investment in the U.S. has benefitted the U.S. as well as Japan. Burdened with a massive trade and budget deficit, the U.S. economy has been strengthened by the jobs Japanese companies provide, the increase in the tax base, and the introduction of new technology and management styles into American society.

Japan's rapid rise to economic power has not always been accompanied by awareness of the effects its success has on other nations. Neither has it made Japan willing to curtail economic expansion and accept responsibility for the global economy by extending support to developing third-world countries. Continued pressures from both first- and third-world countries are forcing Japan to recognize that world leadership includes global economic responsibility.

Japan has benefitted greatly from the international free-trade system. It is belatedly pledging itself to paying its dues as a world leader by becoming an "importing super power," opening its markets to foreign goods. Realizing the vital role of interdependence among nations in determining global economic stability has forced Japan to begin to assume a share of the global economic burden.

Official
Development
Assistance

KAIGAI
overseas

海外

ENJO
assistance

援助

Japan and Thailand will cooperate in the field of environmental protection by building a research and training center in Thailand in 1991. Japan will provide facilities and technical know-how for dealing with pollution. It will be the first use of Japanese governmental aid for environmental protection.

Mainichi Daily News, *April 8, 1990*

The Out-Patient Department of the Philippine General Hospital in Manila was built as a Japanese grant project. Even though the expected patients are from the poor sector of the society, the inside of the building is decorated with a chandelier like a five-star hotel. There are not enough engineers who can work the computer system and sophisticated medical equipment. The Philippine government has to pay a huge amount of money (70 percent of the total budget of National University of the Philippines) for its maintenance and management.

Eduardo C. Tadem, University of the Philippines

Reparations, loans, and grants

Japan's first official development assistance (ODA), granted in 1954, took the form of war reparations grants to compensate for Japanese military invasion of Southeast Asian countries in World War II. These grants also opened export markets for Japan and established economic ties with Southeast Asian countries.

From the mid-1960s, a period of Japanese high economic growth, overseas aid was expanded to include bilateral loans, primarily to other Asian countries. Japan also attained economic leadership in Asia through hosting economic development conferences and taking the lead in establishing the Asian Development Bank.

In the 1970s, grants decreased once war reparations payments were completed, bilateral loans were continued, and contributions to international aid agencies and technical cooperation increased. Recipients of Japanese aid now included not only Asia, but Africa, Latin America, and the Middle East as well. The 1973 oil crisis influenced Japan's ODA policy because Japan depends on importing natural resources to survive as an industrial nation.

During the U.S. economic decline during the 1970s, Japan assumed a share of U.S. bilateral loans to third-world nations and contributions to international agencies. Japanese ODA also began to involve more people—receiving trainees from other countries and sending Japanese technical experts and volunteers abroad. One example is Japan's version of the Peace Corps, the Japan Overseas Cooperation Volunteer Program. Established in 1965 to provide technical services and instruction to developing countries, the program sent 3,582 volunteers overseas between 1965 and 1981. Volunteers serve two years on a subsistence living allowance, working as a member of the host country's government. Recruitment of volunteers and their re-entry to Japanese society is inhibited by Japan's lifetime employment system.

Since the late 1970s, Japan's ODA has increased steadily. In 1989 Japan became the world's top aid contributor, in part because other countries decreased their contributions. Japan's ODA giving totalled U.S. $5.6 billion in 1986, $7.6 billion in 1987, $10 billion in 1988, $11.4 billion (projected) in 1989 (U.S. giving for 1989 was projected at $8.3 billion). Yet this increase still falls for short of the international target goal of 0.7 of a country's GNP; in 1987 it was only 0.31 percent.

Today the three categories of Japanese ODA—loans, grants in aid and technical cooperation, and contributions to international agencies—are approximately equal in funding. A huge trade surplus and international pressure have encouraged Japan to increase its total ODA contributions. These, together with defense expenditures, have steadily increased, despite government cutbacks in most other areas. (Projected defense spending for 1990 will increase 6.35 percent and ODA, 9.4 percent, while the overall budget increase will be 3 percent.)

Does assistance develop or control?

While few people criticize Japan's increased ODA contributions, many question the use and administration of that aid, calling for closer monitoring and greater accountability.

The toppling of the Marcos regime in the Philippines in 1986 was accompanied by charges in Japan of gross misuse of ODA funds.

Critics accused Japanese companies of profiting from ODA, together with persons in high levels of Philippine society. Critics further declare that most aid never actually reaches grassroots poverty levels but instead benefits only the wealthy and widens the economic gap between rich and poor. ODA is said to be used in some cases by oppressive regimes to suppress their people.

Critics also claim that Japan has not dealt seriously with the real purposes of ODA: alleviation of third-world poverty; empowerment of persons restrained economically, politically, and socially; and equalization of the North-South economic imbalance. Many see Japanese ODA tied to Japan's economic interests rather than the recipient country's needs and the voices of the people there. Thus, aid often takes the form of capital-intensive projects requiring expensive equipment purchased in Japan, which the recipient country cannot manage nor maintain after the project is built. An example is the 150-ton fish storage freezer installed in 1986 on Majuro in the Marshall Island group; it has remained almost empty but must be maintained at Majuro's expense.

It is natural that Japanese ODA has focused on Asia, but other countries see this as Japan's attempt to dominate the region both economically and politically, while neglecting critical needs in other third-world countries. In 1989 Japanese ODA funds went for the first time to Eastern Europe, for economic reform in Poland and Hungary.

Only since the late 1970s has Japan's development aid been directed openly for political purposes. With its military role strictly limited, Japan has sought to achieve national and regional security by building a sound economy at home and contributing toward a sound international economic order. To that end, Japan's commitment to double its ODA contributions for the period from 1988 to 1992 is intended to use strategic assistance to shape policy in recipient countries in order to maintain the present Western bloc.

Other forms of ODA include recycling an initial $30 billion trade surplus to international development institutions for the debt crises of developing countries. Japan has also committed funds over the next five years to joint projects in the Philippines and Indonesia to develop technology to cope with deforestation, a condition some claim is partly caused by Japan.

What kind of contributions?

A major borrower from the World Bank in the 1960s, Japan's status as a major creditor nation in the 1980s has produced problems. A small foreign aid staff and the number of government agencies controlling ODA slow the actual distribution of funds. One proposed solution is joint ventures that combine Japanese capital with U.S. expertise. Tensions may arise because the two countries' aid philosophies and regional commitments are different. One example of such cooperation is the Philippine Assistance Plan initiated by the U.S. in 1988 to channel additional foreign aid into the Philippines. However, some Filipinos view the plan as tied to the issue of renewal of leases for U.S. military bases in the Philippines .

Increased contributions to such multilateral agencies as the World Bank and the International Monetary Fund entitle Japan to an increased share in decision-making, which may threaten other donor members' authority. Japan has not had staff to contribute to such agencies because there are not enough experts in this area and those who are qualified are often not willing to step off the career escalator at home.

Today Japanese government ODA contributions are increasing rapidly, but greater private sector involvement in assistance to third-world countries is needed. Japan also can make a valuable contribution in setting ODA policy, because Japan itself was an aid recipient during its own recent development experience. The aspirations of countries currently receiving ODA are expressed by Eduardo C. Tadem of the Philippines:

> To achieve its avowed goals of benefitting the poorest of the poor, ODA must ideally be redirected to projects that will create the conditions for self-generating and self-propelled development dependent mainly on local resources and tapping Filipino expertise. In order to benefit the host population, ODA must make itself eventually unnecessary. Infrastructure development must concentrate on affordable and small-scale to medium-scale projects that will not strain the financial capabilities of government and the people nor destroy the environment. . . .

> It is, of course, wishful thinking to expect major ODA givers like the United States and Japan, who have long been used to promoting their national interests in the guise of "development aid" and "mutual security treaties" to suddenly execute an about-face and stand their present strategy on its head. Given that, the only hope lies in people-to-people exchanges and international solidarity networking to exert pressure on governments to heed the demands of the greater number of peoples for a more humane and just national and global order.

Militarization

GUNBI
*militarization,
armaments*

TAIRA Osamu

An *Okinawa Times* reporter once said that Okinawa's 1,200,000 inhabitants are all on the "list of the dead." If nuclear war came, we would be the first to go. I speak as one who lives in such a place.

The Rev. KINJO Shigeaki, a friend of mine, tells the experience of killing his family during the Battle of Okinawa when he was sixteen years old. We were all taught at that time that it would be shameful for a Japanese to fall into enemy hands. Death, we believed, would be much better. We also thought we would be treated like animals if taken captive. So when young Kinjo and his brother were pressured to kill their mother and siblings to prevent their capture, they did it, believing it was done out of love. They thought the more you love, the more willingly you would consent to kill those you love. So out of love they beat them to death.

But the opposite is true. War is the destruction of morals and ethics. It destroys the humanity of men and women.

Christ enjoined us to love our enemy. By that, he did not mean that to hate the enemy was the true order of things and to love our enemy was the exceptional thing to do. It is the other way around. When we presume we have an enemy, we need to ask ourselves again, is that person really an enemy? Love is the effort to understand the other, to put oneself in the other person's position, to know that person's desires and anxieties. When we look at it that way, we discover not an enemy, but a person for whom Christ died, the one for whom God sent his son. Now we can move past all talk of enemy and ally. That person is neither enemy nor ally, but as human as we are and loved of God as we are.

When we view one another as an enemy, we seek to destroy, to exclude. The reconciliation of Christ, on the other hand, is inclusive. It even includes our "enemy."

117

Just as God used Cyrus of Persia, a non-believer, to deliver the Jews, so God used Japan, a non-Christian nation, bestowing on it the Peace Constitution, in order to show God's will for peace in concrete form.   This should shame and judge so-called Christian nations. I hope that the United States can really stand on the gospel and, instead of waiting ready to retaliate, can take the first step. I hope the U.S. will take the lead, not in an arms-building race, but in an arms-reduction race. I hope it will lead in a peace race.

Some persons say that 1945 was "Year One of the Atomic Era." Atomic weapons have split history. They have brought a new age into being that is unlike any previous one. The day of human enemies has passed. In the nuclear age, the weapon itself has become the enemy. It has forced on us the unprecedented choice of mutual existence or mutual extinction. It is vital to understand this.

The post-World War II economic recovery of Japan is spoken of as a miracle. Japan has become an economic giant. The greatest reason for this is that Japan has held military expenditures to around one percent of its GNP. If we turn this around, we can see what a great burden military expenses are to a national economy.

Some persons are fond of saying that Japan's economic recovery has been made possible by the U.S.-Japan Security Treaty. This is not the case. The growth and the surplus that Japan today enjoys relate to the low military budget.

God loves us all, so we love one another. Christians must stand up against war, which kills the persons God loves so much. To say "No" to war is the Christian's blessed duty. We are peacemakers.

Taira Osamu serves in The Kyodan as pastor of the Sashiki church and moderator of the Okinawa district.

U.S. military presence and Japan's role

No other issue related to Japan's international role today is more troubling than the question of defense and military presence. The Japanese government finds itself caught on the horns of the dilemma of whether or not to rearm, and if so, to what degree. Opposition to rearmament and increased defense spending is expressed on many sides. Chapter II of the Constitution states:

Article 9. Aspiring sincerely to an international peace based on justice and order, the Japanese people forever renounce war as a sovereign right of the nation and the threat or use of force as a means of settling international disputes.

2. In order to accomplish the aim of the preceding paragraph, land, sea, and air forces, as well as other war potential, will never be maintained. The right of belligerency of the state will not be recognized.

The sentiments of most Japanese are strongly against military buildup and increased defense spending. Japan's Asian neighbors live in constant fear of Japan's revival as a military power.

Those people in Japan calling for Japan's rearmament are: 1) ruling Liberal-Democratic party conservatives; 2) arms producers; 3) U.S. Defense Department officials and Japan Self-Defense Forces personnel; and 4) diehard militarists (who fund right-wing sound trucks bedecked with military flags and blaring World War II march music, which speed along the streets appealing for the reclaiming of Japan's "purity" and past glory).

One of these rightists shot MOTOSHIMA Hitoshi, third-generation Catholic Christian and mayor of Nagasaki, on January 18, 1990, because of the mayor's response in a December 1988 city council meeting that "Emperor Hirohito shares responsibility for the war, as well as all of us who lived in that period." After this event the National Police Agency reported that 840 right-wing groups, with 120,000 members, exist in Japan.

The major voice pressuring Japan to increase its defense spending and military role is, ironically enough, the same U.S. government that only forty-five years ago stripped Japan of all military potential and bestowed on the vanquished nation a Constitution forbidding Japan to ever again become a military power.

The 1960 United States-Japan Security Treaty states that "For the purpose of contributing to the security of Japan and the maintenance of international peace and security in the Far East, the United States of America is granted the use by its land, air, and naval forces of facilities and areas in Japan," and that "The use of these facilities and areas as well as the status of United States armed forces in Japan shall be governed by a separate agreement" (the Agreement on the Status of U.S. Armed Forces, which replaced the 1952 San Francisco Security Treaty).

Today the U.S. has 17 military bases in Japan (some bases contain several major facilities) and 65,000 armed forces personnel. At present, Japan pays 40 percent of the U.S. armed forces bill in Japan, contributing U.S. $2.7 billion of the total $6.2 billion needed annually to keep U.S. forces in Japan. Japan's share represents $45,000 per military personnel, the highest percentage paid by any country in which U.S. forces are based. Nevertheless, in 1989 both houses of the U.S. Congress called on Japan to bear all costs related to U.S. military presence in Japan except salaries. Responding to previous U.S. demands to bear a larger share of U.S. defense costs, Japan has, since 1978, appropriated additional funding. In a special agreement to the Security Treaty, Japan pledges to be responsible for pensions and other compensation for Japanese civilians working on U.S. military bases from 1991 on. But Japan now declares that no further increase toward the cost of maintaining U.S. military personnel can be made without revising the Agreement on the Status of U.S. Armed Forces in Japan.

U.S. demands concerning the "defense burden" have increased in direct proportion to economic friction between the two countries, with some Americans declaring that "Japan is enjoying a free ride." Another point of view is that U.S. military bases in Japan form part of U.S. military strategy for the Far East and, as such, do not always necessarily serve Japan's best interests.

Japan Self-Defense Forces (SDF)

In addition to supporting U.S. military forces stationed in Japan, Japan's own 270,000-person Self-Defense Forces represent a major item in Japan's annual budget, one of the few items that continues to increase each year.

The 1989 defense allocation, 3.91 trillion yen, up almost 6 percent over the previous year, represents 1.006 percent of Japan's Gross National Product (GNP). Until 1987 Japan maintained a policy of holding defense spending below 1 percent of the GNP; even so, the constantly increasing GNP allowed defense spending to increase with no major opposition. Although defense spending is such a small percent of GNP and is specified as only for Japan's self-defense, the amounts rank Japan number three in the world after the U.S. and the USSR.

The Japanese Defense Agency announced a 4.168 trillion yen (U.S. $29.77 billion) proposed budget for 1990. This defense budget (up another 6 percent from 1989) is the first to surpass 4 trillion yen. Reasons given for the rise are increases in the cost of crude oil and the depreciation of the yen. The budget includes 35 billion yen for joint U.S.-Japan development of the FSX support fighter plane, and military hardware purchases from the U.S. and other countries, all of which help correct Japan's huge trade imbalance.

Despite recent developments toward U.S.-Soviet detente, including negotiations on disarmament and arms control, both Japanese and U.S. leaders declare that Japan needs to continue its defense capability buildup. When he reviewed the Maritime Self-Defense

Forces on November 4, 1989, Prime Minister Kaifu stated: "The international situation remains confusing and fluid, and it is our job to make our national defense unshakable." Japan is strengthening its defenses on the northern island of Hokkaido, considered by defense strategists to be a potential target for Soviet invasion. A postwar source of contention between Japan and the USSR are four small islands between Hokkaido and the USSR. They have been under USSR control since 1945, and Japan wants them returned.

Troublesome defense questions facing Japan today include: whether Japan's SDF should be allowed to participate in joint U.S. military drills outside Japan; whether the SDF should be sent overseas to engage in peacekeeping missions or to give humanitarian aid; and whether the SDF should be used to escort ships transporting plutonium from other countries to Japan. The present government trend is to establish clearly that all these activities fall within the definition of a purely defensive military force.

While U.S. and Japanese leaders engage in dialogue about defense-burden sharing, citizens' groups continue to appeal for land presently used by military forces to be returned to the original owners. Such appeals are particularly strong in areas with a heavy military presence, such as Okinawa, where U.S. military and Japan SDF installations occupy 26 percent of the total land area. This presence produces serious social problems and frequent military accidents, which inflict property damage, injury, and loss of life on the community.

Peacemaking

HEIWA
peace

HASHIMOTO Eiichi

Hiroshima served as a base for the Japanese invasion of the Asian continent. From 1936 the city's military character was strengthened as Japan opened war on China.

Even our Christian schools were forced to display and pay homage to the emperor's photograph. Activities of foreign missionaries were restricted; they were followed even when taking walks. The eight missionaries at our Hiroshima Jogakuin (girls' school) reluctantly left for their home country in June 1941.

Our school's plan to build and move into a new facility on the Seto Inland Sea was blocked by the army "in order to prevent spy activity." Rightists harassed our school's public meetings and our students by throwing stones. Eventually our enrollment dwindled to half.

The Pacific War brought further oppression. Our key Christian teachers were subjected to religious harassment: "Who is lord, Christ or the emperor?" Even students were interrogated about the content of sermons preached at school. Then, as the war situation worsened, our students were mobilized for compulsory work in munitions plants. To counter the false charge that ours was a "spy school," they worked harder than students mobilized from other schools, until the atomic bomb reduced everything to ashes.

On that August day, the teachers and students of the college were mobilized for factory work; the high school girls assembled for demolition work to clear a wide firebreak in the city's center. That day began with morning worship, and then the bomb exploded—324 students died instantly.

Three months later when school resumed, only 80 students appeared at the opening ceremony, bandages on their heads, arms and legs. They were a pitiful sight.

We began reconstruction of our school with the appeal, *"The tragedy of the atomic bomb must never be repeated,"* but it took twenty-five years for this concern to evolve from an expression of individual teachers to the platform of the total faculty. Occupation censorship of all A-bomb matters excluded them from our educational program. Surviving students, having seen their own parents, brothers, and sisters die in the bombing, instinctively opposed nuclear weapons. A nationwide antinuclear movement arose in response to the March 1954 American H-bomb test on Bikini Atoll, which contaminated 23 Japanese fishermen. This issue also was taken up only by individual teachers. Antinuclear appeals to the entire student body did not occur until 1969, when three of our teachers joined the Peace Mission to the USA and the USSR. When the Kyodan founded the Seireien home for aged A-bomb victims and other elderly persons in Hiroshima as a concrete expression of the 1967 Confession of War Responsibility During World War II, many of our students became active in fund raising and other volunteer services there.

Peace education became an integral part of our school's program in 1970. In 1973 the school teachers' union peace education committee produced a testimonial record of the school's A-bomb experience, *Natsugumo* (Summer Cloud), for use with students. This book was later translated into English to communicate the Hiroshima experience internationally.

Christian education for the present age has been long discussed. With our school suffering particularly tragic experiences, we have to take seriously what form Christian education will take at our school. We forego abstract, idealistic, and sentimental forms in favor of practical expressions of Christ's love in daily life. For us this means education for peace, for solidarity with oppressed minorities, and for international understanding.

Our junior-high peace education curriculum focuses on gaining specific, scientific understanding of A-bomb damage and its effects on human life. First-year students gather A-bomb testimonies from family members and neighbors, which are presented with folded-paper cranes at the annual memorial ceremony for our school's A-bomb victims. Second-year students view the antinuclear film *Prophecy* and solicit contributions to purchase more U.S. documentary footage. Comparison of Hiroshima and Nagasaki experiences by third-year students climaxes with a study tour to Nagasaki.

Students in the high-school peace studies curriculum give guided tours of peace monuments to student groups visiting Hiroshima from other parts of Japan and overseas. In preparation, students visit the various momuments and produce explanatory materials.

Today Hiroshima boasts a lovely 100-meter-wide thoroughfare called Peace Boulevard where, in wartime, mobilized students created a firebreak. On August 6, 1945, close to 10,000 of these students were killed by the bomb, our school's victims among them.

After experiencing the explosion myself, I made my way to the army quarantine station on an offshore island, where I saw two middle-school boys die during a night of excruciating pain. I was baptized on Easter Day two years later and became a teacher at Hiroshima Jogakuin in 1948.

As school principal, the daily life I now share with students cannot be separated from the horrible experience of Hiroshima. We must not forget our students who died working so hard in war factories to erase the stigma of attending a "spy school."

"Blessed are the peacemakers, for they shall be called the children of God." This gospel of peace is our source of strength and vision today; our task is to put it into practice each day.

Nuclear Day One and after

If you ask a Japanese person, "What is the origin of Japan's peace movement?" the answer will not vary.

"Hiroshima—August 6, 1945! Oh yes, and there was Nagasaki a few days later, on August 9. And then we heard the emperor's voice over the radio on August 15, telling us that the war was over. We couldn't fully understand the meaning of his formal speech. Nor could we fully grasp its implications for our lives."

If the person you asked experienced the war or is a student of history, he or she would acknowledge that while Japan initiated hostilities against the U.S. at Pearl Harbor in 1941, imperialistic aggression actually began earlier with the colonization of Taiwan in 1895, Korea in 1910, and the peremptory attack in Manchuria in 1931.

Nevertheless, Hiroshima is "Day One," the starting point from which forty-five years later all peacemaking is still chronicled, and the event that gives voice to the clarion cry, "Never again!" Japanese peacemakers continue to see their task as helping the world to understand the horrors of nuclear war.

If Day One is Hiroshima, then Day Two is March 1, 1954, when the U.S. conducted an H-bomb test on tiny Bikini Atoll in the Pacific. The resulting radioactive fall-out landed on 239 Bikini islanders and 28 American observers. It also rained "ashes of death" on 23 crewmembers of a Japanese tuna trawler, contaminating both crew and catch. After the boat returned to Japan, one of the crew died of radiation sickness. Shock over this new confrontation with nuclear radiation sparked a nationwide protest against nuclear weapons and resulted in the first World Conference Against Atomic and Hydrogen Bombs, held in Hiroshima on the tenth anniversary of the dropping of the bomb. The 30,000 participants included 54 people from 12 overseas countries. This event gave birth to the nationwide Japan Council Against Atomic and Hydrogen Bombs, composed of citizens' movements, religious groups, labor unions, and political parties. Subsequent observances have taken place annually.

As the major powers continued to engage in nuclear weapon testing, concern over the increase in global radiation levels led the U.S., Great Britain, and the USSR to sign the Limited Nuclear Test-Ban Treaty in 1963. Although Japan joined the rest of the world in welcoming this restraint on nuclear testing, divisions of opinion within the Japanese peace movement arose regarding which countries should be restricted, leading to the movement's splintering along communist and socialist lines. The more conservative groups had already pulled out of Japan Council in 1961. Since 1964, separate rallies have been held each August; temporary unity was achieved in 1977 prior to the first U.N. Special Session on Disarmament in 1978.

The effort of memory

The temptation to forget the horrors of Hiroshima and Nagasaki was strengthened by the blanket of secrecy the U.S. occupation threw over all information related to the bombings. "Forgetting" has also been a tactic of the politically conservative Liberal Democratic Party, in power throughout most of the postwar years.

An estimated 18,000 written testimonies of *hibakusha* (A-bomb victims) and many carefully researched scientific documents make forgetting difficult. So does the movement to force the government to provide assistance to Korean, American, and other countries' victims of Hiroshima and Nagasaki.

The Japanese public's aversion to militarism and war in any form, based on recent personal suffering, led to whole-hearted acceptance of the 1947 Peace Constitution, despite criticism that this document was imposed on Japan by its conqueror. Of special significance to war-weary Japan was Article 9 entitled "Renunciation of War," which continues to undergird the peace movement today.*

While the majority of Japanese citizens strongly support the present Constitution, a small minority of conservative militarists

*See pages 118-119.

seek to revise it in order to legitimate increased defense spending and rearmament.

Both victim and aggressor

The Japanese government has continued to make official overtures of friendship toward its Asian neighbors in order to reestablish the diplomatic and economic ties Japan needs for its role as a world power. At the same time, hoping that the passage of time will erase Japan's wartime atrocities from the memory of other Asians and the rest of the world, the government and the Ministry of Education have cultivated a selective domestic memory, gradually deleting from textbooks the most graphic and damning wartime accounts of Japanese brutality toward Asian neighbors. But each time attempts are made to whitewash historical accounts, Asian neighbors lodge diplomatic protests, forcing Japan to reinstate the deleted passages.

From the late 1970s the peace movement's annual August commemorations have focused on Japan not only as wartime victim but also as wartime aggressor. From the early 1980s, many observances have featured personal testimonies by Asian neighbors who survived Japanese brutality. Their stories help Japan reflect on its role in Asia and the Pacific, past and present. For a decade the Japan Evangelical Lutheran church, a leader in the peace movement in the Christian community, has held yearly Hiroshima Peace Seminars. There Christians from Asian and other countries are invited to consider paths leading away from global confrontation and toward reconciliation.

As Japanese Christians have reached out toward Asian Christian neighbors, they too have been forced to reflect on their own role, whether active or passive, in Japan's wars of aggression. Individual Christians and church bodies have confessed their war guilt and sought reconciliation to God and neighbor. Notable among such statements is the Kyodan "Confession of Responsibility During World War II," issued in the name of Moderator SUZUKI Masahisa on Easter Sunday, 1967. It concludes:

> The church, as the "light of the world" and as "the salt of the earth," should not have aligned itself with that effort. Love of country should, rather, have led Christians to exercise a rightful judgment, based on Christian conscience, toward the course our nation pursued. However, in the name of the Kyodan, we issued a statement at home and abroad in which we approved of and supported that war, and encouraged prayers for victory.

> Indeed, even as our country committed sin, so we too, as a church, fell into the same sin. We neglected to perform our

mission as a "watchman." Now, with deep pain in our hearts, we confess our sin and ask the Lord for forgiveness. We also seek the forgiveness of the peoples of all nations, particularly in Asia, and of the churches therein and of our brothers and sisters in Christ throughout the world; as well as the forgiveness of the people in our own country.

Military rebirth

Japan's feet were placed on the path to rearmament in 1950, shortly after the outbreak of the Korean War, by General Douglas MacArthur's order to form a National Police Reserve. In 1952 when the Japan-U.S. San Francisco Peace Treaty was ratified and Japan regained its sovereignty, the name of this body was changed to "Security Forces." In 1954 the name again was changed to the present "Self-Defense Forces." The immediate purpose of MacArthur's order was to secure domestic order in Japan when the U.S. troops were pulled out suddenly and sent to Korea; the long-range purpose was to make Japan a free-world bastion against communist expansion in Asia. Most Japanese viewed MacArthur's order as an arbitrary undermining of the Peace Constitution. Only dyed-in-the-wool militarists and ultra-conservative politicians welcomed it.

The next stage in rearming began in 1960. The U.S. and Japan ratified a revised Security Treaty, under which Japan soon became the launching site for the U.S. war in Vietnam, a war that was to yield huge profits for Japanese companies.

Accompanying the revised treaty of 1960 was an "Exchange of Notes Incorporating Agreed Consultation Formula." These Notes declared that prior to "major changes in the deployment into Japan of U.S. armed forces, major changes in their equipment and the use of facilities and areas in Japan for military operations," consultations between the two governments would be held. Nuclear weapons were in Japan already; the need for consultation would arise only if they were to be taken out.

A basic tenet of Japan's peace movement has been the "Three Non-Nuclear Principles" adopted by the Japanese Diet in 1971, which pledge not to produce, possess, or allow nuclear weapons to be introduced into Japan. Unfortunately, neither the governing Liberal Democratic Party nor the U.S. government appear to value the Principles as highly as do peace-loving Japansese citizens.

Experts claim that many U.S. battleships and bombers visiting Japan are capable of carrying nuclear weapons and no doubt do so. The discovery in May 1989 that a U.S. plane was carrying an H-bomb when it rolled off an aircraft carier on its way back to Japan from a bombing mission in Vietnam in 1965 attests to this. The plane and bomb sank to the ocean floor off the coast of Okinawa.

Japanese peacemakers bear concern also for the extensive software present in the U.S. command, control, communications, and intelligence facilities located within Japan. These facilities are in place to project U.S. nuclear power toward the USSR and close off Soviet fleet access to the Pacific Ocean.

Under the U.S.-Japan Security Treaty, Japan not only provides sites for U.S. military facilities and assists with their maintenance, but also cooperates by sending out Self-Defense Maritime Force ships and planes to patrol the sea lanes.

U.S. military presence in Japan disregards Japanese citizens' voices, their decision-making process, and the many dangers military presence poses to citizens. It also makes Japan a likely target of nuclear attack in the event of either a first strike or retaliation against a U.S. nuclear attack.

Peace crosses borders

Japan's uniqueness in suffering nuclear bombings has meant that often the Japanese peace movement, including Christian peacemakers, operates independently of peace movements in other countries. Acknowledging Japan's war guilt and other peoples' common concerns for peace has led to increased networking with other countries' peace movements on antinuclear and environmental issues. With loyalties to the worldwide faith community, Christians in Japan play a vital role in expanding Japan's horizons beyond striving for a peaceful Japan to joining together with people of other countries to achieve world peace and a shalom-filled creation. The experience of overcoming national boundaries to share a common, inclusive faith with persons of differing backgrounds is unusual in a nation isolated from the rest of the world for much of its history, a nation with a long tradition of exclusive and particularistic loyalties, rejecting persons who are different. Christians in Japan, a tiny minority in Japanese society, realize how crucial it is for them to join hands with other concerned grassroots' citizens groups to raise a common voice in their communities and to make a united peace appeal to the Japanese government.

Environment

KANKYO
environment

We are called upon to boldly proclaim and personally actualize:
   PEACE which overcomes the fear and mutual distrust
      undermining a world facing nuclear destruction;
   RECONCILIATION which overcomes oppression and
      discrimination;
   PARTNERSHIP with all Creation which overcomes
      destruction of nature and the pollution of the environment;
   EQUAL SHARING of the earth's resources which overcomes
      economic disparity.

from the Message of the Bishops' Council
The Anglican Church of Japan, January 5, 1986

Life and nature itself are being defiled, not only human beings. Now the sky, oceans, mountains, rivers, forests, plants, animals and all other living beings are in crisis, their very existence threatened. We clearly hear the voices of those closest to nature. We have realized that we must fight not only to restore the sanctity of human life, but of all life . . . It is significant that we meet in Minamata (Japan), a place which symbolizes to all of us development at its most murderous. As it did to the people of Bhopal and Chernobyl, a giant organization with advanced science technology and production techniques condemned the people of Minamata to fear, sickness, and death, and their beautiful bay to irreparable damage. These three disasters—Minamata, Bhopal, and Chernobyl—can be taken as benchmarks of our time. At Minamata, the industry of a capitalist country poisoned its own citizens . . . . These three tell the story: there is no place to hide.

The Minamata Declaration, August 24, 1989
The Peoples' Plan for the 21st Century,
Non-Governmental Organizations' Conferences.

Nature and the powers-that-be

This cry of the people of the Asian and Pacific regions, issued at the closing session of a series of conferences held throughout Japan in August 1989, summarizes succinctly the environmental plight of Japan today. While the country is abundantly blessed with natural beauty and the Japanese people continue to incorporate their sensitivity to that beauty into their daily lives, the nation's single-minded concentration on postwar recovery and industrial development took precedence over environmental concerns. Grassroots citizen groups are effective in some public appeals; their efforts, for instance, led consumers to stop using non-biodegradable detergents in order to clean up rivers and lakes. But the environmental movement is still quite small in comparison to movements in other countries and also in comparison to the power of the Japanese government and big business acting in collusion to increase productivity.

Another factor in environmental destruction in Japan is the primacy of one's group: people meticulously care for what is their own in sharp contrast to a general careless disregard for public property. For example, individual homeowners and shopkeepers sweep the areas in front of their property each morning. But in all public places litter is casually tossed about. This traditional sense of limits to responsibility has consequences not only in Japan but also for the environmental destruction that Japan is accused of perpetrating in other countries.

Chemicals in the food chain

Minamata marks the beginning of the widespread concern over industrial pollution. In 1907 the Chisso Corporation built a chemical factory in the small town of Minamata, located on the southern main island of Kyushu. Minamata became a company town like others that contributed to Japan's industrialization. By 1925 Chisso was paying local fishermen compensation for damage to fishing grounds. From 1932 Chisso produced acetaldehyde, which required the use of mercury. The mercury waste was dumped into the bay, poisoning marine life. Fish died first, then the birds and cats that consumed the fish. Finally, in the 1950s, it became clear that widespread human symptoms—hand tremors, vision impairment, and general immobility affecting first the Minamata elderly, then adults, children, and finally babies and unborn fetuses—were attributable to mercury poisoning, but Chisso was not yet blamed.

Fishermen demanded and received some compensation from the company, but pollution victims' public appeals were ignored until 1974, when the government acknowledged Chisso as the source of the pollution-caused disease. The company was forced to pay compensation to officially recognized victims. As the forerunner of postwar industrial pollution, Minimata has since served as the rallying point for the citizens' environmental movement, which built networks with movements in other countries.

Proliferating pollution

The increasing number of privately owned automobiles and trucks as well as public buses, with their proliferation of air and noise pollution, has led the government to enact emission code legislation. But these laws have not been enforced uniformly, especially during energy crises. Sound barriers have been erected along heavily travelled expressways to protect residential areas.

In addition to noise pollution created by heavy commercial air traffic, especially over metropolitan centers, noise pollution from U.S. military and Japanese Self-Defense Forces aircraft drills over homes, schools, and communities heightens tensions between citizens and the military and government. In some cases, citizens' persistent protests have successfully forced the removal of military facilities and drill-sites from a community or blocked construction of new facilities. For example, the small island of Miyakejima off Tokyo Bay was designated as a nighttime practice take-off and landing site for U.S. military planes stationed on aircraft carriers. The Japanese government announced the plan in 1983 in response to the U.S. government's request. Local citizens overwhelmingly opposed it on the grounds that such a military facility would not only destroy the tiny island's farming, fishing, and tourism economy, but would also threaten the island's rare wild-bird paradise and the peace of the human population. The islanders' five-year-long appeal was finally rewarded when the government announced that the facility would be based on an uninhabited island.

A long way to go

Similar environmental struggles, to which many Christians and churches lend their support, continue today: 1) in Rokkasho Village, Aomori Prefecture in northern Honshu, a proposed nuclear fuel re-processing and plutonium extraction plant; 2) in Ikego, just south of Tokyo, where the Japanese government plans to build U.S. military housing in a nature preserve; and 3) in Shiraho, on the small southern island of Ishigakijima in Okinawa prefecture. There, to stimulate domestic tourism and the local economy, the government plans to build a larger commercial airport by filling in a rare blue-coral-reef area of the ocean, threatening marine life. In each of these cases Japanese environmentalists have been supported by expressions of concern from individuals and groups throughout the world.

When Japanese industries expand by manufacturing goods and components overseas, they increase their profit margins in part because some countries have minimal pollution control regulations. The health hazards and pollution which are thereby "exported" have not made Japan popular with global and third-world environmentalists. In its recent drive to assume world leadership and avoid isolation, Japan has reversed its seeming indifference to environmental concerns. It has pledged cooperation in international efforts to protect endangered plant and animal species and has committed funding to developing countries' reforestation projects. Nevertheless, Japan has been slow both to respond to warnings regarding the global warming trend, "the green-house effect," caused by high-level carbon dioxide emission, and to agree to implement pollution controls by the year 2000.

Concerned citizens recognize that only as Japan's environmental attitudes and lifestyles undergo fundamental change will environmental protection and restoration be achieved. One symbolic awareness-building program urges citizens to carry their chopsticks rather than to use mass-produced disposable wooden chopsticks. Citizen awareness is the first vital step in eliminating environmental destruction both within Japan and globally.

Part Five

Joining Hands in Mission

DAI-GO
Part Five

SENKYO
mission

KYORYOKU
cooperation

第五

宣教協力

Hands Across
the Land

KOKUNAI
within the
country

国
内

Because only 1,098,108 out of 122,000,000 Japanese are Christians (according to the 1989 *Japan Christian Yearbook*), that is, slightly less than one percent, cooperation among Christians is essential.

National Christian Council in Japan

The roster of the fourteen member and eighteen associate member churches and organizations participating in the National Christian Council in Japan (NCCJ) is a clear indication that solidarity in mission is vital not only for churches in Japan but also for Christian organizations. NCCJ member organizations include those related to international networks, such as the YMCA and the Fellowship of Reconciliation, and those uniquely Japanese, such as the Christian Political League and the Japan Christian Medical Association.

The NCCJ theme for the triennial assembly period 1988-90, "Justice, Peace, and Life," is being put into practice through research, education, and programs that address issues facing Japanese society today. The networks to which NCCJ relates, including the Christian Conference of Asia (CCA) and the World Council of Churches (WCC), enable Christians in Japan to stand in solidarity with people and partner churches throughout Asia and other parts of the world to make justice, peace and the fullness of life real for God's entire creation. Consultations among the NCCJ and councils of churches in Canada and the U.S. have emphasized issues of minority discrimination and of peace.

The NCCJ Women's Committee sponsors the annual World Day of Prayer, celebrated by 230 ecumenical groups throughout Japan. Offerings received at the 1989 World Day of Prayer (¥7,800,000; U.S. $56,286) were directed to programs for women and children in Japan and 6 other Asian countries.

Catholic-Protestant Bible

Eighteen years of epoch-making ecumenical labor in a joint project of the Catholic Church in Japan and major Protestant churches resulted in the publication of *The New Common Translation* of the Bible by the Japan Bible Society in 1987. This new Japanese translation, which includes the Apocrypha, is the first to be officially approved by the Catholic Church. The Bible has served as the introduction to Christianity for many Japanese, and it has been a bestseller throughout the postwar years.

Asian Rural Institute

Asian Rural Institute (ARI) was founded in 1973 in Nishinasuno, Tochigi Prefecture, by TAKAMI Toshiro. Today ARI's goal is to improve the quality of life in the rural sectors of Asian and African countries. ARI brings together men and women rural leaders for nine months to live in a community that makes use of natural energy and practices hands-on organic farming, food self-sufficiency, and socio-environmental balance. Participants gain experience for more effective rural leadership in their own countries.

At the seventeenth annual ARI Harvest Thanksgiving Celebration, ARI director Takami explained:

> We believe thanksgiving is not a mere word—it is a life of sharing. We give thanks not only for the abundant harvest of food but also for the intangible, but real, harvest of experience, insight, wisdom, knowledge, and joy. We harvest these things by bearing burdens together to sustain life now and for future generations, and gain a fresher understanding of creation and of God.

Asian Health Institute

"I was shocked at the number of people who sought medical treatment too late because they were too poor or lived too far from health facilities," said Dr. KAWAHARA Hiromi after serving in Nepal with the Japan Overseas Christian Medical Cooperating Service in 1976. Dr. Kawahara returned to Japan realizing how vital community health workers were to rural Asia. Asian Health Institute (AHI) was established in Nagoya, Japan, in 1980 to provide practical training and encouragement to middle-level health and development workers from other Asian countries. To date 900 workers from 19 countries have participated in AHI programs, which include international seminars, oriental medical and medical specialization courses in Japan; courses for village-level health workers conducted in India,

Nepal, the Philippines, Korea, Kampuchea, and Indonesia; and study tours to India, the Philippines and Nepal.

Christian schools

The current plight of education in Japan poses a challenge for the more than two hundred Christian schools, from pre-school through university graduate school and theological seminary levels.*   Many of these, founded by missionaries and Japanese Christians in the nineteenth century, pioneered in education to develop each student's potential.   Christian schools today are caught up in the intense entrance examination system, which puts heavy demands on students' emotional health and parents' financial resources.   In order to receive government accreditation and subsidy, Christian schools must conform to the guidelines of the highly centralized Japanese Ministry of Education.   In the 1990s, proposed government curriculum revisions will "strengthen Japanese identity among children and prepare them for participation in the global community of the 21st century."   Teachers and parents see these revisions as an attempt to revive prewar values by introducing famous Japanese military figures, previously banned, as models in textbooks and by trying to "make the students think about the nation's security and defense."

An additional concern for Christians is the increased scheduling of public school activities on Sunday morning.   A minister's family recently lost a court case after protesting their daughters' unexcused absences from Sunday public school activities.   The absences become a part of students' permanent records, affecting their future school acceptance and employment.

In addition to introducing students to the Christian gospel, many Christian schools deal with peace education, minority discrimination in Japanese society, and Japanese past military aggression and present economic aggression in Asia.   The NCCJ education division has prepared resources for this purpose.   These concerns are also addressed in chapel programs, courses in Christianity, and through workcamps and tours to other Asian countries.

Schools also address such issues as Japanese affluence, elitism, educational competitition and conformity, and student violence, dropout, and suicide.   They are called on to implement equality in accepting students and hiring teachers without regard to sex, social

---

*The Christian Schools Federation handbook for 1989 counts within its 95 member institutions: 19 graduate schools, 36 colleges and universities, 55 junior colleges, 88 high schools, 67 junior high schools and 19 elementary schools.

status, handicapping conditions, or ethnic origins. National asssociations of Christian kindergartens and schools provide forums for exchange and mutual support in becoming a vital part of God's mission in Japanese society.

After World War II, ecumenical Christian work among students took two forms. Local campus units, often affiliated with the student departments of the YMCA and YWCA, usually did not survive the student struggles in the 1960s and 1970s. The second type of ministry, located near campuses in major university areas, continues in forms adapted to today's needs. Waseda Hoshien began as a Baptist student dormitory in 1908 for students attending a large private university in Tokyo. Its ministry to students continues with support of the Japan Baptist Union and has expanded to include an international hostel for exchange students. Postwar student centers include the Anglican Student Center in Sapporo, Hokkaido, the Sendai Student Center in Sendai, and the Lutheran Student Center and the Student Christian Fellowship in Tokyo. Such centers engage students and faculty in evangelism, in concern for the world Christian community, and in training for Christian leadership. A new ministry is the Tsukuba Christian Center, located north of Tokyo near the new Tsukuba University oriented to science and technology. The center's program includes ministry to a large number of foreign students and scholars.

Tokyo Woman's Christian University was established in 1918 as an ecumenical project supported by several North American mission boards. Today the university is part of a network of Christian women's universities through the Asian Women's Institute. Member schools engage in research in their own countries and share information on issues facing women's education in Asia.

Christian social work

It is impossible to talk about social work in Japan without talking about Christian social work. Today Christian institutions and programs include general hospitals and specialized health-care services for patients with Hansen's disease (leprosy), visual and hearing impairments, physical disabilities, and problems relating to aging and to mental and emotional disabilities. Other special programs include sheltered workshops; physical, vocational, and social rehabilitation in half-way houses; children's homes; and retirement communities.

Other vital contributions include providing leadership and training opportunities to non-Christian staff of private or government social work programs and supplying expertise in drafting government social welfare legislation.   Accredited Christian social work schools and short-term training experiences are open not only to Japanese students but also to social workers from overseas, especially those from third-world Asian countries.   Many members of the Japan Christian Social Work League are leaders in the Japan National Council of Social Welfare and its international division.

A unique educational and social service is provided by the *omoni hakkyo* ("mothers' schools," in Korean language).   These programs teach basic Japanese literacy skills to help Korean women in Japan survive in Japanese society.   Students include older residents in Japan whose busy lives have not allowed them the opportunity to study Japanese and younger women who are newcomers to Japan. The schools, often housed in Korean or Japanese churches, become meeting places where Japanese volunteer teachers, Christian and non-Christian, and Korean women can share their lives and their cultures.

An exciting ecumenical, international ministry of caring was launched in November 1986.   Thirty-five Christians from five Anglican, Catholic, Kyodan, and Presbyterian churches in Tomakomai, located on the southern coast of Hokkaido, began a ship visitation and seamen's club ministry to serve the 15,000 seafarers who enter the port annually.   Because the piers are outside the city and transportation costs are high, most crewmembers do not go ashore. Today 60 missions volunteers visit the ships daily in groups of two or three.   Volunteers also provide transportation and staff the club's open house operated three nights a week in a Maryknoll (Catholic) conference hall.   In 1989 the Missions to Seamen, Tomakomai, visited 927 ships and provided hospitality to 3724 seafarers from 26 countries in the newest ministry to seafarers in Japan.

Among Japanese social workers sent overseas to serve in special projects, invariably one-fourth to one-half are Christian.   One such person is MATSUI Ryosuke, graduate of International Christian University, active church member, and professor on leave of absence from the Japanese Labor Ministry's Vocational Training University.   Matsui is currently assigned by the International Labor Organization of the U.N. as the Asia Advisor for Vocational Rehabilitation of Handicapped Persons.   Headquartered in Bangkok, Matsui visits various Asian countries at leaders' requests to assist in planning and setting up centers and projects designed to meet the needs of handicapped persons in each particular setting.

Thus, Christians play a much larger role in social work than their one percent numbers would suggest.

Hands Across the Sea

KAIGAI
overseas

HOSHINO Masaoki

I went to Canada to encounter the world.

After graduation from the Rural Theological Seminary in 1968, I pastored a small rural church in northern Japan for seventeen years. Hachirogata Church had no members when I arrived. At first only a few high school students gathered for Sunday worship, although many of them seemed to have come to have fun and were not earnest seekers after the truth. When after one year I married, my wife became the first church member.

At first I tried to make the worship services appropriate to the students' needs. Later I felt the need to incorporate more ritual into the service, to encourage congregational participation and de-emphasize the role of the minister in communicating the spoken Word.

Gradually I realized that Japanese farmers do not come to church easily because of the strong feudal traditions in rural areas. Realizing the importance of developing a relationship with the community as a rural evangelist, I started working beside the local farmers in their fields, and thus came to share their daily lives and problems. Only as they came to know and trust me did they talk about the deeper questions of life. And only as the church became involved with the people's daily lives did meaningful worship with the people evolve. When I left Hachirogata Church sixteen years later, the church had grown to twenty-six members and was self-supporting.

My family went to Canada as Kyodan missionaries to be involved for three years in the United Church of Canada's Mutuality in Mission program, working in rural evangelism in the London Conference. I discovered that Canadian farmers and Japanese farmers face identical problems: the need to expand production to survive, mechanization, debt, and urban flight.

I became aware of the similarities in values accorded life, nature, and the total environment by the Native Canadians and the Ainu of

Japan. Both peoples affirm that neither nature nor persons are to be made commodities for exploitation.

Both Canadian and Japanese churches will be strengthened by increased exchange of rural evangelists and of farmers. Churches of the two countries can also join together to address global social issues such as minority discrimination, apartheid, and peace.

When I speak about the continuing tension between church and state in Japan, Canadians are surprised. They ask why church and state have to be in opposition, since the state is the creation of people. Hearing this, I am very envious. In Japan, the church has always been in tension with the state, except when the church relaxed the tension and went along with the state in wartime Japan. In Japan the church has a basic distrust of the state. In Canada citizens always seem to hold positive expectations of the state. It is good to be able to trust the state, but I feel a little uneasy about the lack of tension. I am surprised to see Canadian flags in some church sanctuaries. This would be unthinkable in Japan. I am also surprised to see the Lord's Prayer being prayed in public schools. I wonder about the rights of children who do not come from Christian homes.

Receiving

Throughout the "Catholic century" and the second period of Christian mission in Japan from the nineteenth to the mid-twentieth century, Japanese Christians were for the most part on the receiving end of international mission. Catholic and Protestant mission boards and societies in North America and Europe made major commitments of missionary personnel and financial resources to Japan. These made it possible, within a short time, to purchase property and establish churches, schools and special ministries. It also meant that essential control over personnel and funds was retained by the sending bodies. After World War II, the Kyodan's North American mission partners pledged themselves to continued cooperation in mission. To coordinate the activities, the North American mission boards established the Interboard Committee for Christian Work in Japan (IBC). In Japan the Council of Cooperation was formed, composed of the Kyodan, the Christian Schools' Council, the Christian Social Work League, and the IBC.

As Japanese partners began to call for a two-way exchange of personnel and programs, the IBC was reorganized in 1973 as the Japan-North America Commission on Cooperative Mission (JNAC). Today JNAC is made up of nine partners in mission. North American

JNAC members are: 1) Division of Overseas Ministries, Christian Church (Disciples of Christ) in the U.S. and Canada; 2) The Presbyterian Church in Canada; 3) Global Mission Ministry Unit, Presbyterian Church (USA); 4) General Program Council of the Reformed Church in America; 5) The United Church Board for World Ministries (United Church of Christ); 6) The United Church of Canada, Division of World Outreach; 7) The General Board of Global Ministries of the United Methodist Church.

Japan members are the Korean Christian Church in Japan and the United Church of Christ in Japan (Kyodan). JNAC associate members are American Baptist Churches USA, Board of International Ministries; and United Board for Christian Higher Education in Asia.

The number of JNAC-related missionaries has dropped sharply since the early postwar years because North America partner denominations have found their resources for sending persons overseas diminshed and have re-directed mission priorities and personnel to other parts of the world. Also, large numbers of missionaries who were sent to Japan during the early postwar Christian "boom" gradually have been retiring. In 1970, when North American JNAC mission boards talked of withdrawing mission personnel, Kyodan-related churches and agencies pledged partial support for missionaries to assure some continued presence. In 1989, the Kyodan's shared support funding was ¥143,642,217 (U.S. $1,026,016).

Today approximately two hundred JNAC missionaries are involved in mission in Japan in Japanese and Korean churches, Christian schools and social work agencies. They have been recruited in North America in response to requests from partners in Japan. Christian schools especially have assumed increasing financial support for missionary personnel related to schools, including short-term associates. Thus, in effect, missionaries are sent by two churches. Missionaries to Japan also include persons sent by other mission boards from North America and elsewhere, such as the Methodist Church, Great Britain; German Midnight Mission, the Evangelical Church in Berlin Brandenburg, and Evangelisches Missionswerk in Sudwestdeutschland, all in the Federal Republic of Germany; the Presbyterian Church in Korea, the Presbyterian Church in Taiwan; and the United Methodist Church and the United Church of Christ of the Philippines.

Most Protestant and Catholic groups in Japan have spent time assessing the role of missionaries there. At one point the Kyodan declared a three-year moratorium on receiving evangelistic missionaries until it could work through its position. This process resulted in the Kyodan's formation of "The Basic Understanding Concerning

World Mission" document in 1984, which serves as a foundation for evaluating past mission efforts in order to look toward the future. Discussing the role of missionaries, both those received and those sent by the Japanese church, the document states:

> Recognizing the work of missionaries to be one of the most effective methods of carrying out the various spheres of world mission activity, the Kyodan is engaged in a program of sending and receiving missionaries which emphasizes mutuality, cooperative joint work, and missionaries serving as representatives to and from their respective churches.

Sending

As churches in Japan have grown and matured, they have sought to assume greater responsibility for Christian mission in Japan and have become largely self-supporting. They have also sought to be involved in proclaiming the gospel in other countries, responding to requests from churches in those countries. Today most Catholic and Protestant groups have some part in sending and supporting Japanese persons in mission in Asia and other parts of the world. Some send missionaries in conjunction with other Christian groups, as in the case of the Japan Baptist Union missionary doctor in Bangladesh who works under the ecumenical Japan Overseas Christian Medical Cooperative Service. (The Japan Baptist Union relates to the American Baptist churches USA.) Others send missionaries more directly. The Japan Baptist Convention (relating to the Southern Baptist Convention, in the U.S.) sends missionaries to Indonesia and Thailand. The Japan Evangelical Lutheran Church (relating to the ELCA in the U.S.) has missionaries in Brazil and the U.S.

Since 1957, the Kyodan has sent 102 missionaries overseas to serve in 23 countries. At present 35 missionaries serve in 12 countries. Over half of these are in ministries as chaplains to Japanese residing in that country. A new program ministers to those who are in the greater New York and Chicago areas on short-term job assignments. These ministries, which offer support during cultural adjustment, language assistance, Bible study, and house meetings, are jointly sponsored by the Kyodan and 5 U.S. denominations.

The largest number of missionaries from Japan are at work in the U.S., Taiwan, and Canada. In addition to ministry to Japanese residents, these missionaries are involved in education, agriculture, community development, ecumenical ministries, theological education, and Christian education. Their support comes from several sources: the Kyodan, the receiving body, and a support group or individual congregations in Japan. Today the Kyodan seeks to send missionaries who can both interpret Japanese church mission concerns and can work effectively with local colleagues, especially in third-world countries.

The Korean Christian church in Japan, though a small denomination which itself suffers a shortage of pastors, is beginning to take some tentative steps in sending missionaries to other countries. A few are ministering with Koreans in North America, and the KCCJ is considering a missionary to work in a ministry with Native Canadians.

As their vision has broadened to include the whole world, Christians in Japan have developed a variety of short-term mission experiences: overseas home-stay and mission tour study programs, church-to-church exchange groups, overseas work camps, and Christian schools overseas exchange. Christians from other countries have been invited as short-term partners-in-mission to live in community with and learn about the churches of Japan and to introduce the concerns of their countries' Christians.

Christians in Japan today seek to recreate mutually supportive relations with such Asian neighbors as Korea and the Philippines, as the people of those countries continue to suffer in their struggles for unity and peace. The church also seeks to extend its circle of concern to oppressed sisters and brothers in such distant countries as South Africa—Japan's primary relationship with South Africa has been as its number-one trading partner. Churches in Japan have welcomed South African church leaders, translated and published anti-apartheid leaders' writings, joined anti-apartheid citizens' groups, and boycotted South African products in solidarity with the black community's struggle there.

What shall we give and receive?

Over one hundred years of Protestant mission efforts in Japan have succeeded in establishing churches, Christian schools and social work agencies, and such other special ministries as Christian audio-visual communications, publishing, and the arts—even though the number of Christians never reached two percent of the total population. What unique experience does this tiny Christian community offer Christians in other parts of the world?

First is sharing what it means to live out their commitment as a small but faithful minority in a non-Christian society. Second is the experience of making a united witness, although that unity in Japan is incomplete in many ways. A third contribution Japanese Christians have to offer is their war-time experience, coupled with the confession that they failed to speak out prophetically or resist state pressure to participate in Japan's brutal aggression of other Asian countries.

Out of that last experience the Japanese church has reflected seriously on its failings, sought to uphold the constitutional guarantee of separation between religion and state, and dedicated itself anew to being God's faithful, prophetic voice in Japanese society. Christians are especially called to witness to the urgency of peace-making and peace education. These are among the gifts Christians in Japan have to share.

And to receive? As tiny Christian communities in a society that long remained isolated, Christians in Japan desperately need the support and fellowship of Christians in other countries. They need to be reminded that the Christian church exists beyond national boundaries. They need constant reaffirmation that the community of faith is not intended to be a gathering of like-minded persons but that its doors must ever be open to all persons and to the winds of the Holy Spirit. In truth, Christians in Japan cannot be truly Christian apart from the rest of the world.

Facing challenges together

An NCCJ ecumenical dialogue held in Tokyo on May 30, 1990, discussed challenges facing the Christian community in Japan and Japan-North America cooperation in mission. Representatives of NCCJ member churches and organizations gathered to share not their church/organization's official policy, but their personal concerns. They invite North American sisters and brothers to join them in envisioning and creating new Japan-North American mission networks for tomorrow.

NAKAJIMA Masaaki (John), general secretary, Kyodan (nearing completion of third four-year term): The Kyodan will focus on its fifty years of existence at the General Assembly in November 1990. Also taking place in November is the enthronement of the emperor, which is of deep concern to us. Our assembly will occur between the two main ceremonies of the enthronement, so we must work not to get "caught" between them. The Kyodan came into being by imperial edict. When the denominations were thus brought together by force, some of us discarded fellow Christians who stood up against the emperor. We continue to reflect on these actions and repent the stance we took. We reexamine also such subsequent occurrences as the union of the Japan Kyodan with the Okinawa Kyodan in 1969. In these and other concerns, we must keep being concerned about how majority groups relate to minority groups. In the same spirit, we are finding ways to acknowledge the discrimination that exists in the Christian community, symbolized by the writings of KAGAWA Toyohiko. The main issue for the Kyodan is what it means to be one of Christ's churches today in a non-Christian country of many religious faiths and ideologies.

Our cooperative mission relationship with the 6 North American denominations to which the Kyodan relates is undergoing a radical change right now. After World War II, we received a tremendous amount of assistance from them, especially through mission personnel. We've been benefitting ever since. But now most of the 150 to 200 missionaries in Japan have either retired or will soon. We have maintained exchange and cooperation through them, but what form will our partnership take when they are gone? Although we've thought of our partnership as one of equality, realistically speaking there have been many more missionaries coming to Japan than we have sent overseas. Now there is a more even balance with the sharp decrease of North American missionary personnel.

We talk about partners as *aibo* in Japanese (one of a pair of palanquin-bearers or litter carriers). This refers to the two persons who carried the *kago* (palanquin, litter), who worked together and carried a load in tandem, each using the same amount of strength. What was important was not the weight they were carrying but that they worked together in a balanced way. If the bearer in front is weaker than the one in back, the load would shift and the balance be lost. Of course there are ways to compensate for this and not lose the balance. I think our task now is to search for ways to do just this.

YOON Chong-Un, pastor, Yokohama Church, Korean Christian Church in Japan (KCCJ): Our KCCJ, which ministers primarily to Koreans living in Japan, is 83 years old. It has 75 churches and about 10,000 members (including all who attend worship). Our most important concern today is the lives of Korean residents in Japan.

Our work began when the Korean YMCA in Japan was founded. We often experienced discrimination. Then, in 1940 we were forced to join the Nihon Kirisuto Kyokai (Japan Christian Church) and the Kyodan in 1941. Just five months after the war ended, the Korean churches withdrew from the Kyodan, and became the KCCJ. Soon our home country was divided into north and south Korea.

Even today Korean residents are divided into two groups, and the church is caught in the middle, although it has leaned toward the south Korea-related side. The church has expended its energy in building congregations and churches and has left undone the vital work of reconciliation. To be a real witness we must become an open church, not the closed, church-oriented church we are today. We must be concerned about the lives of all the Koreans in Japan— more than a million people. And we must deal with several different kinds of discrimination and minister so that we can be a cleansing agent in Japanese society.

In terms of our mission relations, we Koreans must remember that we are in Japan as a result of World War II. Both Japan and the U.S. are related to the reasons we are here. The problem is not only in the church but in the political realm, too. U.S. and Japanese churches must become involved in appealing to their governments to work for reunification of Korea. When we look at what has happened in Germany, we are surprised by the tremendous power when the people rose up. Right now both Japan and the U.S. stand in the way of reunification of Korea; historically we see that Japan has done what it has done for its own profit, and America has done the same thing. The appeal of the KCCJ and churches in Korea to American churches—and also the churches in Japan—is to think seriously about this problem.

KYUNG Hae-Jung, pastor, Shinagawa Church, KCCJ, and first KCCJ woman pastor: We are one of the churches that needs the most help from the NCCJ. At present we are aiming to grow to one hundred churches, and we need all your help as we work toward this goal. I feel that in order for there to be real peace in Japan, all Koreans in Japan must come together. I hope that you will join us in praying for this reconciliation and unity. Only the governments can bring about unification, but we believers can do more to enable the Koreans in Japan to become one.

NAKAMURA Ryujiro, general secretary, Japan Baptist Union (body related to the American Baptist Churches in the USA): This year a world meeting of Baptists will be held in Seoul. We have wondered if we could easily participate in such a meeting. In preparation, we have decided to present a special apology to the Baptist churches in Korea when we go.

In other relations, a few years ago we were able to cut the aid we received from the American Baptist Church to zero. In principle then, we can stand by ourselves, but we are still dependent on them in many ways. We have set a goal to increase our number of churches from 70 to 100 by the year 2000, doing our part to increase the percentage of Christians in Japan—if we don't, we won't really have the power to change our country. Something else I'm personally concerned about is that church school attendance is going down every year, despite a slight increase in Sunday morning worship attendance. We need to stop this trend as soon as possible.

MATSUKURA Osamu, general secretary, Japan Baptist Convention (body related to the Southern Baptist Convention): The JBC celebrated its 40th anniversary in 1987. Today we have about 300 churches and preaching points and 30,000 members.

In 1984 we sent a representative to Korea with our church's apology for the part we played in World War II and in 1988 we very belatedly admitted our church's responsibility for World War II. Examining our war responsibility helped us to see the presence of greed that we, including the church, possessed at that time.

In this process, we have been seriously searching for the real message of Christ that we should proclaim in today's world. In the midst of this, we've been considering how little we can do because Japan's Christian population is only one percent of the total. So we would like to increase the number of our churches from 300 to 500 by AD 2000. To do this, we must become self-supporting. Each congregation must become stronger. At present I don't know that many of our churches could build or remodel their own buildings, and only about half can fully support a minister.

At the same time that we emphasize church development, we must also focus on the problems of Japanese society: the emperor system, discrimination, conservatism, and pollution. Some say we can't be involved in both emphases, but I wonder how we could be involved in social issues without also being involved in evangelization.

We have to determine how the church is going to deal with the secularization of society, both its positive and negative aspects. We need to look at the lifestyles of salaried workers, who spend so much time commuting to work, and re-examine our own lifestyles and morals as Christians to be able to struggle in today's world.

In terms of mission relations, no matter what else is said, we like American missionaries. But often we aren't operating on the same frequency. It's like the O'Henry short story, where a woman sells her hair to buy a watchchain for her husband, who has sold his watch to buy a comb for her hair. But I think we and our co-workers love each other very much. One benefit of working with those from a different culture is that we Japanese tend to get caught up in ourselves, and missionaries seem able to view some things with the objectivity we lack.

Our church may have one of the largest groups of missionaries, about 200; in recent years, many are Korean-American or Taiwanese-American. We are going to have to develop new ways to be in mission together. North American children learn about other countries and people, and are challenged when they are young to become ministers or missionaries. We in Japan fail in this—people don't volunteer for missionary service. I would like to see common projects established to enable us to engage in ministry together, both in Asia and in North America.

MAEDA Teichi, moderator, Japan Evangelical Lutheran Church (JELC moderators are limited to one four-year term): Our church began with the work of missionaries from the U.S. in 1893. Later, missionaries arrived from Europe also, and after the war, other Lutheran denominations from the U.S. As we approach our centennial, we are a small denomination with about 140 churches. Although we tried to become self-supporting many times, we did not succeed until the 1970s. Of course, laypeople worked hard to achieve this, but membership has not grown much nor has an effective method of planning emerged; rather, all four Lutheran bodies achieved self-support only as we rode the crest of the Japanese economy.

When I attended a Lutheran General Assembly in the U.S. last year, I was not asked about what the tiny Japanese church thinks about Japan's politics or government—the person knew that as Lutherans and Christians in Japan we are small and powerless. Instead, I was asked about American society and about how I view the people of Southeast Asia. I think the first question has to do with the trade problems between Japan and the U.S. The second is very difficult. At a regional Lutheran meeting, we presented funds from a special offering to dig wells in an area of Southeast Asia, money our Lutheran women worked hard to raise. Afterwards, some people said they didn't need "left-over" money from Japan. I guess they equated Japanese Christians with Japanese business.

We are a small group and have experienced persecution at times, but we are not seen from that standpoint today. And we must accept the reality that we in the church were among the wartime perpetrators, not the victims.

Today, because we are self-supporting thanks to the Japanese economy, we have to ask, "So where is it that the church is standing?" Is this where we want to be in order to preach the true and living message? This is a big issue for our church today.

UEDA Jintaro, general secretary, Nippon Seikokai (Anglican Church of Japan): Our church is small—29,000 baptized members, 58,000 if you count all the registered members. Much of what we have is an "inheritance" from missionary work, such as 5 or 6 universities and about the same number of junior-senior high schools.

We have a rich heritage from the Anglican tradition, which we have copied and translated directly from abroad for our purposes. This begins with ministries, liturgy, and hymnal and extends throughout the church. Unlike the Kyodan, I think we are not really a national church yet. I think our biggest task today is making our church into a truly Japanese church.

But like the Kyodan, our church has been forced to enter a new era whether we are ready for it or not. At the end of the 1960s there were more than 100 missionaries from overseas, most of them American. Today there are only 4 or 5. This leaves a tremendous hole in our labor force. At the official level, the national church (ECUSA) doesn't plan to send any more missionaries to Japan, but when we visited North America, we found that some local congregations and small mission agencies are still enthusiastic about sending missionaries. When I was in the U.S. last year, one of my requests was that they not send us missionaries who communicate a "cheap gospel," for this would lower the credibility of Christianity in Japan. Just sending missionaries to attract Japanese people to Christianity doesn't fit with what we consider to be the real mission of the church.

The fact that churches in Japan and the U.S. really are not equal partners is a difficult point. What is necessary is that we have common issues to work on together. We ought to be able to say to each other that we need help on a specific focus. Our churches need to ascertain where their strengths and weaknesses lie. Then we can say: we can do this by ourselves, maybe we can help you with that, we need your assistance with something else.

SAITO Fusae, former director, YMCA of Japan: The YMCA of Japan is 110 years old. Today we have 29 city YMCAs, over 70 university YMCAs, and a membership of about 140,000. From the beginning we have sought to be self-supporting, and this was achieved in the 1960s. Among YMCAs of the world our budget is the second largest, next to the U.S.

Although we have achieved our goal of self-support, we are going through an identity crisis. It has become difficult for us to see just who we actually are. In the YMCA tradition, we have program-related and movement-related activities. But I think our organization has become tied to its buildings and programs, and the excitement of a "live" program has become harder to find. In all of this, we seem to have less movement-related emphasis.

Another concern is recruiting new leadership to replace older leaders who came out of university YMCAs or local churches. We cannot expect much of them today. Perhaps also we have not put so much emphasis on working together with our suffering neighbors. We need to work harder to develop better relationships with other YMCAs of Asia, including those of Korea and China. We emphasize education on development, the environment, and peace today.

SHIMADA Reiko, general secretary, YWCA of Japan, member of the Nippon Seikokai (Anglican Church of Japan): The YWCA of Japan, founded eighty-five years ago, from its inception worked for the liberation of women, to help women be treated as honorable and respectable human beings, so they could work and be educated in the same way as men, and with men. We participate in the NCCJ, but since 1970 the YWCA of Japan has had an open membership policy, which means that members no longer have to be Christians to belong. So one of our major issues is how we can work together as Christians and non-Christians while keeping Christian principles at the center of our work.

After World War II the YWCA went through a difficult, heavy time of self-examination, reflecting on our contribution to the war. It is true that these women really had no power at that time, but the fact that they didn't stand up and oppose the war was very embarrassing to them. Since then, we have worked very hard for world peace and the rights of all human beings, strongly supporting the Peace Constitution from its inception. Since 1970 the YWCA of Japan has stood on an antinuclear platform. That was not a popular stand at the time but we persisted. We began annual pilgrimages to Hiroshima and thought about the problem of nuclear power in other ways. I realize now that our stand on this issue has actually helped the YWCA to grow and become stronger.

From this base, we are moving into concerns for energy, the environment, human rights, Korean atomic victims, freedom of thought and religion, the emperor system, and Korean residents in Japan. In our 25 city YWCAs we are working to achieve a nuclear-free society and respect for the human rights of all persons. Concern for these issues has come from within our movement, as we stood before God and struggled to see what we should be doing as an organization based on Christian principles. Another pressing issue is our aging membership. We have just added a youth coordinator to our national staff.

We have much to learn from North America in terms of program development skills, and we plan to take a study tour to the U.S. to learn these techniques.

I feel that both Japan and the U.S., as developed countries, have to take more responsibility in the world. I wonder how concerned members of our churches are about people around the world who are suffering from hunger and other causes. I also am concerned that the top priority of Japanese salaried workers—even for those in our churches—seems to be the company. Indeed, the company is their god. Is this really O.K. as a way of Christian life? What would it mean for each of us to put our faith on the line?

YAMAYA Shinko, NCCJ vice-moderator and chairperson, Peace Committee, Japan Woman's Christian Temperance Union (JWCTU), member of Kyodan: The JWCTU was founded 104 years ago when American WCTU representatives visited Japan. JWCTU has always worked to prevent alcohol and tobacco abuse. At the same time we have worked for peace and the human rights of women—that focus came from concern for young rural women sold into prostitution. In prewar, wartime, and postwar years, JWCTU worked to abolish legalized prostitution. After women were elected to political office, they worked together for the passage of the Prostitution Prevention Law in 1956. But prostitution continued in Japan. Japanese men also began visiting other Asian countries on sex tours to "buy" women. JWCTU campaigned to eliminate the sex tours. Next, when women came to Japan from other Asian countries in search of jobs, they were put to work in Japan's entertainment/sex industry. The JWCTU again got involved.

In 1986, on its 100th anniversary, JWCTU established HELP Asian Women's Shelter to address the sexual exploitation of women in Japan. HELP is supported also by other Protestants and by Catholics, women's organizations, individuals, and citizens' organizations. NCCJ was the first ecumenical group to support HELP.

Last year NCCJ and NCC/USA sponsored a joint Peace Consultation. I hope this can be done on a regular basis to consider how Christians in Japan and North America can cooperate in bearing responsibility for peace and justice in Asia.

TAKEUCHI Kentaro, Nippon Seikokai (Anglican Church of Japan); moderator, National Christian Council in Japan (NCCJ): Spreading the gospel is our calling. The issue is what the specific content of that gospel is, and how we relate to it.

The church of which I am a part, the Anglican Church of Japan, has been greatly influenced by the North American church. We must acknowledge this influence and express our gratitude to those who brought it. Japanese Christians, however, have experienced the same history as non-Christians, including the war and the emperor system. Looking back on these experiences, we begin to comprehend their serious implications. As we look at what the issues are for the church today, we are forced to search for the true meaning and form of Christian faith for Japan today: For whom is the message intended? What should we affirm? What should we deny? I feel this is our main assignment at present.

An example of how we have not yet dealt with this history is shown by the emperor system. It may be that God is giving us a chance to deal with it seriously now.

Another ongoing concern of mine is whether it is possible for victimizers and victims to cooperate in mission. And if so, under what conditions? With reference to colonization, America should face some of the same issues that Japan faces, for example, in the Philippines. England should also be doing the same. The continuing results of colonization need to be faced on a global scale.

Someone here has mentioned the word "partner." We often use the term "partnership in mission," but what posture or attitude must we adopt for true partnership to happen? When we talk about cooperative work with churches in North America, we also use the term "resource sharing." This has evolved from a situation where one group has become settled and is now able to share its resources with another group. Although this sounds rough, it can reflect the sentiment: "When we have some left over, we'll share it with you." What I think is necessary is something quite different, something that might be called "poverty sharing," sharing out of our lack. Until we can do this, we can't participate in the real meaning of "resource sharing." I think North America and Japan stand in similar places today, and so I have great hopes for our cooperation in world mission in the future.

Aiko CARTER, Women's Committee staff, NCCJ; member of Kyodan: As I participate in the activities of the church, I concentrate on ways in which women can more fully participate in church life and make a meaningful witness in the world.

I would like to see the NCCJ receive more young people for involvement in mission in the future. I think this process will greatly benefit the education program of the North American church. I think the Japanese church also needs to think more seriously about creating opportunities for Japanese youth to work and learn in churches in other countries.

Japanese church-school curriculum needs to be revised to include the concept of serving others as a major tenet of the church, to emphasize that serving God means serving others. I feel this concept is generally lacking in our curriculum resources today.

YAWATA Akihito, Youth Division staff, NCCJ; member of Nippon Seikokai (Anglican Church of Japan): Church leaders need to talk together about the actual situation of youth in the church today. Almost everyone refers to "since 1969" [the period of university student unrest] in talking about youth in Japan, but youth like me were only elementary school children in 1969. As long as the church is not able to focus on where youth are today, to ascertain what their needs and interests are, it will not be able to develop a program relevant to youth. The entrance exam system has changed tremendously, for example, since then.

To those of us who want to organize young people, development of leadership among youth is very important. As one who has been involved in youth work in the '80s, I can tell you that many youth are assuming leadership roles in citizens' groups today. They are searching for the kind of involvement that will change and renew society and are finding places to do this outside the church. Why aren't they satisfied with or involved in church activities? Their energy could be such a large plus in building up our churches. It's not that there are no youth available, but the kind of involvement the church offers doesn't appeal to them.

A great many changes have been occuring in the latter years of the 1980s, and many youth have been deeply involved in these changes. Even if they don't read newspapers, they are still exposed to much information and world news. And many Japanese youth are traveling abroad, often on their own. While this has both positive and negative effects, youth today have many opportunities to reach out to what is happening in other countries. When they get to meet and know the youth of other countries, especially those in third-world countries, for the first time they realize that they are persons whose lives, although very different, are nevertheless related to their own daily lives. These experiences will greatly affect our ecumenical movement for international exchange.

YAMANO Shigeko, secretary, Urban Rural Mission, NCCJ, member of Nippon Seikokai (Anglican Church of Japan): The NCCJ Center for Christian Response to Asian Issues publishes *Ajia Tsuushin* (Asian News) and *Japan Militarism Monitor*. We sponsor seminars and events to help Christians in Japan understand problems in Asia and discover ways to relate to them. We have had a number of young mission interns from North American churches working with us. One thing that Japanese and North American Christians can do is to join the peoples and churches of Asia in working to achieve justice, peace, and the integrity of creation. With the help of the mission interns, we can publish more materials in English to reach more persons concerned with peace and justice issues. We can become a "window" for North American youth so that together we can learn about the issues in Asia.

MAEJIMA Munetoshi, general secretary, NCCJ; pastor in Kyodan: I would like to re-emphasize the importance of holding regular NCCJ-NCC/USA peace consultations. I also feel that the U.S. and Japan really stand in the way of Koreans' work for reunification. Some of you have mentioned what churches in the U.S. and Japan must do. At summit meetings, the problems of the stability of the Korean Peninsula and the Philippines are always raised. I don't think we as neighbors fully understand the real situation in those countries. It's important for us to understand that the people of Korea seriously wish for reunification. The same is true in regard to other countries in Asia and throughout the world. Christians in Japan and North America must carry the burden, including the responsibility for working toward the achievement of "Justice, Peace, and the Integrity of Creation." Will you, our North American sisters and brothers in Christ, join us in this quest?

Conclusion

NAKAJIMA Masaaki (John) talked about partnership between churches in Japan and in North America when he spoke at the 1985 General Synod of the United Church of Christ (USA), one of the denominations to which the Kyodan relates.

Today missionaries are rarely principals, presidents, or chairpersons of church institutions as they once were. Rather, they work with Japanese colleagues under Japanese leadership. Yet we Christians treasure their presence among us.

When Jesus called the twelve disciples he wanted twelve different people. If the twelve had anything in common, it is that all responded immediately; when they were told to come, they came. I believe this is what Jesus expects of us today. The church should never be composed of the same kind of people. It ought to be a place where different kinds of people come together to respond to the call of Jesus.

We all tend to feel happier when we are with like-minded people than with people of different tastes. In the Kyodan, as almost everywhere in the 1960s and 70s, sharp voices criticized the establishment. One group thought that the people expressing radical opinions should be thrown out of meetings where they had no right to be present. Another group felt that these people ought to be given a chance to speak and be heard. I firmly believe that the effort to include different voices was the right one. There are other places where law and order must be strictly maintained. There may be cases when unwanted people should be kept away by force. But the church is different. The church is not kept by law and order, but by the call of Jesus. And Jesus is calling everybody. You may not particularly like some people and feel they don't really belong. But it's not up to you or me to decide who should be in the church. It's Jesus who decides. The church that rejects someone because he or she is different doesn't represent the spirit of Jesus. The church should be the place where we have a foretaste of Jesus' declaration that "People will come from east and west, from north and south, and will sit down at the feast in the Kingdom of God."

155

The presence of missionaries among us is essential because of this truth. We have a duty to show the world that in the church, unlike secular institutions, all kinds of people are called together to be one.

During World War II, when my country and your country were fighting, most of the missionaries returned home. But some remained in Japan among Japanese Christians. I think this is significant. It shows that even when the rest of the world is divided, the church can be one.

On January 12, 1945, my father was shot to death by the strafing of American Grumman fighters on a plain of Luzon in the Philippines. He had been a Congregational pastor of a tiny Japanese congregation in Manila since 1933. As the war progressed, high-ranking Japanese military officers frequently visited him trying to recruit him into the army They wanted his language ability. They came sometimes with sweet words and promises of high rank, sometimes with threats. But my father refused, saying, "I am here as the pastor of my congregation. Even if most of my members are taken away, I must be here when my people need me."

Finally the military lost patience and conscripted my father. He had never had any military training and as his unit began to move north the strafing took place. He was forty-two years old.

When I look back on my father's life I can see that he tried to be with Jesus, tried to be faithful to his calling. But in the end he yielded to a power other than Jesus. I remember his preaching to us Sunday School children just before Pearl Harbor. As Japanese residents in a country under U.S. control, we were restless and anxious about the future. He assured us that a war would not take place, but even if it did, that Japan would be fighting for a just cause, and since "God is always on the side of righteousness, you don't have to worry."

How could a Japanese pastor who had access to English information, denied to people in Japan, still believe in the holy-war theory of Japanese imperialism? He was indoctrinated by a demon called national interest. People in many nations are deceived into thinking that protecting national interest is being on Jesus' side.

It is very difficult to be sure who is on the side of Jesus and who is with forces other than Jesus, particularly when you are isolated within your own people. We all need someone who can look from outside to give advice and provide perspective. The mutual exchange of information and experience can help us to differentiate between being with Jesus in faith and being with demons out of our own interest. For this reason we *all* need the presence of missionaries from another culture. Missionaries exist not only to communicate to the people to whom they are sent, but also to bring back messages to their own people out of their experiences, so that their own country's people can deepen their commitment to Jesus and make their decision to stand only with Jesus.

Jesus sent the twelve disciples out to preach. Sometimes people equate the gospel with material prosperity. They feel that missionaries should be sent only to poor countries, that preaching the gospel is no longer needed in affluent countries, and that sending missionaries in such cases is a waste of money. This is wrong. I am not proud to have to say that only one percent of the population of Japan is Christian. There are many opportunities yet for preaching, and we both need the other's help in achieving the goal of preaching to our own countries' people.

Jesus gave the twelve authority to drive out demons, then thought to be the source of all unhappiness and suffering. The disciples were commissioned by Jesus to drive out all sources of human suffering; this is expected of the church today, too.

There are demons throughout the world today. I hear about the suffering of North American farmers. It is not that farmers have stopped working or that the soil has suddenly become barren. Rather, farmers are suffering because of demons that control the human social system. It is the church's task to tackle this issue together with other people.

We hear of hunger in Africa. It is not that the world produces too little food to feed everyone. Some places have huge surpluses, other places extreme shortages. Surely demons are in control and the church is called to attack and drive out those demons, not stopping with benevolent gifts of food to those who are hungry.

Some of your missionaries are expressing solidarity with Korean residents in Japan by refusing to be fingerprinted, a practice reserved in Japan for criminals and foreigners. Korean residents are resisting fingerprinting, and I believe that missionaries who join them are responding to Jesus' call to drive out demons from Japanese society.

All Christians—Japanese, American, Canadian, German, Russian—are called to be engaged together in the battle against demons. And for this purpose the missionary presence is needed everywhere, be it Japan, Korea, Canada, or the U.S., as we seek to be with Jesus together.

Glossary

Buddhism: religion originating in India practiced in Japan

buraku: originally, "small village or group of houses"; also refers to an area or a person subject to discrimination

butsudan: Buddhist ancestral altar found in the family room of a Japanese home

Confucianism: philosophical, ethical, and political teaching from China that has great influence on Japanese education, ethics, political thinking and daily conduct

daimyo: local lord in feudal Japan

fumi-e: image of Christ Japanese were forced to trample on in feudal times to prove they were not Christian

hibakushi: surviving atomic bomb victims

hinomaru: rising sun flag, used by Japan in World War II and used unofficially today

juku: "cram schools" that prepare students for entrance examinations

kami: god or spirit found in nature, in certain persons and in deceased ancestors

kamidana: Shinto household altar found in kitchen of Japanese home

Kimigayo: ancient court song in praise of the emperor; used as national anthem in World War II and unofficially but widely today

Kojiki: eighth-century mythical account of Japan's origin and history

Kyodan: Nihon Kiristo Kyodan, United Church of Christ in Japan

mukyokai: "non-church movement" of Christians independent of formal church organizations

Nihon-shoki: eighth-century mythical account of Japan's origin and history

Nisei: second generation Japanese-American(s)

obon: late summer festival when families welcome souls of deceased relatives

samurai: member of military or warrior class in feudal Japan

shaman: religious leader with special counseling and healing powers

shinko shukyo: "newly arisen religions" active in modern Japan

Shinto: indigenous religion of Japan

shogun: strong military general who served as leader of feudal Japan

sutra: Buddhist scripture narrative

tenno: emperor

torii: gateway at the entrance of a Shinto shrine

Yamato: another name for Japan

Major Sources of Information

Some chapters were written by the authors based on written source material. Some chapters or sections of chapters, including most first-person accounts, were written by various persons for this book.

PART I: Christianity in Japan

Christian Beginnings: The Catholic Period

Cary, Otis. *A History of Christianity in Japan*. First edition, New York: Fleming H. Revell, 1909; second edition, Tokyo: Charles E. Tuttle Company, 1976.

Japanese Religions

Kodansha Encyclopedia of Japan. Tokyo: Kodansha Ltd., 1983.
Reid, David. "Japanese Religions" in Hinnels, John R., ed. *A Handbook of Living Religions*. New York: Viking, 1984.

Protestant Beginnings

Cary, *A History of Christianity in Japan*, cited above.
Kirkwood, Dean R. and Gano, Glenn G., eds. *Followers of the "Son."* Valley Forge, PA: International Ministries, ABC/USA, 1984.

A United Church

Phillips, James M. *From the Rising of the Sun*. Maryknoll, NY: Orbis Books, 1981.
Shoji, Tsutomu. "The United Church of Christ in Japan: Its Sin and Rebirth," in *Mid-Stream*, journal of the Council on Christian Unity of the Christian Church (Disciples of Christ), April 1988.
"One Sunday Morning" section is by Margaret Warren, missionary, United Methodist Church; Kyodan (United Church of Christ in Japan).

PART II: The Group Society: Inside the Group

Family and School chapters are by SHOJI Rutsuko, Division of Education, National Christian Council in Japan.

Nation-State and Emperor

"Hirohito and His Legacy," a special issue of *Japan Militarism Monitor* on Japan's Emperor System. Center for Christian Response to Asian Issues, No. 38, Feb. 1989.

PART THREE: The Group Society: Outside the Group

Ainu

"Mission Prototype," from keynote address by KOYANAGI Nobuaki, presented at the NCC/Japan-NCC/USA Human Rights' Issues Workshop, March 27, 1987.

Korean Residents

CHOI Sun Ae interview by Philip Park, missionary, Presbyterian Church, USA; Korean Christian Church in Japan.

OH Soo Hae quote from *LINK*, WCC Programme to Combat Racism, No. 5, 1989.

Okinawa

YOSHIDA Teiko section from her presentation at NCC/Japan-NCC/USA Human Rights' Issues Workshop, March 27, 1987.

Persons with Disabilities

Information on MIZUNO Genzo and translation of his poem by Marnie Tunbridge, former missionary, United Church of Canada; Kyodan.

Outside the Group—American Style

NOGAMI, Yukiye interview with Ruth Reames, former missionary, United Methodist Church; Kyodan.

PART FOUR: Japan's Role in the World Today

Official Development Assistance

Eduardo C. Tadem quotes from "Philippine Assistance Plan: A Mockery of Aid," in *AMPO: Japan-Asia Quarterly Review*, Vol. 21, Nos. 2, 3.

KANEKO Fumio. "Japanese ODA: Politics of Strategic Assistance," in *AMPO*, Vol. 20, Nos. 1, 2.

Stallings, Barbara. "Increased Japanese Role in Third World Development," in *Policy Focus*, Overseas Development Council, 1988, No. 6.

Peacemaking

HASHIMOTO Eiichi section from *Shinto no tomo* (Believer's friend), Aug. 1985, and *Kyodan Newsletter*, No. 198.

Swain, David. "Peacemaking and National Identity: A Case Study of Japan," in *Powers and Principalities: Outside Intervention in Asian Affairs*. Hong Kong: Christian Conference of Asia-Ecumenical Peace Program in Asia Workshop Report, 1988.

PART FIVE: Joining Hands in Mission

Hands Across the Sea

HOSHINO Masaoki section from *Kyodan Newsletter*, Nos. 212, 228, and *Mandate*, United Church of Canada, Oct. 1987.

Household
of
Power

Household
of
Power

The Task and Testing of the Church in Our Time

Oliver Powell

A PILGRIM PRESS PUBLICATION

UNITED CHURCH PRESS

Boston • Philadelphia

Library of Congress Catalog Number: 62-18361

Printed in the United States of America

To Eleonore

Contents

"You are no longer outsiders or aliens, but fellow citizens with every other Christian — you belong now to the household of God."

— *Ephesians 2:19**

"I now remind you to stir up that inner fire which God gave you. . . . For God has not given us a spirit of fear, but a spirit of power. . . ."

— *2 Timothy 1:6–7**

Introduction

A couple of years ago, a British astrological journal announced to its readers that it was giving up publication " because of an unforeseeable future."

It made me think of the recent announcement by Columbia University that it had suspended its compulsory sophomore course in contemporary civilization. " The action came," said *The New York Times*, " as a regretful admission that contemporary civilization has become too complicated and specialized to be taught by the ordinary teacher."

Let's face it: It's a tough time to be living. To try to live as a Christian makes it tougher!

There's no point in trying to minimize the seriousness of the condition of our world. But I am struck with the fact that so many church members seem to be as grim as everybody else about it all. They exhibit the same kind of tenseness and anxiety. Ministers become grim in their sermons about " the crisis of our time," and the fact that " it is later than you think," apparently believing that we can be scared into doing something about these conditions. Denominations become grim and ponderous in their massive and often unimaginative efforts to let the people in the churches know how serious things are, and how the " local church " should be stirring its stumps. They devise " emphases " from time to time to dramatize the urgency of the task. These are apt to succeed in creating quite a gust of enthusiasm at the upper levels of denominational life, but may end up barely rippling the pond of the local parish, where, of course, the job really gets done. Perhaps our grimness is simply our frustration showing. Or, the grimmer we can get about a matter, the more likely we are to have the feeling that we are doing something about it!

At any rate, I am struck by the fact that all this is something different from the kind of religion you find in the New Testament, our primary source for understanding what Christianity is and how Christians are expected to perform. Have you read lately about the hard-pressed people of the church in New Testament times? Believe me, that is exactly what they were, hard-pressed, backed up against a wall. The Roman government had thrown the book at them. You can sense their realization of how serious things were, but what strikes you more forcibly is how radiantly happy they were in the middle of it all. It's not that they were living in a fool's paradise. They knew things were bad. But what they knew best was that they and the world were in God's safe and holy keeping. God would manage; he always had. He would again. They talked about the *end* of things (and we in our day catch glimpses now and then of the possibility of the " end "). But what they mainly had in mind was Christ's return in triumph. The world was not headed for disaster, a dead-end street; it was headed for God's victory!

If we believe the same things about *our* time, is there anything we can do about it?

The following pages are an attempt to answer the question in part. They are intended for Christians and church members like myself who are anxious that in these times the church be at its best, that it muster all the vigor at its command, that it assert itself with all the life it possesses, and that it renew itself wherever its enthusiasm has flagged. These words are written by a working pastor, deep in the involvements of an ordinary parish. Little, if anything, of what is said is bright or new, but it is said by one who, like most of his fellow-members of the household of God, ministers and laymen, cares enormously what happens to this enterprise to which so many of us have given our lives. It is written by one who knows, too, that in the end the renewal of the church, if it is to take place, will be the work of God, speaking to us all through his Holy Spirit.

Chapter I

Giving the Critics a Hearing

EVERY SUNDAY, as the hands of the clock in my study crawl toward eleven, I stand at the window and watch the stream of worshipers arriving for the morning service. Now and then I find myself, preacher-like, appraising the volume of traffic, and crassly calculating the size of the assembling congregation. And, just as often, I find myself strangely moved, my heart touched. Some of the arriving people, of course, are strangers, newcomers, and I have little to go on. Others, however welcome they are made to feel, are people who will never have more than a marginal interest and concern. But most of them are men and women who come on warm, sunny days, or through driving snow across treacherous icy pavements, out of fierce loyalty, with love and pride and affection. It is a humbling, sobering sight. Just the other Sunday I found myself in a silent prayer of thanksgiving.

For these are the people of Christ's church, and part of the secret of its strength, not many of them wise, according to worldly standards, or powerful, or of noble birth, as the apostle Paul would say, but faithful over the long years, serving, sometimes sacrificing, standing loyally by in hard and in hopeful times.

1

Most of us know a church that we can call " home." We have found love there, acceptance and understanding — a place to lean our weariness, to dry our tears. It may be a meetinghouse, chaste and white against a green New England hill. It may be a stone structure at a busy downtown intersection, on the outside grimy gray, but within, soft shadows, the glint of brass, and richly grained woodwork, luminous and glowing in the sunlight that pours through jeweled glass. It may be a clapboard chapel on a treeless plot at the edge of town, with the winds from the great plains roaring round its eaves like thunder. It may be a sprawling, spreading, low-roofed, glass-walled building, new-smelling still, new-echoing.

Colonial, Gothic, Georgian, Romanesque, or Contemporary in architecture, this is the " House of God," a sanctuary of the spirit, a covert from the storm, an anchorage in eternity in the midst of time, and I celebrate it! Over the years it has been the true and faithful church of Jesus Christ. Here the word of God has been spoken, here the sacraments rightly administered, here hungry sheep have looked up, and in gracious compassionate words have been bountifully fed. Here young men and women have looked into each other's brimming eyes, and have spoken deathless vows. Here families have brought their dead, and bowed as a benediction was gently laid on their grief. Here enduring friendships were first knitted. Here a lonely, frightened man got hold of life again. Here words were spoken that brought courage to stand in God's name against wrong and injustice.

But, for all its faithfulness, for all the glory of it, for all the affection we have for it, there is no denying that the church of Jesus Christ is under heavy fire these days. And if we love it and take it seriously, we will listen to what its critics are saying.

This will be hard for some, especially ministers, who are not always the best listeners. But let's face it: Churches are

under fire these days. People who ought to know what they are talking about are making charges that are not easy to take. Some of them, of course, are exaggerated; some of them are just not true. But a lot more of them, like the proverbial shoe, really fit!

Maybe you haven't heard much of this criticism in your church. Maybe you haven't been listening very hard. Or maybe you and your minister are so busy running what is often called a " successful " church that even if you pick up criticism now and then, you're sure it can't possibly apply to you.

It's easy, of course, to criticize and complain. And it is easier to point out all the things that are wrong than it is to indicate what must be done to set them right. It goes without saying that some of the criticism leveled at Christian churches has been extreme and irresponsible. Furthermore, although it's necessary to talk about all the things that are wrong about a church, it's more important to look at the positive side, to call attention to all the good things a church does — the lives it helps to hold steady, the aid it gives to people in trouble, its ministry to children and to young people, and all the rest.

Even so, having made a number of allowances (which we are awfully good at doing!) let's give serious attention to what our critics are saying.

Who are these critics? They are people outside the church, all sorts of people — writers, civic leaders, sociologists, historians, journalists, artists. They are also people inside the church — ministers, denominational executives, seminary professors, rank and file members.

What are they saying about the church? They are saying a great many things — in books, magazine articles, speeches, and sermons. Here we are sketchily summarizing.

1. *Many critics are saying that Protestant churches often act like chameleons, those small lizards that take on the*

color of whatever background they are set against. This, say
the critics, is exactly what churches do: They assume the
color, the shape, the style and habits of the community in
which they find themselves. They seldom stand out against
it; they have become part of it, merely an echo of its voice.
There is little that's distinctive about churches any more.

G. Paul Musselman in his book, *The Church on the Urban Frontier,* says that the church has become simply " one
of the normal adjuncts of a good community in the same
category as good schools, a good library, good police force,
good streets, and good commuting service."[1]

Typical examples of this chameleon-like trait of
churches can be found in suburban communities. In *The
Suburban Captivity of the Churches*[2] Gibson Winter declares
that many churches have let themselves be taken prisoner by
the style of life that marks the typical American suburb. A
church is just another piece of suburbia with a strong religious flavor. And, in the main, as suburbia goes, so goes the
church!

It is not only in suburbia, of course, that we discover
this tendency of church and world to look and to be more
and more alike. There is danger of making suburban
churches scapegoats in such matters. To be sure, they face
particular temptations in this regard, but what is happening
in America is happening to us all, to one degree or another.
In city churches, suburban churches, small town churches,
and open-country churches we are becoming more and more
a part of what Theodore Matson in his fine book, *The Edge
of the Edge,*[3] calls a " homogenized, pan-urban culture," all

[1] G. Paul Musselman, *The Church on the Urban Frontier.* The Seabury
Press, Greenwich, Connecticut, 1960. (P. 50.)
[2] From: *The Suburban Captivity of the Churches,* by Gibson Winter.
Copyright © 1961 by Gibson Winter. Reprinted by permission of
Doubleday and Company, Inc., Garden City, New York, 1961 and Student Christian Movement Press Ltd., London.
[3] Theodore E. Matson, *The Edge of the Edge.* Friendship Press, New York,
1961.

in the middle-class style. It's like homogenized milk: wherever you dip into it, it is of the same consistency, the same quality, consistently checking out to the same standards of excellence, or of mediocrity.

The standard is set by the pattern of life in big cities: that of material well-being, seemingly the almost divine right of Americans to be comfortable and secure.

Newspapers and magazines provide plenty of evidence of the lengths to which Americans will go to cushion their lives, to fill the chinks and crannies of their snug existence against the cold winds of risk and failure, packing them tight with all sorts of kitchen-tested, foolproof products, predigested opinions, and even packaged religion. An advertisement in a widely known publication expresses this: in a picture one executive is saying to another, " Of course I'm sure; I read it in *Newsweek!* " Or mark the slogan used by an insurance company: " Simplified Security."

A sobering documentation of what is happening all over the American scene in gratifying this hunger for comfort and security is provided by Alan Harrington in his book, *Life in the Crystal Palace.*[4] The " Crystal Palace " is a typical, large business organization which handpicks its employees, expects them to stay in its employ for life, and builds around them a towering wall of immunity. The book is a record of Mr. Harrington's experiences with all this, of a terrifying and mounting fear of losing his individuality and, thereby, his essential dignity. He tells how, finally, in order to preserve his life, he left the enfolding arms of the company for more precarious but essentially human working conditions elsewhere.

Then as he rides to work one day in the meticulously arranged car-pool, he meditates on the meaning of his rigidly

[4] Alan Harrington, *Life in the Crystal Palace.* Alfred A. Knopf, New York, 1959.

structured way of life. "We know exactly where we have been," he says, "and where we are going; we could set our watches by the arrival of stoplights. . . . Thus you ride for years over the same road in the back seat of someone else's vehicle. . . . Looking around at all the passive faces, I think what a peaceful load of humanity we are, so innocent, so sure of the years ahead. If one of us, willing to be a disturber of the peace, would rise from his seat and cry out: ' Wake up! Prisoners of Benevolence! ' " [5]

Now, ask our critics, how are the churches managing in this " homogenized " style of life? They are managing very well indeed, they will say. With very little difficulty, they have fallen in with the whole scheme of things. Except for an occasional protest, which is usually laid at the door of some ill-advised " radical," the churches of America, by and large, exist to supply a kind of spiritual plastic coating to the surface of contemporary life. They baptize it, if not always in the name of the Trinity, certainly in the spirit of a God who wants people to be happy and who admits that there's quite a bit to be said for the Golden Rule and for brother-hood — generally speaking, that is.

In short, our critics conclude, the church has turned its back on the very quality of its essential life which would give it the right to speak with authority — the quality of " the Other." It has lost the sense of having a word to speak which is not merely the echoing of man's words, lost the awareness of being " a colony of heaven," an outpost of another king-dom by which it claims the right to say, " Thus saith the Lord! "

As the result of a steady accommodation to the ways of the world, the church has become so much *of* the world that it is not really *in* it with any degree of power or effective-ness. Chameleon-like, churches have so effectively blended

[5] *Ibid.,* p. 37.

into the background of the communities in which they live that it gets harder all the time to tell where the church leaves off and the community begins.

A second charge of the critics is that churches substitute organization, " program," and a variety of activities for real, bona fide fellowship, which is what people need more than anything else.

If this is true it has come about not because churches have deliberately set out to establish themselves on a new basis, but because of the nature of so many of the communities in which they live, and because they have become so much a part of them. That is to say, many modern American communities are not real " communities " to start with; they are simply residential areas. And these two things are not necessarily the same. So many of the elements that make neighborhoods real " communities " have disappeared: long and cherished tradition with its accompanying festivals and celebrations; national and racial rootages; economic and social bonds forged in a common occupation or service.

The effect of all this on the style of religious life in a community is described by Dr. Winter. In many instances, he points out, the " natural," organic ties between people are dissolved. " The basis of congregational integrity dissolves; in fact, the human materials of friendship and familial ties are no longer available. The churches try to create fellowships without any common base in long-standing association and familiarity. The only common elements among residents of the new type of neighborhood are a relatively similar position on the economic ladder and some similarity in style of life. Where these common elements are missing, . . . the congregation simply dwindles and dies or develops some special field of interest. Where the common elements are present, a new style of religious life emerges — the organization church." [6]

[6] Winter, *The Suburban Captivity of the Churches*. (P. 82.)

The " organization church "— the program-centered or
activity-centered church — is a type that most of us are
familiar with. Most of our churches follow a fairly conventional pattern. We have a weekly service of morning worship
on Sunday, and occasionally a second service in the evening.
We have a church school, one or more youth groups, an organization for the women of the church, a men's group, and
other auxiliary bodies to serve people of various ages and
interests. There is the usual structure of boards and committees to carry on the necessary business of the church. Our
critics do not imply that this is inherently bad, or that this
familiar structuring of church life should immediately be
abolished. Indeed, in many communities where the opportunities for social intercourse are scanty, where the possibilities for establishing interpersonal relationships are bleak, the
conventional church program with its multiplicity of programs and activities has helped to make community life
bearable.

But our critics raise a very important question: What
does all this, commendable as it may be, have to do with the
essential nature and purpose of the Christian church as the
loving community of God's people in the world? The problems that Dr. Winter and others see in connection with the
" organization church " are these:

1. *In the organization church, activity tends to turn in
on itself.* It becomes activity for its own sake. In the mind of
a participant, what goes on may have very little to do with
the fundamental purpose and mission of the church of Jesus
Christ in the world. It may be little more than religious
" busy work," or an effort to hold a member's interest.

2. *In the organization church, the planning of more
and more programs becomes almost an obsession.* Stereotypes
develop simply because of the pressure to maintain an unbroken succession of good programs, usually the presentation of a speaker, who may or may not allow time for ques-

tions and answers or other opportunities for participation by those present. If the program is preceded by a meal it is assumed that the opportunities for fellowship are heightened. This may or may not be so, particularly if we test our concept of fellowship by what the New Testament means by it — a kind of free and relaxed exchange of thoughts and feelings about important things, down at a deep level.

It is all too true that many church organizations have become what are referred to good-naturedly as " Knife and Fork Societies." You may not have been personally acquainted with the busy lady described in the following lines, but you probably know her first cousin or her great-aunt:

On Monday she lunched with a Housing Committee,
    With statistics and stew she was filled;
Then she dashed to a tea on " Crime in Our City,"
    And dined with a Church Ladies' Guild.

On Tuesday she went to a Babies' Week lunch,
    And a tea on " Good Citizenship ";
At dinner she talked to the Trade Union bunch
    (There wasn't a date she dared skip).

On Wednesday she managed two annual dinners,
    One at noon and the other at night,
On Thursday a luncheon on " Bootlegging Sinners,"
    And a dinner on " War: Is It Right? "

" World Problems We Face " was her Friday noon date
    (A luncheon-address, as you guessed),
And she wielded a fork while a man from New York
    Spoke that evening on " Social Unrest."

On Saturday noon she fell in a swoon,
    Missed a talk on the youth of our land. . . .
Poor thing, she was through! She never came to,
    But died with a spoon in her hand.[7]

---

[7] Quoted by C. W. Gilkey in *Present Day Dilemmas in Religion*. Cokesbury Press, Nashville, 1928. (Pp. 61–62.)

3. *The organization church, with its endless activi-*
ties, raises the question of loyalty. For whose sake and in
whose name is it all taking place? Are church members
enlisted merely to perpetuate the life of a particular
church, to hold it together by a network of faithfulness to
a multiplicity of jobs — raising money, putting on church
suppers, teaching in the church school, working in the
office, serving on a board or a special committee? Or,
somehow, through their involvement in Christ's work in
the world, are they brought closer to him, to his mission
to the world, and to their fellow members in his living,
working body? And are they brought closer to one another as children of God, accepted, and released from their
dreads and frustrations through the liberating force of work
done in love, nothing held back, and without expectation of
praise or reward?

These questions are the kinds we need to ask about the
organization church, the program- or activity-centered
church.

A third common criticism of churches is that they are
sadly out of touch with so much of what is important and
exciting in the affairs of the world. For all their busyness
within their churches and organizations, so many church
people actually are out of touch with the currents of contemporary life. And a church that is out of touch with the
world around it is the saddest sight in creation.

Several years ago the city of Boston added a new res-
ervoir to its water supply system. As often happens, a
whole village had to be moved to another site. Everything
was demolished except an old stone church which pur-
posely was left standing — for aesthetic reasons, the city
fathers said. People driving by enjoyed the lovely sight —
the curving shoreline, the arching trees, and the Gothic
tower raised against the sky. But the structure rapidly
deteriorated until it was little more than a shell, its roof open

to the rains, the foundation sagging a little more each year.

This is a parable about some churches. Swiftly flowing tides of change have flooded their communities but, turned in on themselves, they live lonely lives shut up with their memories of a dear, dead past, holding fast to ancient forms and practices, often beautiful, but seldom, if ever, engaged in spirited, pointed conversation with the new world that is running with such vigor and excitement past their tightly closed doors.

Churches can get to be a little like Laura and her mother, characters in Tennessee Williams' play, *The Glass Menagerie*. For a long time they tried to keep going a genteel, cloistered kind of life that had become a museum piece in a fast-moving age. At the end of the play, Tom, the son, says to his sister, " Nowadays the world is lit by lightning! Blow out your candles, Laura." [8] A candle-lit church in a lightning-lit world simply won't do!

It is depressing to realize that a church is not relevant any more, that all it is doing is giving pious answers to a flock of questions that very few people are asking. Such a church is a little like Victor Borge's grandfather, back in the old country. He was a medical research man, says Victor, and working in his laboratory one day, he discovered a cure for which there was no disease! This, he said, was disconcerting enough, but even more so was the fact that a few weeks later his grandmother caught the cure and died!

Lots of people feel strongly about our churches. They feel that they are poorly equipped to deal with the tough realities of a tough time. They feel that, although their intentions are the noblest and their members selfless and devoted, they are enterprises that are not hooked onto reality. They are not hooked onto the social changes that are taking place at their doorstep. They are not hooked onto what con-

[8] Tennessee Williams, *The Glass Menagerie*. Random House, New York, 1945. Scene VII.

temporary novelists, dramatists, and painters are saying about
our world through their creations, sometimes simply because
their Puritan sensibilities are shocked by certain words and
images. They often are not hooked onto teenagers, to their
bewildering world and what they feel and say about it. They
are not even hooked onto some of the exciting experiments
and advances that Protestant denominations are making in
carrying out Christ's mission in the world.

A minister friend of mine, serving with distinction in a
rural area, writes to tell me of his disappointment that the
church is not doing more to help farmers face the questions
they should be raising as Christians. Most of their figuring
as to whether or not they should participate in the government's farm program has to do, he says, with the dollars they
can expect to make. There is no consideration of what is
best for the soil or for the needs of future generations, no
consideration of conserving God's gift, or of the needs of
the hungry two-thirds of the world.

*Again, critics of the church say that it does not pay
nearly enough attention to individuals, to men and women,
boys and girls, young people, taking them one by one,* which
is the only way you can " take " anybody. The church, they
say, is long on group activity, on services of corporate worship, on organizing people into planned, carefully structured
programs, but short on getting to know people in their soli-
tariness. It does little to help them come to know themselves,
to help them discover a sense of personal worth, to put them
in touch with the great reservoirs of spiritual power.

In the long run, what people want almost more than
anything else is for another human being to take them seriously. And when they come to church, whoever they may
be — the cynical, the critical, the embittered, the offended —
that is what they want, to be taken seriously, whatever they
may have done, however they may look on the outside. As

somebody put it once, there is nothing more important in the world than to give another person your whole, undivided attention. Churches engrossed in elaborate programs of group activity often do not have time for this, and that is a tragedy.

We have been outlining some of the most frequently heard criticisms brought against Protestant churches from the *outside:* that churches, like chameleons, have taken on the color of the communities in which they live; that they have substituted organization, " programs," and activities for bona fide Christian fellowship; that they often are out of touch with the world; and that in their busyness with corporate activities they have neglected people as individuals.

Now, let us turn to two criticisms that are more likely to be heard *inside* the church, coming from sensitive members, from ministers and other leaders. Actually what they say is not so much criticism as confession — admissions which explain, in part, the reasons for the other charges brought against the church.

Of all the things the Christian church has forgotten down through the centuries, two have been most devastating. It has forgotten, first, that its essential character is that of mission; and, second, it has quite forgotten exactly what justifies its existence, namely, the hard core of the religion of the Bible, the gospel of the love of God, made plain in Jesus Christ.

Let our confessional begin, then, with the recognition that many churches have lost their most distinctive mark — that of being *part of a mission operation.* Actually, a church does not *have* " missions " as part of its program, as we sometimes say; a church *is itself* a mission. (If you are interested in that kind of thing, the word mission comes originally from a Latin root meaning " to send.") This is the kind of language Jesus used: "And he called to him the twelve, and began *to send them out*, two by two " (Mark 6: 7). Ever since, this has been the classic language of the Christian church. To talk about a church correctly, then, you have to talk about it as *a company of people on a mission*.

Moreover, it is always a mission on behalf of a cause — not for selfish profit. Its people are under orders, so to speak, working for somebody else. They are accountable to headquarters located elsewhere. Specifically, the people of a Christian church are recruits who have signed up to further the cause that God has been advancing in the world for centuries. It is embodied in a particular institution which transcends all the usual distinctions of place, nationality, race, social position, and even of time.

Discerning people in all parts of the church are saying that it is precisely the loss of this sense of mission — of being sent into the world to do a job for somebody else — that describes its real problem, its lack of effectiveness. Many a church has become just the opposite kind of institution, not one that is sent at all, but one that stays home and takes awfully good care of itself!

The second confession — underlying the first, and actually the root cause of it — is simply that by one means or another, over a long period of years, churches have drifted away from the hard core of biblical faith and have accepted all kinds of substitutes.

One of these substitutes for authentic biblical faith is the *cult of spiritual health*. This reduces Christianity to the notion that faith (if not God himself) exists for its practical, utilitarian value — that is, for what it can do for you. Religious faith works; therefore, acquire religious faith! There is continual counsel on *how* to do and to acquire all kinds of things: how to eliminate fear, how to stop worrying, how to be a success though a Christian, and all the rest. This cult has little or nothing to say about the hard things in the New Testament, the scandalous, shocking things, the impossible things that Jesus expects of people. It wraps religion up in a pretty package and advertises it with an attractive folder, outlining how you can make it your own in five (or, at the most, six) easy lessons. And it is an empty and foolish distortion of the religion of the Bible!

A certain type of popular evangelism offers another substitute. Actually, it is much closer to biblical religion than the " how-to-be-a-successful-Christian " versions. It comes right out and says that modern man is in a mess because of his pride and a built-in perversity about him. It says that if he is ever going to get anywhere he must do a lot of confessing, give up his old ways, and start fresh. But it tells only part of the story. It stops too soon. It talks about sin mainly in terms of individual, private wrongdoing. It bypasses the giant sins of nations and of people in the mass. And, like the " success " schools of religion, because it, too, is anxious to show that religion works, it packages its faith in a formula.

Recently, still another substitute has appeared. It is what Martin Marty calls *The New Shape of American Religion.*[9] This new religious style, Marty says, is a compound of a number of things: patriotism, motherhood, common sense. It rests on the belief that faith is *a good thing.* It boils down to a kind of " faith in faith." This, says Dr. Marty, is currently the popular religion of American democracy. Actually it does not require very much of a person. And it is eminently respectable!

What all this commentary adds up to is the imperative of rediscovering the hard core of biblical religion. Or, to say it differently, before we do another thing, we must get back on the main highway of the Christian faith. Many of us in the Protestant churches of America have been on a long de-

[9] Martin E. Marty, *The New Shape of American Religion.* Harper and Brothers, New York, 1959.

tour. Our route has taken us through gently rolling country, up easy slopes, and through pleasant valleys. On the whole, things have gone well. The road surfaces have been in good condition; there have been notably few collisions, and the rest stops along the way have been frequent and satisfying.

But there is another road, a very old one, running back over the centuries for nearly two thousand years. It is poorly paved in places and along the rocks at the roughest spots there are stains of blood. Along this road has traveled a re-markable and gallant company — the people we know as the saints and the martyrs, the heroes of Christian history. But there are also numberless ordinary men and women, lay people and ministers, who, as someone has put it, in season and out, in good times and bad, have preached the gospel, have lived the life, have kept the faith. Many of these people are living and working in our own time. Some of them are serving on exposed, dangerous frontiers of the church's mis-sion; some of them may be in your own church. Most of them are plain people like the rest of us, with the normal quota of faults and weaknesses. The one notable thing about them is that they are still on the main highway — this road of faithful, costly witness.

The next part of our discussion, therefore, leads us straight into a fresh examination of exactly who we are — we who make up the membership of these churches of Jesus Christ — and what we are called to be and to do in his name. This will be a project in self-understanding. Any genuine renewal of the churches must start with exactly that kind of exercise!

	The Church
Chapter II	**Is Knowledge**

ONE OF THE GLARING weaknesses of churches is that not enough of their members really understand exactly the nature and business of the organization to which they belong.

I relish Amos Wilder's story of the church and the architect.[1] The church engaged him to design a new building for them. He was one of the top men in his profession. Having agreed to do the job, he immediately asked the building committee to tell him, first, how they envisioned the new building being used, and, second, how the members understood the ultimate meaning of the church and its worship.

The committee and the minister were struck dumb, says Dr. Wilder. They had not expected this second request. But the architect was simply asking the question underlying all other questions. The committee knew that they wanted a sanctuary, accommodations for a church school, an assembly hall for meetings and church dinners, a kitchen, a gymnasium, a study for the minister, rest rooms, and all the rest. But they were hard put to tell the architect what they thought a house of God was for, or fundamentally what their

[1] Amos N. Wilder, *Theology and Modern Literature*. Harvard University Press, Cambridge, 1958. (P. 41, paraphrased.)

17

particular kind of church was for. This discerning architect knew, however, that he could design neither a court of justice without an understanding of the meaning of law in our Anglo-Saxon tradition, nor a church without an appreciation of the faith of the particular congregation in question and how they thought it should be expressed in their day.

This *is* the question underlying all the other questions about the church and the renewal of its life and mission in these times: How thoroughly do Christians understand and appreciate exactly what a church is, what its unique role in society is?

The next three chapters, therefore, are addressed to this question. They sketch three ways in which a church is uniquely a church and not simply one more serious, well-intentioned social organization. (Remember what the critics say — that one thing that is so wrong with churches is that they are not distinctive, there is nothing special or unusual about them, and they look just like the rest of the community.) In the next three chapters, then, we shall point out what is unique about the church:

First, the church is *knowledge;* that is, knowledge of what God has done for man. This is knowledge of something unique, of something of life-and-death importance, something that no other human institution or organization pretends to know anything about.

Second, the church is an *experience* of this knowledge; that is, the experience, firsthand, not by hearsay, of a special brand of human relationships, of a special kind of fellowship that cannot be found anywhere else, the kind that accepts people and reconciles them to themselves and to one another.

Third, the church is *mission* in putting its knowledge to work in the world; that is to say, it has an assigned task, a special work in God's name that nobody else will do.

Obviously, there is something artificial and misleading about such an arrangement. The three ways of describing the essential life of a church are, of course, interdependent. Each is incomplete without the others. In one sense, we have no business separating them. For instance, we may say that the church is knowledge, but it is empty and useless knowledge unless (a) what it talks about is known and felt in actual experience among people; or (b) the knowledge gained is put to work in some practical way; or (c) there is a constant returning to the spring of all our knowledge, namely the ultimate wisdom which is God, and the most practical demonstration he has ever given of it in Jesus Christ. But, so long as we keep this in mind, for purposes of definition, we can safely talk in turn about certain specific aspects of the work and witness of a Christian church.

Turn, then, to the first of these ways of saying what a church is: that *it is the knowledge of something that can make a life-and-death difference in the lives of people and society*. It is the knowledge of what God in and through the person of Jesus Christ has done for man, how he has acted decisively on man's behalf, and how man, when he responds to this action, is able to start living a new life right in the middle of his old one, no matter how discouraging his situation may seem to be.

Before we go any further we should consider the crucial role of knowledge in the Christian life. Many of us, because of the kind of lives we lead, the kind of community we live in, and the kind of church in which we were brought up, are inclined to think that the *knowing* part of the Christian religion is relatively unimportant. At least we do not consider it nearly as important as the *doing* part. Christianity, people will say, is, after all, a *doing* kind of religion; it is practical. Jesus went about " doing good "; he did not go about asking all sorts of hard, intellectual questions, organizing group discussions, or writing books on theology. All of which may be true. But to suppose, as many people apparently do, that

Jesus or any other of the great figures who have shaped Christian history disregarded or looked with disdain at the importance of knowing, of thinking, is a grotesque distortion of the truth.

Jesus said, " You shall love the Lord your God with all your heart, and with all your soul, and with all your strength, *and with all your mind* " (Luke 10: 27). Unless I do not understand him, this means that along with all the other things that God requires of us, he expects us to use the brains he gave us! The plain fact is that in this life and in this tough age there are a lot of hard, tough questions that have to be thought through. Just thinking about them is, of course, no proof of your worth as a Christian, but it is evidence that you are taking things seriously. And it may also help people who put a premium on thinking to take Christianity seriously. As George Buttrick put it once, the doorways of churches must be built high enough so that people will not have to leave their heads outside!

Because many people take such a dim view of Christian brainwork, we have occasional outbreaks of anti-intellectualism, and theology acquires a bad reputation. People are leery about theology. They imply that it is for " eggheads," for the " professionals," and that it is a lot of dry and irrelevant speculation. According to these people, the clear waters of primitive Christianity (supposedly found in the basic simplicities of the Man of Nazareth as he is pictured in the four Gospels) got muddied by the apostle Paul and his writing, and we would really be better off, in a way, without his complicated theological discussions.

A few Christmases ago, the chairman of the program committee of a certain church women's organization went to her minister to ask if he would help her select some Christmas carols which would be " free of all those awful theological references." The minister had the wit to say to her kindly, but quite properly, " But, Mrs. M., the birth of Jesus was, after all, a very theological affair! " So, indeed, was his whole life, his ministry, healing, and his death and resurrection. There can be no real understanding of it any other way.

To dismiss theology as irrelevant, unnecessary, and as abstract wool-gathering is mere nonsense. Theology is basic to everything we believe and do as Christians. Theology is simply the intellectual aspect of Christian faith. As Roger Shinn writes, " With a special kind of effort we might try to imagine a religion without any intellectual content. It would be an emotional blur, with feelings never clarified or directed to any goal. Such a religion could never be explained to another person because words require thought. It could never persist consistently in the life of even one person, since such continuity also demands thought. Probably it could not exist even for a brief time, for man is (among other things) a thinking being.

" Certainly the Christian faith gives major importance to thought. It stems from the word of God and the words that convey that word. It interprets written Scriptures. It has a mission in a complex modern world, which it seeks to understand. Far more than most religions, Christianity asks every believer to use his mind. And every thinking Christian is to some degree a theologian." [2]

So much for that. Come back to our main theme now: What does the Christian church know that is so crucially important? Can it be summed up in a few plain words? That is difficult, but, at the risk of oversimplifying things, it is worth a try.

A safe place to start is the Bible itself. Here and there in the New Testament you come on a number of short, terse statements which try to put in summary, nutshell form what its writers are driving at. Look at three of them:

[2] Roger L. Shinn, *The Educational Mission of Our Church*. The United Church Press, Philadelphia, 1962.

" God so loved the world that he gave his only Son, that whoever believes in him should not perish but have eternal life " (John 3: 16).

" If any one is in Christ, he is a new creation; the old has passed away, behold, the new has come. All this is from God, who through Christ reconciled us to himself and gave us the ministry of reconciliation; that is, God was in Christ reconciling the world to himself, . . . and entrusting to us the message of reconciliation. So we are ambassadors for Christ, God making his appeal through us" (2 Corinthians 5: 17-20a).

" But we have this treasure in earthen vessels, to show that the transcendent power belongs to God and not to us " (2 Corinthians 4: 7).

All this says four things, at least, as to what the religion of the New Testament is all about:

1. God loves to the limit the world and the people he made. His love is unbelievably great. It goes far beyond anything a man ever believed possible. It is over him and under him and around him all the time. It enters the deep places of his life and goes clear around the corners of the things he is ashamed of and has been afraid to look at.

2. This love of God can best be understood in such a term as " reconciliation," which means " bringing together again." Thus, God's love can bring together whatever has got separated — people, man and God, or the various parts of a man's own life. Whatever else God may be trying to do in the world, the most important job he has is to bring together, to restore, to heal, to give people who are lost and mixed up the chance for a fresh start.

3. But his love does not stop there: The people who have experienced the joy and the peace of a fresh start, of having their broken, unhappy lives put together again, are expected to pass the good news on to others. They are to

become " ambassadors for Christ." In other words, the message of Christianity is something you cannot keep to yourself. It has to be shared.

4. The sharing of the good news of the love of God takes place through a very imperfect instrument (an "earthen vessel "), through a fellowship of very ordinary people who, for the most part, are like the people you find in your own church.

But before we do any more theorizing, let us see how the good news is likely to work out in the lives of people — of two particular kinds of people, to be specific. Their experience with it is told in the New Testament. But you can still meet them — during the morning coffee break, or over the back fence, or at the P.T.A. meeting.

One is the young man we know as " the prodigal son." (If you need to refresh your memory about him, read Luke 15:11–24.) He was obsessed with the notion that whatever else life might be good for, it was meant to be enjoyed, to be used up, and anybody who did not drain it to the last drop was not only cheating, but was also likely to be a stuffy bore. God had made him a free man and he was determined to act like one. His theory was an old and familiar one: It's today that counts; eat, drink, and be merry, for tomorrow you die!

The prodigal's father most likely did his best to point out the folly of the boy's intentions, but, in the end he did not try to stop his son from doing what he insisted on doing, which was to cash in his inheritance and leave home. For a time the young man " had a ball." He went through his resources like a drunken sailor. He was really " free " for the first time! He was running his own life; he had liberated himself from old-fashioned morality and religion.

Then one day he hit bottom. He was still " free " (or so he insisted), but he also grew to hate himself a little more every day. Besides, he was getting all he could take of pigs and garbage. His moment of truth came one gray morning when he knew he couldn't stomach himself any longer. As Jesus told the story, " he came to himself " — that is, he was ruthlessly honest with himself, admitted that he had " had it " and that his life had gone bankrupt. He confessed that he had to have help, slammed the gate on the pig stye, and started the bitter journey home.

Now, all this time his father had been waiting for him, refusing to intervene, for he knew that the boy had to have it out with himself. When he saw him turn the bend in the road, however, he knew that everything was going to come out all right. With a hoarse cry of joy he hurried out to meet him, threw his arms around him, and handed him back the dignity he had lost.

That is one example of the way this love of God works: It works with people who suppose that they really can run their lives on their own, who kick over the traces and set up their own little world.

The good news works with a second kind of person, too; conventionally good people, who have a very proper and respectable religion, who are pillars of church and community. But, said Jesus, sometimes people like that are just as lost, in their own way, as the prodigal son was in his.

Read the story of Nicodemus (John 3:1–15), quite the opposite from the prodigal son who wanted to be free (but whose " freedom " finally tightened around his neck like a noose). Nicodemus looked for the meaning of life in strict, rigid adherence to the religion of the Jewish Law, where everything was put down in black and white; no guesswork, none of this freedom of individual choice. The Law told you how to live the good life, and that was that!

But behind the mask which Nicodemus was able to hold snugly in place most of the time (some people are not as successful at this as he was), he was uneasy. He had the unsettling feeling now and then that his life was empty, that he was going through a lot of motions that were not adding up to much. He had heard a lot about Jesus, and decided to have a talk with him. He arranged for an interview with him late one night. In that unforgettable encounter he got the shock of his life, of course.

Instead of discussing the Law, Jesus started right in to talk about Nicodemus and his need to be born all over again. He said that religious faith is all a matter of the movement of God's Spirit on a man's life, and that you cannot be any more sure of it than you can be sure of the wind. Nicodemus was shaken and went off in a daze. But for the first time somebody had thrown open a window in his stuffy life and given him room to breathe and the chance to acquire a vital religious faith that was truly his own!

What we are trying to make clear here lies at the very core of Christianity: a message announced to the world, a message of unbelievably good news about what God, because of his love for man, has done for him. It is the good news that God has shown man the way to live a new life right in the middle of the old; that man can be " saved," that is, rescued from a life of futility, of triviality and boredom, of empty show and strain.

The tangible evidence of all this is the person of Jesus Christ, who, says the New Testament, is actually God himself in person, in human form, sharing the life of the world, entering it right down " at ground level," as J. B. Phillips puts it, experiencing its tragedy and pain, even letting himself be killed by its hate and viciousness — all to the end that from that moment on men would know that everything Jesus did and stood for was real. It was not just theory; it happened right here in this life, where people saw it happen and told others about it. As Dr. Phillips says in another place, this is the center, the foundation on which Christianity rests, this fact that God lived in this world in the person of Jesus Christ. And, says he, this " historic fact remains, and we in the twentieth century . . . may have to short-circuit the cen-

turies and let the startling truth break over us afresh — that
we live on a visited planet."[3]

But Christianity goes still another step. It not only possesses and announces the crucial knowledge that in Jesus
Christ God broke open for people the way into new life; it
says that centuries later, right in the middle of our own time,
of our own hesitant, troubled lives, God keeps offering to
people the opportunity for that same experience. It is not
just something that happened in the far away and the long
ago; it can happen here and now when people accept in faith
what God has done and throw themselves into the life and
work of the Christian church which, in its truest definition, is
Christ's living body.

Now it is important to keep in mind, in this connection,
the way the Christian church came into existence. Nobody
brought it into being. Nobody said, " Come now, it's time
for those who believe in Jesus and want to follow him to
get together and organize a church." It did not happen that
way at all. Rather, the church sort of "exploded" into being.
A few thoroughly defeated followers of Jesus suddenly were
convinced that he was not dead, as everybody supposed, but
very much alive, though in a different form. Almost overnight they were turned into excited, enthusiastic ambassadors
of everything Jesus had believed and taught. (You can read
about it in some of the most important verses in the New
Testament, in the second chapter of the book of Acts.) It
was the Holy Spirit of God let loose again, like the wind,
blowing where it will, and this time in a most unlikely place,
among some discredited, unsophisticated folk from up-
country!

This, then, is the core of the knowledge which the

[3] J. B. Phillips, *God, Our Contemporary*. The Macmillan Company, New
York, 1960. (P. 63.)

church possesses, which it prizes so highly, and which it preaches wherever it gets a chance:

God, in his love, so vast and deep that we have trouble comprehending it, acting on his own initiative, entered our human life in and through Jesus Christ and showed how it is possible to have "eternal life" here and now.

God had guaranteed the possibility of this happening in every age of history by calling into being a very special kind of community or fellowship, made up of those who have responded in faith to what he has done (the way the prodigal son responded, and the way Nicodemus wanted to but could not).

This special community — the church, comprising those who have become part of its life out of sheer gratitude for what God has done for them — is commissioned to carry on the reconciling work of God. The church, therefore, in the strictest sense is not the voluntary association of those who take Jesus seriously and want to follow him and find mutual help in being together. The church is itself part of the good news, part of the life-giving gospel of God.

Theodore E. Matson sums it up by saying that we modern Christians do not make our witness in an alien world. We make it in one which God has re-claimed, which he loves, which he once lived in as a man, for which he still has the same purpose. And, most astonishing of all, God has entrusted to us the work of reconciliation. " We are ambassadors for Christ, God making his appeal through us."

Now, there is a very practical side to all this. It is all very well to describe a church as a company of people who possess the special kind of knowledge that we have been describing. But, as a matter of fact, people who know our churches intimately will be saying: " Look here; what you say may be true enough in theory, but to get down to cases, we don't know very many churches that think of themselves in those terms at all. For one thing, they don't aspire that high. And, granted that they can understand all the fine language that's used, there's no assurance that they either are interested in or capable of assisting in God's work of reconciliation. They think of themselves, rather, as quite ordinary people, hard-pressed by the demands of making as decent a living as they can in a highly competitive society, and providing a home and education for a family. Besides, just like everybody else, they share the anxiety of an age where periodically somebody nervously fingers the fuse of a hydrogen bomb. These people believe in churches; it's hard for them to think of communities without churches. They want their children to have the benefits of a Christian education, but, frankly, they are embarrassed and even a little annoyed when Christian educators tell them that the church can't do the job by itself, that it requires the informed and unfailing assistance of home and parents. Perhaps they feel that if churchmen were really on the job they could somehow, by thorough research, find a way to package a person's Christian education the way almost everything else can be packaged these days."

In short, what people are really saying is this: "We want Christianity, but we're not sure we want, or can afford to pay, what Christianity apparently costs in time and effort."

This honest though dismaying confession brings us to face squarely *the whole process by which the people of a church really become the possessors of the knowledge of who they are and the job they have to do in the world.* The fact that they have such a skimpy acquaintance with it much of the time can largely be explained by a faulty way of going at one of the main-line jobs of any church, the Christian education of its people — *all* its people, boys and girls, young people, parents, grandmothers and grandfathers. We shall give our attention to this matter for the balance of this chapter.

Straight off, we need to make an elementary but very important observation: When we say " Christian education " we mean, in the broadest sense, everything that happens in a church to condition the thinking and action of its members. The educational life of a church is not simply what goes on in church school classes on Sunday. In some instances *that* may be the least effective form of education. If we are talking about the education of children and young people, then the opinions that children hear their elders expressing in a church, or the things they see them doing, may be molding them more effectively than what is printed and used in the curriculum material on Sunday morning. If, for instance, they witness a lot of feuding and in-fighting among church members, the fundamental lessons of brotherhood, of forgiveness, however effectively treated in the church school curriculum, have only a slim chance of taking hold. Or, if the officers of a church stoutly resist even the discussion of racial integration as a live option for their church and community, the children and young people of that congregation are being effectively " educated " on the subject of " the body of Christ " and who makes up its membership.

The minister's sermons educate; the programs of the women's organization educate; the way church business is conducted in boards and committees educates; the day-to-day personal relationships of individual members educate. Everything educates!

But we can speak of Christian education more specifically. It is an organized effort to train children, young people, and adults in the Christian faith and in Christian living. How a church conceives its job in this area is of pivotal importance. Sometimes it conceives its job too narrowly, as consisting mainly of transferring a body of material from the pages of the Bible, or the creeds of the church, or the records of heroic Christian lives to the minds of pupils. This is like saying that you " learn " religion in the same way that you learn the multiplication tables or important dates in American history.

This is the " Gradgrind " theory of teaching, the way Schoolmaster Thomas Gradgrind, of Dickens' *Hard Times*, taught his pupils. He thought of them as little pitchers waiting to be filled with facts. His job as their teacher was to pass among them, open their mouths, and pour in the information! Too much so-called Christian education still is based on this misguided, long-disproved theory that if you are able to cram enough facts about the Bible and Christian beliefs into children and young people, Christian character is bound to result. Certainly, having children recite reams of scripture, or drilling them in reciting the books of the Bible or the kings of Judah and Israel in their proper order serves only a limited purpose. As Roger Shinn has said, by such methods children may acquire information that has some value for them, but they are more likely to be better prepared to win Bible quizzes than to make Christian decisions!

At the other extreme, the task of Christian education may be too broadly conceived if it consists only of taking children seriously, of listening to them, of encouraging their questions, of getting them to accept themselves, and, if possible, other people, of developing a tolerant attitude toward other religions and races, of becoming responsible citizens.

Now, commendable as all this may be as accents in the Christian style of life, it may end up being simply education about religion in general as an important phase of human culture, rather than specific education in religious living.

Important as our knowledge of people may be — who they are and how they learn — essential as it is that our teaching be rooted in the Bible, Christian educators are trying, as Dr. Shinn says, to define the goals of Christian education more adequately than by calling them either " Bible-centered," or " child-centered." He offers the following as a

statement of the purpose of Christian education: " *to introduce persons into the life and mission of the community of
Christian faith.*" It is the business of " inviting them to share
the common life of Christians. In personal relationships with
other people they can enter into the worship, the moral discipline, and the study that characterize Christian faith."[4]

This conception agrees, he says, with what scholars have
been saying for some time: that " the Bible is not a collection
of teachings about religion set down in logical order." It is
rather " the story of a people and their activities. It tells of
God's deeds from the time of creation down through centuries of Hebrew history and on into the life of the early
church. God made covenant with his people through Adam,
through Noah, through Abraham, through Moses. The Old
Testament records the history of the covenant people in their
faithfulness and unfaithfulness. Through the prophets God
called his people to fidelity and offered them new opportunities. In Jesus Christ he made a ' new covenant.' The Bible
tells of the life of the community that, whether obeying or
disobeying God, responded to his unique revelation with a
peculiar faith. . . . Christian educators, therefore, stand on
biblical grounds when they assume that the doorway to
Christian education is the effort to introduce persons into the
life and mission of a community of faith."[5]

Randolph Crump Miller says essentially the same thing
in *Christian Nurture and the Church*. There has to be a supporting community, he says, a locale in which what has been
" learned " is really accepted, and, to some degree, practiced.

" Christians become such," writes Dr. Miller, " within
the Christian community. The crucial factor is not information as such, not the capturing of the mind, not the passing of
an examination. The significant factor in Christian education

[4] Shinn, *The Educational Mission of Our Church.*
[5] *Ibid.*

is helping the individual, by God's grace, to become a believing and committed member of the community of the Holy Spirit, obedient to Christ as his Lord and Master, and living as a Christian to the best of his ability in all his relationships."[6]

Let me put this in story form, which is the Bible's favorite way of stating things. I call your attention to a remarkable passage of scripture in the fourth chapter of the book of Joshua. At this point in the narrative, the children of Israel are nearing the end of their fateful journey to the " Promised Land." They have just made a successful crossing of the Jordan River, thanks to God's faithfulness and to his intervention on their behalf. We read:

When all the nation had finished passing over the Jordan, the Lord said to Joshua, " Take twelve men from the people, from each tribe a man, and command them, ' Take twelve stones from here out of the midst of the Jordan, from the very place where the priests' feet stood, and carry them over with you, and lay them down in the place where you lodge tonight.' " . . . And Joshua said to them, . . . " When your children ask in time to come, ' What do those stones mean to you? ' . . . Then you shall tell them that the waters of the Jordan were cut off before the ark of the covenant of the Lord. . . . So these stones shall be to the people of Israel a memorial for ever."

Consider the essential ingredients of this narrative. *First, there is the people, the community* — in this case the twelve tribes of Israel. *Second, there is God's decisive action on their behalf* — here his provision for a safe river-crossing. *Third, there is their response in the erection of a memorial,* their grateful acknowledgement of what he has done for them. *Finally, there is their testimony,* in their own words, to their own people, in their own time: " When your chil-

[6] Randolph Crump Miller, *Christian Nurture and the Church*. Charles Scribner's Sons, New York, 1961. (P. 4.)

dren ask in time to come, ' What do those stones mean? '
. . . you shall tell them. . . ."

Translate that into Christian language – first person
plural, present tense. It does not comprise a formal theory of
Christian education, I grant you; but it is a vivid statement of
our commission.

First, whatever else we are in the world, we are the Christian community, the " people of God." We are not just any
collection of serious-minded, well-intentioned citizens. We
are not just earnest seekers after religious truth in general. We
are a special people with a special history. We are men and
women on a mission. We are, to be sure, members of the civil
order, but we hold a second citizenship in a community that
spans the centuries and the continents, cutting across the
lines of race and caste which in our pride and awful insecur-
ity we draw to keep us safe, or so we like to think.

We are *in* the world, responsible to it and for it, but
never fully *of* the world. We have been gathered out of all
our brokenness and isolation into a healing, redeeming kind
of fellowship. And we are not our own; we are marked
people; and the sign upon us is the mark of the cross!

Second, there is at the center of our common life the
haunting memory of what God has done for us, something
of life-and-death importance: his accepting us, his taking us
as we are, even though we often cannot accept ourselves; his
breaking open for us a path through the tangled underbrush
of our cramped and cluttered lives. And all of it is made so
very plain in the life, the death, and the resurrection of Jesus
Christ!

Third, there is *our* grateful acknowledgment of all this:
our memorials, the songs of faith to be learned and sung, our
prayers, our symbols, our gathering for supper at the Lord's
table.

Finally, there is our testimony, our witness, in our own
words to our own time – *our educational task,* if you will.

For " When your children ask in time to come, ' What do those stones mean? ' . . . you shall tell them." And for each of us it must be a personal reply. " What do those stones mean? " The quiet sanctuary, the open Bible, the service of baptism, the clear, honest word spoken without fear from the pulpit, the table with its bread and its cup — what do they mean? None of us can teach, really, until he can answer that for himself, at least in part; until on some Communion Sunday, for instance, he has knelt with other pilgrims in the memory-haunted silence, heard the word, received the bread, and with trembling hands lifted the cup of God's redeeming, healing love!

The Church Is Experience

MANY OF US who are ministers are deeply troubled. The reason is that, so much of the time, the churches we serve seem to fall short of embodying the warm and living expression of the message of love and reconciliation that we preach regularly from our pulpits and teach in our classes.

Why is this so? Let me try to make clear what I mean. The amount of work is not what gets us down. I am not one of those who feels that the average minister is overworked. But many of us have not learned how to work with maximum efficiency, with a quiet mind, with an inner poise and relaxation, " with the strain off," as James Cleland put it once.

I do not believe that the fault lies primarily with church members. I do not have the feeling that the members of the church keep working against their ministers, that because of spiritual dullness or crass materialism they are constantly undermining our efforts. Occasionally, a minister may dramatize his situation beyond all recognition, posing as the misunderstood, persecuted upholder of the truth, and regarding the members of his flock as Pharisees, the forces of anti-

Christ. There have been, of course, tragic situations in which ministers were crucified by certain members of the congregation who never once got within a thousand miles of what the Christian gospel is about. But few of us have crosses like that to carry. And if we should ever have to carry them, there is still always the possibility that, as with Brutus, the fault is not in our stars, but in ourselves!

My experience as a minister has taught me that, on the whole, the members of our churches are what we expect them to be, a healthy cross-section of the human race, certainly no worse than their non-confessing neighbors, and often a whole lot better! Few of them, to be sure, are saints. (Nor is the proportion among the clergy any higher!) But a great many of them are making notable, and, in some instances, heroic efforts to be good disciples of their Lord Christ. I celebrate the members of my church; I'm all for them! And I'm convinced that it is sheer dishonesty, mere bravado, or the mark of spiritual cowardice when Christian ministers single out laymen as the chief offenders and the root cause for the lean days upon which the church has fallen. Such a minister, I'm sure, has not been reading his New Testament!

The reason lies deeper. It is deeper than any dullness or villainy on the part of church members, deeper, also, than any professional ineptitude or spiritual blindness on our part as ministers.

Actually there are two reasons. One of them is what Lesslie Newbigin in his book, *The Household of God*,[1] calls an overintellectualizing of the content of faith. That is to say, putting all the stress on knowing what correct religion is, without sufficient attention to the importance of enjoying a firsthand experience of it.

[1] Lesslie Newbigin, *The Household of God*. Friendship Press, New York, 1954.

Dr. Newbigin says that there are three indispensable elements in the make-up of a church whereby you can test how
real it is. These elements are: to regard the church (1) as a
continuing historical body; (2) as the congregation of the
faithful; and (3) as a special kind of community.

The first is to regard the church as a continuing historical body, properly constituted, properly representing to the
contemporary world the ancient and classic claims of Christianity through traditional forms, sacraments, and symbols.
In this case, one can say: *where the true order is, there is the
church.* (This, of course, is the stress of the Roman Catholic
Church, and because of extreme stress, its heresy — the notion that true and proper order constitutes ultimate and unquestionable authority.)

The second element is to see a church as the congregation of the faithful, where man makes response to God's
grace, makes proper confession of his faith. In this case, as
Dr. Newbigin points out, one can say: *where the true witness
is, there is the church.* This, essentially, is the major stress of
main-line, evangelical Protestantism, and also its temptation
to heresy in thinking that once the faith has been formulated,
whether in " liberal," " neo-orthodox," or " existential "
form, the church has done its job. It is the heresy of which
most of our churches are guilty — thinking of themselves
mainly as centers of instruction or " spiritual guidance,"
places where the knowledge that the Christian gospel possesses is expounded, interpreted, and endorsed.

The third decisive element in the description of an
authentic church is to see it as a special kind of community,
gathered, empowered, and constantly being renewed by the
Holy Spirit. In this case one can say, *where the Spirit is,
there is the church.*

This brings us to the crux of the matter. This is the
source of what troubles me, and what occasions anxiety and
frustration in more than one Protestant minister: We serve

churches that have intelligently planned, skillfully operated programs of study, fellowship, and service, *but we are not at all sure what it means to be members together of " the community of the Holy Spirit."*

A great deal is being said these days about the renewal of the church, and most of it is focused on this very need — to restore a lost excitement; to recover the sense of being a participant in a community that can turn things upside down; to be able to talk about forgiveness and acceptance and faith, and grace and inward peace, not as abstract qualities which correctly describe the Christian life, but to be able to say: " I know about those things; they have all happened to me! "

If we are interested in this business of church renewal, and for the life of me I cannot see how we have any choice in the matter, the place to begin is with Paul's question, " Did you receive the Holy Spirit when you believed? " Like the Ephesians Paul was talking to, we may have to answer, " No, we have never even heard that there *is* a Holy Spirit." (See Acts 19:2.) But this need not be the end of the matter. It can be the start of something new and exciting. It could even be the salvation of the church you love!

The second reason that our churches are falling short is what the critics of the church rightfully say is its biggest liability — the blight of institutionalism, the " organization church " that we talked about in our first chapter. Real renewal cannot take place, says John W. Meister, until we recognize the "vicious nature of ' institutionalism ' in the contemporary church. In much the same way that clericalism has historically plagued Roman Catholicism, modern American Protestantism is plagued by institutionalism. That is to say, we have reached a time when conventional American Protestant churches are inordinately concerned with upholding the existence, the authority, and the sanctity of their own organizational structures. Forms of organization which originated as *means* to enable the church to function ' decently and in order ' in performing its redemptive mission, have become *ends* to be served." [2]

Take a look around the church you know best. Do you see any *means* that have become *ends?*

This is all well and good, say some of my friends and critics, but, to be quite honest about it, nobody is really prepared to take the radical steps that are required if the church is again to become an effective force in society. What is needed is complete re-tooling, a scuttling of existing structures, organizations, and methods. What is needed is a wholly fresh start.

This, of course, can be a neat way to dismiss the whole matter. For the plain fact is that a wholly fresh start is not possible. Christianity itself was not a wholly fresh start. It began as an attempt to reform Judaism. The Protestant Reformation was not a wholly fresh start. Its point of departure was the accumulated experience and wisdom of the Christian centuries. What it sought to do was to purify them, restate them in terms adequate for the new day. The separatist movement of sixteenth-century England was not a wholly fresh start. Nor is the modern ecumenical movement. These have all been *reform* movements, re-claiming and re-stating principles and ideas that had got lost or been forgotten beneath the steady wash of the years.

You and I are part of the American Protestant church at a time when a special kind of reform is desperately needed: the recovery, not of the New Testament church itself (we cannot recover that), but of the idea that motivated it — the idea of a loving *community*, a fellowship of mutual acceptance and trust, a place where, in an age in which the individual gets lost in gigantic masses of thought and emotion, he

---

[2] John W. Meister, "Requirements for Renewal," *Union Seminary Quarterly Review,* March 1961. Copyright, 1961, by Union Theological Seminary, New York. (P. 254.) Used by permission.

can be found again, believed in, his dignity restored, and his hope and faith and sense of accountability renewed.

In such a time, says Lesslie Newbigin again, men are asking an important question, " Is there, in truth, a family of God on earth to which I can belong, a place where all men can truly be at home? If so, where is it to be found, what are its marks, and how is it related to, and distinguished from, the known communities of family, nation, and culture? "[3] Then he reminds us that " What our Lord left behind him was not a book, nor a creed, nor a system of thought, nor a rule of life, but a visible community."[4] The really crucial question before us is this: Can people see in the life of our churches these signs of this priceless heritage, or have they been obliterated by the stereotyped structures of our organizational life?

A few years ago there appeared in the press a poignant parable about the hunger people have for community, for a place to belong, and how, in our impersonal, organization-centered lives, even in Christian churches, they can be denied it. It was the story of a Chinese student at the University of Michigan who — confused, worried, and ashamed — hid in the attic of a church near the campus. He lived there for four years, never once leaving the building. He lacked the courage to face his problems. He saw people come and go. He ate what was left over from church suppers and social events. He could hear the choir sing on Sunday morning. He often longed desperately to cry out to those who were so close to him, yet so very far away. But he could not.

Now, asks Gerald Jud, commenting on this poignant incident: " How many people are hiding in our churches, *in* the church, but not really sharing its life or hearing its message; longing for the true bread and getting the scraps left over from suppers and social events? How many are hearing the worship, but not really sharing in it? How many are

[3] Newbigin, *The Household of God*. (P. 4.)
[4] *Ibid.*, p. 20.

hiding in the church; wanting to cry out to those who are close, wanting to tell of real, unmet needs, but somehow never doing it? "[5]

The church is community, whatever else it is, and where that quality is lacking a congregation has to work at finding and creating it by deliberate, self-conscious experimentation. The church is a firsthand experience of the gospel of the love of God. Where mere organization has replaced real participation in the kind of community which the gospel creates, a church must find new patterns for communication and interpersonal relationships within it.

Out of this deeply felt need for Christian community, and the recognition that traditional patterns of organized church life have failed to provide for it, there has arisen a growing interest in the organization of small, personal groups within the life of the church. Here in small numbers, in intimate, face-to-face contacts, Christians are able to talk with each other, without apology, without embarrassment, about the deep things of their common faith. Churches that have experimented in this field testify that deeper levels of faith have been penetrated, people reached who have not been reached before, the quality of churchmanship lifted, new and hitherto unsuspected reserves of spiritual power discovered and used. Men and women have found, through firsthand experience of it, that the gospel does make exactly the kind of life-and-death difference that the Bible claims and that ministers have talked about for years. " The widespread appearance of small personal groups may be seen, in years to come, as one of the most significant religious movements of our time,"[6] writes John Casteel in his book, *Spiritual Renewal Through Personal Groups.*

[5] Gerald Jud, " Lenten Letter 1960."
[6] John L. Casteel, *Spiritual Renewal Through Personal Groups.* Association Press, New York, 1957. (P. 17.)

Dr. Casteel reports on nine different experiments in the small-group approach. Each of them is illustrative of its basic purpose which, as Dr. Casteel writes, " is to help members come into a primary personal relationship with God, with other persons, and with themselves. The commandment to love God, and our neighbor as ourselves, is taken here to be not so much a responsibility laid upon us as a description of our deepest spiritual need. Against so much in our life today that reduces our relationships to impersonal ' contacts ' . . . the personal group seeks to bring us back into those primary associations and relationships best implied in the phrase ' face-to-face.' " [7] Dr. Casteel points out that in the revival of small, face-to-face groups, the church has been returning to the kind of intimate life that marked the earliest years of its history. The church's own beginning was " in a group of Twelve, called by their Master, ' to be with him and to be sent out . . .' (Mark 3 : 14)." He says that the church's " history might be written as the account of the church's regeneration through the rise of small, tightly knit, deeply dedicated bands of people." [8]

Personal groups take a variety of forms; no two are alike, and certainly the experience of one church cannot be copied in another. But such groups can aid in the business of renewal in several ways.

(1) *Small personal groups can aid in renewal by helping people come to a deeper understanding of the Bible and the central beliefs of the Christian faith.* Many groups start by acknowledging the biblical illiteracy in most congregations. People want to know what the Bible is all about, and what it is that their Christian faith affirms. They may have other types of opportunities to learn — formal classes, lectures,

[7] *Ibid.,* pp. 19–20.
[8] *Ibid.,* p. 20.

sermons. But the particular quality of a small face-to-face group studying the text of the Gospel of Matthew, for example, lies precisely in the fact that each member of it is in an exposed position. Soon or late, he must become involved personally. He cannot hide behind the minister's eloquence or a textbook's fine phrases. He is expected to say what he believes a certain passage means, to react by reporting something out of his own experience. There is a kind of primitive, even frightening quality about Christians gathered around the word of God without a lot of propping up by the professionals.

I have started several such groups on their way, beginning usually with either Matthew or Mark. Basic requirements are minimal: a few concerned people, willing to give their time faithfully, consistently, regularly (this is important), and one solid reputable biblical authority, such as *The Interpreter's Bible*. Ministerial or other "professional" guidance may be needed in certain groups, but the need for it may soon diminish. Weeks may pass before lay people overcome their initial hesitancy over their apparent unfitness to dig out the meaning of biblical passages on their own.

Some of the groups that I helped to organize later sagged and finally died, for a variety of reasons. There is no formula for success in this kind of experience.

Other groups wanting to get at the essentials of Christian faith have used books other than the Bible as a starting point; books such as those in the *Layman's Theological Library*, the highly readable works of J. B. Phillips, or contemporary novels and plays, with a view to exploring their theological implications.

But, as Robert W. Lynn and Carl R. Smith, ministers of the Montview Boulevard Presbyterian Church in Denver, Colorado, put it in describing their venture in small groups, "The choice of the first book or the first topic of discussion is not of any great consequence. The actual starting point is that moment when a study group becomes a Christian community, a center of trusting love that frees each person to argue and dispute, to check and criticize the other. Sometimes God's gift of liberating trust comes after months of meeting together. Sometimes it comes only after a group feels ' blocked ' and constrained to start all over. (Then, perhaps, a group understands how the phrase ' God as Holy Spirit ' is really shorthand for the myriad times God stands astride our path and forces us to a more radical confrontation.) And sometimes the gift never comes and the group remains a gathering of earnest people stumbling around in the darkness of individual isolation." [9]

(2) *Small personal groups, particularly as intimacy deepens, as " God's gift of liberating trust " is accepted, can provide people with the chance they may have waited for all their lives to air all their doubts, to say some things about religion they would never dream of saying anywhere else, for fear of being misunderstood or criticized.* Many church people have been conditioned to give " Sunday school " answers to questions; to say the things they think ministers expect them to say. But, says Paul Tillich, all genuine faith runs the risk of serious doubt, or it is not bona fide faith. Real faith never eliminates doubt; it supplies the courage to face it and live with it. For many people the doubts they live with can be the threshold of illuminating insight, of genuine faith, and somewhere, somehow, sometime they simply have to get them out into the open. Unexamined doubt can corrode faith; examined doubt may stoutly reinforce it.

(3) *Small personal groups can aid in renewal by doing an utterly necessary thing for individuals: to prove that there are some other human beings who take them seriously, who accept them.* This is one of our fundamental human needs — to be taken seriously, to be accepted.

[9] Casteel, *Spiritual Renewal Through Personal Groups.* (P. 156.)

Sometimes it is a matter of getting behind the masks people wear. Experienced, sensitive school teachers can help us at this point. They know how to listen to the " inside " words of their pupils and get behind the masks of what they are saying. They listen to hearts, not simply to mouths.

I read recently about one teacher who, wanting to know her youngsters better, encouraged them to write short compositions about themselves. She gave them a choice of titles, including " Who Am I? " or " The Person Most Like Me." Some of the results were startling. One shy boy of eleven, whose confidence always seemed in need of a boost, wrote under the influence of a child's biography he had been reading. "Leonardo da Vinci was a man like me," he wrote. " He had all kinds of ideas. They didn't always work. He started lots of things he didn't finish. . . . Some of his inventions are used today, like tanks. He was also good at art and many other things. I am, too." His teacher said she learned a lot from that. Instead of taking him as a boy whose ego needed constant reinforcement, she discovered he had a basic self-confidence, and she decided to accept him at his own evaluation.

This teacher went on to say that she learned something else about a boy of the opposite type, brash and brassy, the " Big I am." She found that he was really quite disgusted and discouraged with himself. He wrote in his composition, " I am a big tease. That is what everybody says except my father who says I am a bully. Sometimes I tease people on purpose but not always. Sometimes I can't seem to help it. . . . Sometimes I tease my mother. I say I will be Ruler of the World in twenty years and my brother will be the first to go! I can always make her mad saying this. She should know that I'm not that kind of person really! "[10]

" She should know! " You and I should know people

[10] Dorothy Barclay, " The Child in the ' Mask '." *The New York Times Magazine*, March 27, 1960. (P. 80.)

better than we often do. Really to be listened to; really to be taken seriously — this is every man's basic need.

Another minister friend writes: "From my twenty years in the ministry I feel the greatest need of the people in the Christian church is for them to find the strength, the healing, and power which only real Christian sharing can bring. We have experimented with this to some degree. We have had six or seven small groups of folks over the past three or four years. The objective has been to come to really know each other; to be willing to learn how to share hopes, frustrations, dreams, failures, and all the rest.

"Some wonderful things have happened. . . . One woman was brought through a serious illness because of the hope she found at the hands of a small group of women who kept loving her. . . . Another woman finally came to see that her marriage really was impossible and found the courage to separate from her husband."

Other groups in which there has been a grappling with reality far below what is the usual surface level of human relations have been gathered around vocations. A minister in Indiana writes: " Our Doctors' Seminar really began when one physician and I were discussing in my study this question: ' What are the implications of being a *Christian* physician? ' Later on he and I raised this question in conversations with small groups of doctors. A study series resulted. At the close of the series, about twenty-seven of the men who attended arranged for a two-day retreat to bring their thinking to some tentative conclusions."

(4) *Small personal groups provide the kind of climate and sense of mutual support needed by people who are interested in working on the disciplines connected with developing a rich and fortifying inner life.* Prayer needs a lot of working at; cultivating the art of meditation takes time. (We

shall have more to say in a later chapter about this all-important matter of renewing life at its roots.)

(5) *People who are active in a church where small personal groups are part of its life say that such groups help enormously to maintain integrity of church membership.* By this they mean that people are helped to have the kind of experience they rightfully expect to have because they are part of the church — the sense of being renewed people, forgiven people, empowered people, thoroughly committed people.

The minister of a United Church of Christ in the East reports the experience of a young woman who had found in this particular congregation exactly this kind of experience. " It was made clear to me when I joined [the church]," she said, " that I was choosing a way of life which if I followed it faithfully might not always be easy or pleasant. This aspect of the Christian faith is one which many churches seem reluctant to bring out. They seem almost afraid to present anyone with this kind of challenge or to ask anyone to make such a definite choice. But this was exactly what Christ himself asked of his followers when he said, ' Whosoever would come after me, let him deny himself and take up his cross and follow me.' I think many of us do not want to recognize that real commitment is involved in becoming a Christian. . . .

" If we do not dedicate our lives to God, what do we do with them? One of the works of T. S. Eliot that has long been a favorite of mine is *The Cocktail Party*, in which he describes two ways of life. One is characterized by the cocktail party with all its superficialities and meaninglessness, and attended by people who neither care for nor understand one another. The other, in his play, leads eventually to death by crucifixion in a Christian mission in Africa. When I first read this play, I did not want to believe that there were only these two ways of life. I wanted very much for there to be a middle road, one which would include some of the more attractive aspects of them both. But I have never been able to find such a middle path. It seems that we must choose either the cocktail party or the Cross."[11]

Now, someone is objecting: " This is all very well; the idea of developing small groups is a fine idea. But how do we find time and energy to launch a new venture like this while it takes everything we have now to keep the church running as it is? Besides, personal groups, at best, reach only a small fraction of the total membership."

This, of course, is really the whole point: The idea of small personal groups in a church is based on the ancient New Testament idea of leaven — the quiet, secretive working of little noticed, unadvertised power. It is precisely because churches are often so thoroughly " organized," so saturated with formal " programs," so involved in the intricate structures of institutional life that a breakthrough in a wholly new direction is imperative. There comes the day when a handful of discerning people, caught in the organizational "busyness" of the church, pull themselves and a few others up short and say: " We love this church; we believe in it; we want to stand by it. But it is slowly becoming exhausted with ' programitis.' It is caught in the cogs of its own machinery. Time runs out before we get round to the really important things that ought to have first place in a church's life — prayer and worship, Bible study and thoughtful discussion of what a Christian's role in society is, helpful service to those in need. Our church is well organized, but is it organized for its primary mission — *to be the bearer to the world of the good news of the love of God?* "

It does not, of course, mean wholesale scrapping of existing patterns and structures. But it does mean " setting some dough " as my grandmother in my boyhood home used

[11] Beverly Cosby, "A Covenant Community in Action," *Union Seminary Quarterly Review*, March 1961. Copyright, 1961, by Union Theological Seminary, New York. (Pp. 283–284.) Used by permission.

to do every Friday night before she went to bed, entrusting the outcome of her favorite recipe for bread to the quiet working of the yeast during the hours of the night. What we are talking about is a little like that. It means a focus on depth for a change, rather than so much broadcasting of seed on the surface. It means shifting for a time, at least, from extension to concentration.

You begin, of course, where you are, with what you have, certainly not with the creation of a whole new structure of organization. You begin with an invitation to a small group of individuals who are ready to take some extra time. In our church we've had a group of women use the days of Lent for this purpose, meeting in the morning for reading and study of the fine book *Great Phrases of the Christian Language*.[12] It may be an invitation to a group of businessmen. In a church near ours a group of them meet early in the morning one day a week for prayer and meditation, and then breakfast. It may mean suggesting to your official boards and committees that the minister be given an amount of time regularly at the beginning of each meeting to deal briefly with some aspect of the life and mission of the church. It may mean proposing a spiritual life retreat, overnight, away from the church. It may mean asking a few people to open their homes on a Sunday evening and inviting members of the congregation who live nearby to discuss the minister's sermon for the day, and, at the same time, themselves draw closer together.

My own experience with small personal groups has been limited — a few trials (including some errors) in two parishes — Bible study groups, small discussion units, a prayer circle. Though limited, the results have been more than promising, and have convinced me that such opportunities need to be multiplied. More courageous and inventive col-

[12] *Great Phrases of the Christian Language*. United Church Press, Philadelphia, 1958.

leagues, and others whose experiments have been reported in books and journals have unfolded greater possibilities than I have personally experienced.

But words of caution have come along with heartening testimony as to the renewing power of small groups.

1. Particularly for those who are looking for such things (and, unfortunately, there are a good many) the small-group approach may be seized upon as the latest, sure-fire gimmick to restore ailing churches to health.

2. Others in their enthusiasm may lean more heavily on the potential and the effectiveness of small groups in the church than is justified. Is not this, also, another indication that often we look for " a sign," but, deep down, know that none will be given? To be sure, small groups with their face-to-face contacts are meeting one of the urgent needs of contemporary Christians to have their faith pin-pointed to the frustrations, the despair, and the brokenness of everyday life. At best, however, they can be only one facet of the total life of the church. I have friends who talk solemnly and with considerable awe about this approach almost as if they were quoting from the manuscript of a hitherto un-known Fifth Gospel!

In short, it is possible to claim too much for these groups. As a friend of mine, one of the outstanding ministers of our fellowship, wrote me recently on the subject: " There seems to be the notion," he said, " that whenever you get small groups together in non-judgmental, accepting relationships, there is an accompanying guarantee that the Holy Spirit will be let loose in their midst. I am a little cynical about this. I am not cynical about the possibility of the Holy Spirit being there, but ofttimes the evidence of his presence seems to boil down to nothing more than the chumminess among those who have shared their shortcomings. This is not to disparage the effectiveness of the small group in terms of its ability to experience certain insights of faith which would not be possible under other circumstances, but I have not yet read an account of a program or a project or adventure which says with discriminating clarity what the difference is between human companionableness and divine presence. . . . This small-group stuff is bunk if it does not deal realistically with the community beyond the cozy circle of self-concerns within the group and fails to lift its worship experience beyond the intimate congeniality of the group."

3. Unless guarded, there are two spiritual dangers in the development of small groups in a church. One, as my plain-speaking friend indicates, is the possibility of a group maintaining a private sort of cult off in a corner by itself, " a perfectionist possibility for the few," as another has phrased it. Whatever course such a group may follow, its only end can be to serve the spiritual well-being of the whole of Christ's church.

A second danger is the failure to make an honest appraisal in advance of what the deeper dimensions of such an experience are likely to be. One must speculate as to what it means to leave oneself and one's relations with others wide open to the operation of the Holy Spirit of the living God on our carefully guarded, well-groomed lives. Without doing so, it may be unwise to venture very far, as Nicodemus discovered to his dismay. Participation in an intimate face-to-face group could save our lives, perhaps; but before it does it may very well send them scurrying for shelter in all directions like scared rabbits. " It is a fearful thing," said the writer of the Letter to the Hebrews, " to fall into the hands of the living God! "

In many instances, however, reports reveal that small groups, quietly organized, skillfully tended, carefully interpreted, have quickened the life of the church, have made available to people the kind of experience of the love of God which brings them to say with Job, " I had heard of thee by the hearing of the ear, but now my eye sees thee."

All such projects as these are, after all, ventures of faith. They mean pushing out in a fragile craft beyond the safe, snug harbor of the known and the familiar and, as a friend of mine puts it, unfurling a sail, hopeful, trustful that it will catch the fresh wind of God's Holy Spirit which is forever blowing across our cramped and crowded lives.

What God can do with us and with our churches, once we set out with courage, cannot be calculated. He works in the most surprising ways, often in the most unlikely places. Our best hope, after all, may be these surprises of God. Surprise, says the French poet, Charles Péguy, is one part of the nature of God's grace. " When [grace] doesn't come from the right," he says, " it comes from the left. When it doesn't come straight it comes bent. . . . When it doesn't come from above it comes from below; and when it doesn't come from the center it comes from the circumference. . . . When it doesn't come like a bubbling spring it can if it likes come like a trickle of water oozing out from under a Loire dyke." We may finish a way we never began, he says, but we shall finish. " This age, this world, this people will get there along a road they never set out on! "[13]

How is it in your church? Are doors and windows open? Are people looking skyward? Are they giving attention to little nooks and crannies? Or is it all statistics and reports of organizations? At any moment God may be ready to spring one of his surprises!

[13] Daniel Halévy, *Péguy and Les Cahiers de la Quiuzaine.* David McKay Company, Inc., New York, 1947. (P. 184.)

The Church Is Mission

Chapter IV

EXCEPT FOR ITS worship and teaching, most of the real task of the church lies outside of it, beyond its walls, off its property, out where a need is waiting to be met.

A church that forgets this is headed for trouble, inevitably. And it is easy to forget it, especially when things are going well, when a church is comfortably situated and equipped. As a minister on the West Coast put it, " The very beauty of our chancel window and our total plant attracts people so effectively that we can afford to let up on our evangelism program without feeling a sense of neglect."

In short, *the church is mission.* This is its very genius. It is sent into the world by God to act out what it knows about his love, to get involved in his unceasing task of reconciliation. When it talks a lot about having to take care of its own needs on home base before tackling a new project on the outside, before considering an increase in its support of the world-wide mission program of its denomination, then it is not only being disloyal to its commission from its Lord, Jesus Christ, but it has also taken a big step toward its decline. For, as someone has put it, " The church exists by mission as fire exists by burning."

53

Of course, we have a job to do *inside* the church, and it must be done well. The church plant which we love must be maintained at its best. Here we dream dreams, see visions, make plans. Here through worship and a mutually sustaining fellowship we find strength for the task. This is important. But what is more important is the job to be done *outside* the church. This is what counts; this is the definitive hallmark of authenticity as a church of Jesus Christ. So, as Roy Pearson expresses it in one of his books, what God asks of the church today " is that it get out of the harbor and sail on the open sea, that it get out of the briefing room and head for the battlefield, that it give up its place on the sidelines and get out into the game itself." [1]

Unfortunately, churches are found all too frequently on the sidelines, out of the main current, carrying on a pleasant little operation all by themselves. To talk about the church as *mission*, therefore, means, first, to be sure that we are in touch with the world to which we are sent in Christ's name, to listen to what it is saying, to read what it writes, to be familiar with its images and its symbols. I am sure that the world, which, we must remember, is one that God has visited and one that he loves, would pay more attention to what the church has to say if it really felt that it was being listened to, was being taken seriously.

Therefore, in moving out beyond its walls into the world that Christ calls it to serve, the church's first responsibility is to be a good observer of the contemporary scene. That is not always easy or even pleasant, particularly if you have not done much of it. You will hear a generous sprinkling of four-letter words, and will find it hard to keep your eyebrows horizontal. Some things will strike you as sheer blasphemy.

I recall two New England matrons who gathered up

[1] Roy M. Pearson, *This Do — and Live.* Abingdon Press, New York, 1954. (P. 81.)

their bonbons one Wednesday afternoon and in their inno-
cence set off for Boston to see *Death of a Salesman* by Ar-
thur Miller. They went because they always went on the
days their subscription tickets said they were to go. They
had heard nothing about the play, and, consequently, were
wholly unprepared for the dose of surgical and shattering
realism that Mr. Miller administered across the footlights.
They came home shaken and shocked, bewailing, as they put
it, the " immorality " of the modern American stage.

Now, while *Death of a Salesman* is not a " nice " play,
it is a very moral play, ruthless in its honesty and unsparing
in its commentary about us all. I suspect that what had happened to the two ladies was that Mr. Miller succeeded in
getting behind their pleasant suburban masks, their well-
groomed exteriors, and had done a little painful probing in
the depths of their comfortable, busy, but rather empty lives.

The point is that you need a " third ear " and a " third
eye " to listen to, to see, and to appreciate many of the forms
of expression used in the world of contemporary arts. The
reason is that we are so heavily conditioned by traditions and
stereotypes in aesthetics that new and different artistic forms
of expression often succeed only in shocking and unsettling
us. But with persistence and by courageously returning for
further exposure, we can find increased understanding.

The composers who introduced new harmonic patterns
in music had this effect on people at first. They were using
conventional notation. Their scores were written in the
usual manner, and could be played on the usual instruments,
but the sounds that resulted had not been heard before on sea
or land, and were therefore rejected with ridicule and jeer-
ing. The same is true of painters who are not bound by the
convention that every self-respecting painting has to *look*
like something. Still, these painters use the same colors that
traditional artists use, apply them to canvas with the same
kind of bristle, but because they are attempts to portray, not

what something *looks* like, but how they, as people, *feel* about it, their efforts are often rejected.

Writers have the same experience. Many of them deal with subjects that everybody knows about, talks about, or enjoys hearing discussed, but which, again by certain long-established conventions or " ground rules," are considered, at best, " in bad taste " or, at worst, plainly immoral. To suggest that any of these so-called literary or artistic works could possibly have anything to do with religion or faith is out of order.

We are still under the heavy thumb of a traditional order of aesthetics. Many still feel that the only legitimate basis for writing is (a) to get across in " inspirational " style a solid moral principle, or (b) to elevate the mind and gladden the heart with a wholesome tale in which " spiritual " values emerge victorious over the forces of darkness and evil. If anyone wishes to paint a picture, people say, for heaven's sake, let it be recognizable, and preferably let it illustrate some of " the finer things of life." If an architect is going to design a church, let it look like a church and not like a laundry or a hen house. The real question that these people should be asking, of course, is: " But, do I know what a church *should* look like in this third decade of the atom, in this broken, scared world? " Who said it has necessarily to look like a Gothic cathedral or a New England meetinghouse?

The moralistic aesthetic code implies something else: that a writer or artist dealing with strictly " religious " subjects has free rein. He can do no wrong, so long, of course, as he handles his subject in the traditional manner, making things come out "right" in the end, and generally advertising the virtues of sound, respectable religion. Standards of craftsmanship are often blithely overlooked, and hearty hallelujahs arise from ministers and others rejoicing in the popularity of spiritual soap operas and the latest " religious " film.

Now, there is something terribly wrong with all this moralizing through books, paintings, movies, and plays. A lot of it is just so much pretending — that things are going well in the world when we know they are not. Deep cracks have showed up in the walls of contemporary society. We can see them. They are signs of a serious moral and spiritual sickness. It is a highly questionable business to use religion as a thin coat of plaster and paint to cover them up. There is, of course, room for pure " escapist " entertainment, musical comedies and the like, which have no pretensions other than to divert, to help people shift into lower gear, and to enjoy the holy gift of laughter. But to exploit serious art forms — literature, drama, painting, simply to illustrate or to shore up pious preaching and teaching is to degrade them.

Furthermore, an artist, a writer, or a dramatist has to be honest. He has to " call the shots " as he sees them. If what he sees is ugly, he cannot pretty it up with a paintbrush. If it is sordid, he cannot mask it with hopeful homilies. If it discloses a great emptiness, he must write about it, sketch it, or put it on the stage with such power that we shall be moved to look inward ourselves and to see our own spiritual poverty laid bare.

The plain fact is that many writers and artists are making a more accurate, more telling diagnosis of the spirit and nature of the times in which we live than are many church leaders, some of whom still think, apparently, that people can be " inspired " into genuine faith.

Think for a moment of your church. What is its listening capacity, its involvement index, its participation rating? Is it in touch with the world outside the doors? Or does it leave the impression with people that its message just is not relevant to the tough situations they are facing?

Kaj Munk, the faithful Danish pastor, who was killed by the Nazis, said that he was sure that when many people thought about the church they had the feeling of someone tricking them into a bad deal. " They live well inland, far from streams of any kind and here we come breathlessly dragging cement with which to build bridges! " [2] Does your church make it a point to listen to things it probably would rather not hear? Robert Spike says that every wall which tends to separate the church off from the pressures of secular culture must be broken down. Because, as he says, " it is possible for the church to exist as a privileged craft tossed about on the froth of this culture. It is possible to use the institutional church and also ' spiritual ' sentiments to ride the storm, never . . . confronting the real demonic elements in this age, but masking ourselves for protection. Choosing an antiseptic gospel of the good life and gentility of spirit, the church can exist in the midst of cultural crisis almost as a decoration." [3]

And, as he says, the only safeguard is to be in close touch with the world, to be involved in it. It means turning our back on those who would like to keep the church prissy and dull. In the words of Father Kilmer Myers, " The church must ' go native ' in everything except faith and morals."

I am sure of this much: We in the churches need to identify ourselves more closely than we have in the past with the pain and the anguish of the world. I think this is why so many sensitive and intelligent people outside the church have little to do with us. They get the feeling that we are like the priest and the Levite in Jesus' familiar story of the good Samaritan. We come upon evil and suffering, say how sorry we are that such things have to happen, then pick up our skirts and hurry by on the other side to look after our institutional needs.

This has a lot to say about what we call our program of " evangelism." Too often, I am afraid, we are content to sit in our comfortable, well-equipped churches and teach each

---

[2] Kaj Munk, *Four Sermons*. Lutheran Publishing House, Blair, Nebraska, 1944. (P. 20.)

[3] Robert Spike, *Safe in Bondage*. Friendship Press, New York, 1960. (P. 19.)

other. But what of all the sincere, alert people on the outside whom Christ loves as much as he loves us? Why are we out of touch with them?

For example, take the kind of people personified by the leading character in the novel *The Fall*, by the late Albert Camus. Jean Baptiste is a young man whose life is haunted by a terrible sense of guilt and judgment. But since, in his way of thinking, God is out of style, and having no one to whom he can unburden the awful load, he cannot find spiritual healing. All he can settle for is a kind of uneasy acceptance of the fact that, at least, he shares a common guilt with all mankind. The point is that such people, as Jesus observed once to a man, may not be very far from " the kingdom," may be a lot closer to a state of grace than many conventional churchgoers who have never been this honest with themselves, who have never admitted their own vulnerability to the Christian gospel.

We who are inside the church have a lot to learn from such a person as Simone Weil, the French philosopher and mystic who spent all her life outside the church, and who could never bring herself to join it. She was afraid of " church patriotism " she said, afraid of substituting a loyalty to it as a social institution for loyalty to what it stands for. The church as a social structure frightened her. She believed her special vocation was to move and mix with people in the crowd, not in any " official " or representative way, " disappearing among them, so that they show themselves as they are, putting off all disguises with me. It is because I long to know them so as to love them just as they are. For if I do not love them as they are, it will not be they whom I love, and my love will be unreal." [4]

Question: Do we in our programs of evangelism and

---

[4] Simone Weil, *Waiting for God*. G. P. Putnam's Sons, New York, 1951. (P. 48.)

outreach seek new members for the church because we, too, want to love them as they are, want to share their anguish, and want to bring them into a loving fellowship? Or do we do it because (a) we have a goal of so many new members to reach, or because (b) we think our church is a friendly place that people will enjoy, or because (c) we need more members to cover rising costs of operating the church? I do not mean to be cynical. But these questions are the kind we must raise.

Simone Weil said that the most important thing to be done is to show people the possibility of a truly incarnated Christianity. She said she was sure that she could help in doing this better by remaining right where she had been since her birth, "at the intersection of Christianity and everything that is not Christianity."[5]

So, says Leslie Fiedler in a biographical note about her, "Simone Weil finally remained on the threshold of the church, crouching there for the love of all of us who are not inside, all the heretics, the secular dreamers, the prophesiers in strange tongues, ' without budging,' she wrote, ' immobile, ... only now my heart has been transported, forever I hope, into the Holy Sacrament revealed on the altar.' "[6]

I wonder, sometimes, if people like Simone Weil do not "crouch" there also for the love of us who are *inside* the church. At any rate, I am sure that is where many of us need to be — on the *threshold* of the church, at that place where its life, worship, and witness can spill over into the life outside.

Jesus said once that he had " other sheep that are not of this fold " (John 10:16). " God's incognitos," someone has called them. How many of them do you know? With how many of them is your church in touch?

It is strange how easily we forget God's own deliberate

[5] *Ibid.*, p. 9.
[6] *Ibid.*, Introduction by Leslie Fiedler, p. 28.

use of the unfamiliar, the " outsider," the scandalous. Actually, this is the way Christianity found its way into the world. Paul summed it up in these words in his First Letter to the Corinthians. " God," he said, " chose what is foolish in the world to shame the wise, God chose what is weak in the world to shame the strong, God chose what is low and despised in the world, even things that are not, to bring to nothing things that are " (1 Corinthians 1:27–28).

As far as we can tell, God has not given notice of any change in strategy. He goes about his real business quietly, without advance press notices, without fanfare, without benefit of the services of Madison Avenue. That is the way he came, there at Bethlehem. People were looking for him in another direction, scanning the skies for a real production — glittering angels and a lordly conqueror. They *never* would have thought to look inside a stable in a sleepy country town! They were listening for trumpets; they had no ears for the choked cry and the heavy breathing of a peasant woman in labor!

Our calling requires us to let people know that we are one with them in their unhappiness and their despair, and to engage in a dialogue with them. Christian communication cannot be all one-sided: prophetic pronouncements or helpful bits of advice from the pulpit, and respectful attention in the listening pews. Christian communication is conversation. Christianity is mission; and mission begins by being in touch with the world and the people to whom Christians are sent!

THE CHURCH'S MISSION TO THE WORLD

Is a church organized for mission, or is it just organized? This is the important question to ask.

Canon Wedel's familiar and widely told parable of the lifesaving station puts it succinctly. It was a lifesaving station built at an especially dangerous spot along the coast. Its only purpose, ostensibly, was to save imperiled lives. It saved

a lot of people, but as time went by the saved assumed more
and more of the management, and being much more im-
pressed by the beauty of the spot than by the importance of
saving lives, they gradually turned the station into an elegant
beach club.

The renewal of our churches could well begin here,
with a fresh examination of this basic concept of the church
as mission, and not, as we have said earlier, as a religious society that has a program of "missions" as one aspect of its life
— and one for which the minister and a few others have to do
battle at budget-making time!

A sensitive minister in a New England church writes:
"I believe that the most critical issue facing our churches
today is the one of mission. As the church defines and dis-
covers its mission, and gears itself toward fulfilling it, I believe that signs of renewal will begin to be visible."

To take this seriously, as he goes on to say, means asking
questions like these: What *is* Christ's purpose for his church,
anyway? And how is the church to be a reconciling influence in the world over which he is Lord?

The people of a church in trying to answer such questions are bound to come upon new insights and, probably, as
this minister puts it, wind up with " more people doing the
work of the church and fewer doing ' church work.' " Indeed, trying to answer such questions will help a church get
out into the open its feeling of guilt because so much of the
time it appears to be putting its own survival before its mission, that so much of the energies of its members are used up
in merely maintaining the life of the organization. And our
assignment is not maintenance. It is *mission:* " We are ambassadors for Christ, God making his appeal through us "
(2 Corinthians 5:20).

Take time, then, for a review of the whole matter. Arrange conversations between the church officers and other
concerned people. Be sure to include people who make no

bones of the fact that they consider " missions," especially
" foreign missions," an invasion of the religious freedom of
other peoples, and, at best, a kind of luxury item in the church
budget, something that's nice to include provided all the
" home " expenses are cared for. Be sure, also, to include
people who zealously carry a torch for the world-wide mission enterprise of the Christian church and who, in their enthusiasm for it, are sometimes not realistic about the proper
care of property and facilities on home base.

Ask people to read a good book on the subject of the
church's mission. We think of two, *Edge of the Edge* by
Theodore E. Matson,[7] and *God's Colony in Man's World* by
George W. Webber.[8] The latter is a compelling statement of
the meaning and nature of mission which has the authentic
flavor of on-the-spot reality, being worked out in terms of
one particular example of mission, the East Harlem Protestant Parish in New York City.

Begin the discussions with a consideration of this statement from Mr. Webber's book, a crisp definition of just what
a church is.

"A true church," says Mr. Webber, " is an outpost of
the kingdom of God, placed in a particular spot in the world
to bear witness to the lordship of Jesus Christ. A church is a
mission living by the foolishness of God in a world that sometimes hates it, sometimes is indifferent, and sometimes seeks
to take it captive. Any church that does not recognize the
basic purpose for its existence is in jeopardy of its life. The
predicament of the church in America is precisely that it
does not recognize that it is in a missionary situation. Missions are seen only as a special project of the church, through
which men and women are sent overseas to preach in distant

[7] Matson, *Edge of the Edge.*
[8] George W. Webber, *God's Colony in Man's World.* Abingdon Press,
New York, 1960.

lands. Even the local mission of the church is a home missionary venture off somewhere in Indian territory or in the
world of the inner city. We have forgotten that mission is
the task of the church wherever it finds itself." [9]

Turn now to a discussion of the mission of the church,
and, first, to what it is *not*.

1. *Mission is not ecclesiastical charity*. It is not Christianity's " Community Chest." It is not simply giving out of
our plenty to relieve the suffering of the world's poor and
disinherited. Mission is not simply American big-hearted-
ness, particularly the kind for which you are entitled to
claim exemption in paying your income tax!

2. *Mission is not a spiritual " Point IV " program*. It is
not the religious counterpart of American democracy. It is
not part of our nation's face-saving program in certain parts
of the world. There is no denying the fact, of course, that
Christian missions have had this practical effect more than
once. Ruth Isabel Seabury used to say that in many parts of
Africa, until the missionaries came, the average African's
concept of the white man was summed up in three things: a
whiskey bottle, a deck of playing cards, and a gun! But in
essence, the mission of the church is not an accompaniment
of anything. It is the prosecution of a cause all its own.

3. *Mission is not a weapon against communism*. It is
not a weapon *against* anything, for that matter. It is *a testimony for* the reconciling, life-giving love of God who loves
individual Communists as much as he loves anybody else. In
fact, there is a sense in which we must regard communism as
a Christian heresy, as historians have indicated. It started and
flourished, in part, because of the preoccupation of the Christian church with its own affairs, its identification with one
particular group in society, and the neglect of its responsi-

---

[9] Webber, *God's Colony in Man's World*. (P. 29.)

bility for social justice, one of the most ancient of biblical teachings. And although the cruelties and the denial of basic human rights as practiced and spread by modern totalitarian states must be opposed, we cannot " use " the spread of the Christian gospel in the struggle to find a tolerable balance of power between East and West.

4. *Mission is not just " foreign missions "* nor an " overseas mission," a service rendered at some distant point, far from the bounds of the church's parish. It is not the business of sending a few consecrated, self-denying people to work with benighted or otherwise " inferior " people in a far-off and exotic corner of the globe. Mission is the church engaged anywhere and everywhere with the forces of secularism (which somebody has skillfully defined as " this-worldism "), blight, and with plain human suffering. The engagement may be no farther away than the next city block where several families of Puerto Ricans are desperately trying to make their way with all the odds of the neighborhood stacked against them. It may be as close as the next county where hundreds of migrant farm workers live in squalor, walled in by hostility and suspicion. It may be as near as the nearest college campus where the faith of a keen-minded student teeters on the knife-edge between belief and unbelief.

Move on, now, to develop a rationale for Christian mission. Give consideration to the following:

1. *Mission is the way Christians explain and act out their biblical tradition.*

This tradition shows up in the earliest parts of the biblical record. Abraham, hearing a far call, turned his back on safety and security, and went out, " not knowing where he was to go." Then came the days of bondage in Egypt. The children of Israel could have made some kind of tolerable arrangement with the government; things undoubtedly would have improved. But the far call came again, and with it the wilderness, and the suffering, but always over the horizon lay the Promised Land. Then days of exile and disgrace in Babylon. This time, surely, they could have settled for security. But again the call, and there followed the weary business of repairing the wasted city of Jerusalem. And, finally, Jesus himself, never supposing that anything he taught could be kept as a cozy cult for Jews, but sending the disciples out into a hostile world: " Go therefore and make disciples of all nations " (Matthew 28:19). Then the apostle Paul turned it into a one-man crusade, putting in at the dirtiest, scabbiest ports of the Mediterranean to preach " Christ and him crucified," and giving Christianity a foothold in Europe.

Always the call! It came to Luther and Calvin, to Zwingli and Knox. It came to Pastor Robinson and the Pilgrim company, who turned their backs on the warm hospitality of Holland to battle the late autumn gales of the North Atlantic and barely to survive a cruel New England winter. Always the call! It came to a group of Williams College students, dedicating their lives in a meeting under a haystack on a summer afternoon a hundred and fifty years ago to take the good news of Jesus Christ to men they knew nothing about.

" The church exists by mission as fire exists by burning! "

2. *Mission is the way Christians express the ultimate wisdom about their lives* – that they own nothing, that all that they are and have is God's property, that they are simply caretakers of his bounty for a few brief years, stewards of his wealth. In the deepest sense, they have no choice whether or not they will give their treasure and their time to support the work of Christ's church. Their treasure and their time belong to God to start with. They are simply employing and enjoying what belongs to him.

3. *But most profoundly, mission is the way Christians*

express their gratitude to God for what he has done for them.
This is the ultimate motivation for the whole enterprise:
" Freely you have received; freely give! " Freely we have
come to know God's forgiveness; freely this must be shared
with all who are locked in a sense of guilt. Freely we have
been led to newness of life in the liberating fellowship of
Christ's people; freely this must be shared with any who are
lonely and cut off. Freely we have received courage for our
daily lives; freely this must be shared with those who still live
in fear of their enemies, without and within.

Mission is our response to God's decisive action on our
behalf. We do not carry on a world-wide mission enterprise
because we feel sorry for unfortunate people, or because it
is sound strategy; we do it because we cannot help doing it!

THE CHURCH AND SOCIAL ISSUES

Differences of opinion about its role in dealing with current social issues often cause tension in a church. Here, frequently, a wide gulf between pulpit and pew shows up. In
many ways, the hardest thing a minister has to do, particularly among people he loves and respects, is to say things to
them with which they sharply disagree, or which they feel
he has no business talking about in the first place.

The minister, of course, has no choice in the matter.
When he was ordained he gave himself up to the business of
speaking, not as fancy might strike him — though there are
some preachers whose sermons appear to be developed on
this heretical theory — but as he honestly believes God requires him to speak. However clumsily he may speak at
times, through it all he is trying to be a spokesman for God,
and if he is to be that — which is never easy — it simply is not
relevant to ask whether what he has to say is popular or not.
Most of us ministers are grateful that we serve churches with
truly free pulpits. This can never mean license to sound off
on purely personal prejudices or crackpot theories; but it

does mean the privilege of being given a hearing whenever, under the guidance of the Holy Spirit, a man has something to say which he honestly believes God wants him to say.

Every church, particularly one concerned about renewing its life, must come to terms with the prophetic role of the minister, and that is what I am talking about. The modern minister has to be all sorts of things — a pastor, a priest, an administrator, a teacher, a counselor, and, not least, a loving husband and father. But there are times when he must also be a prophet, the speaker of some hard, angular things which he knows will not sit well with the congregation, and which may stir them up to charge him with being " visionary," " radical," or even " communistic," but which, nonetheless, must be spoken.

But the prophetic responsibility of a church cannot be left to the pulpit alone. It must find its way up and down the aisles and into the pews. The people sitting there must also be prepared to speak hard and unpopular truths when necessary, truths that will cut across the grain of majority thinking in community and national life, truths that unsettle and disturb. In short, minister and people are in this business together, even though it spells trouble, to discern and to declare God's will for the world he made and loves.

Jesus frequently saw himself in the role of prophet, a spokesman for God. He said lots of things that hurt and distressed people. " Do not think," he said once, " that I have come to bring peace on earth; I have not come to bring peace, but a sword " (Matt. 10:34). As George MacLeod said once, after all, " Jesus was not crucified in a Cathedral between two candles, but on a Cross between two thieves." [10]

A classical statement of the Bible's prophetic word, and the subsequent prophetic role of all who propose to take it seriously, is found in the sixth chapter of the book of the

[10] George F. MacLeod, *Only One Way Left*. The Iona Community, Glasgow, 1956. (P. 38.)

prophet Micah. " Hear, you mountains, the controversy of the Lord, and you enduring foundations of the earth; for the Lord has a controversy with his people, and he will contend with Israel " (Micah 6:2).

It shocked the people of Micah's time. It is likely to shock the people of our own time. We do not like to think of God as an adversary. We prefer to think of him as one whose love shelters us, whose forgiveness is assured us, whose patience bears with us. But, says the Bible in its blunt way, this same God takes sharp issue with us from time to time, engages in controversy with us. It may be a personal issue, one with which God faces a man in the seclusion of his private life. One of the most sobering facts about all our human relationships is that none of us knows when he may be talking with a man who is being hard pressed in some lonely battle of the soul, having it out with God!

But just as frequently, certainly as the Bible talks about it, the controversy is a social one: God speaking in terrible judgment upon social injustice; God defending the rights of some of his children who have been disinherited or exploited because of the color of their skin; God tiring of our beautiful ceremonials, our refined liturgical practices because they have become substitutes for doing his will.

Now, it is understandable if there are times when we wish that this were not one of the requirements of Christian discipleship, particularly if things are going well in a church and it is especially important that a certain membership goal be achieved. We would not want to turn people away; surely the minister can soft-pedal some of his views!

But, however we hem and haw about it, the prophetic role is laid upon our churches, and perhaps never more urgently than in our contemporary world. Furthermore, to be quite honest about it, other institutions and agencies in society frequently fill the prophetic role more courageously than the church. In some areas of social concern the church is lagging behind, way behind, and I suspect that part of what makes the business of handling controversial subjects such a touchy matter in some quarters is a deep, underlying feeling of guilt.

There is no question that the times of greatest health, of sturdiest witness, of maximum effectiveness in the history of Protestantism have been times when Christians and the church were dealing with public issues, and were often engaged in controversy with the world.

A perusal of the history of the church in colonial days is instructive, for instance. As Ola Winslow expresses it in her book *Meetinghouse Hill*, dealing with New England life in the years of the Revolution: " Under stress of perilous events town and parish were again one as in the earliest days. The meetinghouse once more became the center of community life. . . . it was the town arsenal. . . . The Rev. John Adams of Durham, New Hampshire, preached Sunday after Sunday with the town's supply of powder directly under his feet. . . . The meetinghouse was also the recruiting center, the place of rendezvous for troops, the point of departure when it came time to go." [11]

For many of us the memory of heroic Christian resistance to Nazi tyranny is still fresh — the memory of those men who met the diabolical threat to human freedom head-on, who refused to fall back on the soft claim that religion is, essentially, a private matter, that churches should learn not to meddle in affairs that do not concern them. This spirit of gallant resistance was voiced in a classical way by Kaj Munk, who said in a sermon one Sunday, right into the teeth of members of the Gestapo sitting in the congregation: " It is better that Denmark's relations with Germany should deteriorate than its relations with the Lord Jesus." [12]

[11] Ola Winslow, *Meeting House Hill*. The Macmillan Company, New York, 1952. (Pp. 273–274.)

[12] Kaj Munk, *Four Sermons*. (P. 8.)

Or, you will recall how ordinary Christians in Denmark and in the Netherlands reacted to the order given by the Nazis to all Jews in those countries to sew the star of David to their sleeves as a public badge of ignominy and shame. In a few days, thousands of Christians also sewed the star of David to their own sleeves in order to affirm their oneness with their persecuted brothers!

Take some time in your church, as we have done in ours, to examine the prophetic role of Christianity. Give thought to the following statements as an attempt to summarize its chief aspects.

First, there is the basic insight, so characteristic of the whole biblical record, that *history is the locale of God's dealings with men.* The Bible goes so far as to say that a nation's rise or downfall can be explained only in the light of its faithfulness to or its denial of God's determination to establish justice and righteousness in human society. In other words, when a nation is in trouble economically, socially, internationally, the chances are that what it has run into is not bad luck, or fiendish enemies, or blind fate, but God!

Second, religious ceremonial can never be substituted for fulfilling God's demands for justice among men. But we sometimes try! A beautiful, dignified service of worship on Sunday morning may be a piece of artistry, but it is also a piece of mockery so long as hateful relationships or unjust conditions exist among the people. Jesus lifted this up into permanent and disturbing visibility in his words about churchgoing, and we need to heed them each time we bow in prayer at the beginning of a service of worship: " If you are offering your gift at the altar, and there remember that your brother has something against you, leave your gift there before the altar and go; first be reconciled to your brother, and then come and offer your gift " (Matthew 5:23–24). And if we recall how inclusively — even " promiscuously,"

some people would say — Jesus used the word brother, we
have a stringent condition, indeed, laid upon our churchgoing!

Two ministers we know, one of a Negro congregation
in the city, the other of a white congregation in a suburb,
each troubled that the people of his church knew so little of
the ways and the thinking of the other, have arranged for a
small group from each congregation to meet together once a
month. They alternate their meeting place from one parish
to the other, not to talk about " the race problem," but
simply to share a common meal, to engage in conversation
and discussion, but mostly in simple, human ways to try to
make real their oneness in Jesus Christ.

*Third, there are times when the church and church
people humbly but resolutely have to take a stand against
prevailing community opinion, no matter what the reaction
is likely to be.* As John Bennett says, one of the things that
makes the church's role as prophetic critic difficult is the
habit we have of viewing everything from the standpoint of
" public relations." We Americans have made a fetish of this.
It is one of our " sacred cows." Good public relations are
important, of course, especially for an organization interested in communication. But, says Dr. Bennett, there is a
false type of public relations which attempts to apply to human beings and groups the methods of advertising which
may be appropriate for selling soap, but which become ab-
surd when we apply them to the Christian gospel.

*Fourth, the prophetic role of the church is not simply a
negative attack on social evils.* Its aim is redemptive — to
heal, to bring together, to reconcile. For beyond the judgment of God there is always his forgiveness, his grace, his
love. The full Christian message is never one-sided.

*Finally, arrange for a discussion in your church of the
" Call to Christian Action in Society "* issued by the General

Synod of the United Church of Christ.[13] Ask your minister to make it the subject of a sermon. If you have a social action committee, urge its study there. If your church does not have such a responsible group, suggest that one might be gathered around the discussion of this statement.

Here are a few sentences from it, a kind of New Testament letter of the twentieth century, addressed to us all:

" In the midst of this abundance, we are beset by much that is trivial, dehumanizing, and vulgar. Prodigious plenty tempts us to selfish indulgence while millions of people in our land and abroad live in want. Private consumption has reached unprecedented levels while public services on which all of us depend are starved. . . . Much of our leisure time is devoted to forms of entertainment and escape that dull us to the world's problems and our neighbor's needs. . . . We are tempted to love things and use people when we should love people and use things. . . .

" Now as always God calls us to a new life that offers genuine meaning, faith, and community. He sets before us goals that are higher than comfort and success. He summons us to develop our capacities for mental and spiritual growth. He frees us from our bondage to the networks of opinion and taste. He saves us from calling good evil or evil good. He searches the streets of our cities and the by-ways of the countryside — not for the church that takes pride in its popularity, its wealth, or the splendor of its buildings — but for the church that does justice and seeks truth, that cares for people and loves the gospel, lifting up family, community, and world."

The church is mission, in all areas of human need. " We are ambassadors for Christ, God making his appeal through us! "

---

[13] "A Call to Christian Action in Society," Council for Christian Social Action of the United Church of Christ, 289 Park Avenue South, New York, N. Y.

Chapter V

ALONG THE MAINE coast, which is our favorite vacation haunt, I never grow tired of watching the twice-daily miracle of the incoming tide. Miles from the open ocean, along one of the long arms of salt water that probe far inland, I like to watch it quietly, irresistibly pushing its way through the marshes and up the tiniest brooks, inching up wharf posts, turning oozing mud into shining crystal pools, obliterating littered rubbish, and lifting boats from off a hundred sand bars. It is the deep calling to deep, day after day, in ceaseless cycle, linking the shallowest, driest creek with the fathomless depths of the sea!

Whatever else may be said about renewing the life of the church, it is upon a force, a process such as this that eventually we depend. And thus we humbly acknowledge that God alone can renew his church, just as he called it into being in the first place. And he is renewing it all the time, flooding it with increments of power, winnowing it in the wind of his Holy Spirit, clearing our rubble, making waste places fertile. In the end, the most and the best that we can do is to make ourselves accessible, to leave ourselves and our

74

churches open-ended to the influence of his quickening spirit which moves at his will and in his good time.

This is to say that there is a real risk in our self-conscious discussions of the renewal of the church. There is the subtle temptation to believe that it could happen when an ingenious denominational secretary devises and packages the right set of procedures for it, or that a book, such as this, could generate enough interest and concern to accomplish the job. I am under no such illusions. All I have tried to say thus far is that if a church cares about the renewal of its life, there are a number of areas in which it will be doing some hard digging, some honest stock-taking, making a sobering re-evaluation of itself. In these areas especially: in a fresh understanding of what the church uniquely knows through its possession of the good news of the love of God; in an examination of its corporate life to discover to what extent it embodies and engages people in the life-giving truths of that gospel; and in an appraisal of itself as an enterprise in mission, carrying these truths out into the life of the world around it.

Beyond this, a church can simply trust that the deep will answer to its own depth of sincerity and desire to be faithful. "The unshackling of the Holy Spirit," says James A. Farmer, Jr., is the decisive element in this business of church renewal. Beyond this a church can only pray that God's Holy Spirit will do with it what it will — confirming what is right, shoring up what is weak, and ruthlessly pruning what needs to go. We cannot minimize the importance of this last function of the Spirit. As an amateur gardener, I have learned that my rose bushes bear the best blooms when I have severely pruned them in the early spring, cutting the canes back to the main stems. Churches need the same treatment, from time to time, and often get it. There are some things happening in our churches that should not be renewed, that should be allowed to die.

This brings us to the most important part of this whole

discussion — the sheer necessity of being faithful, in season and out, to what is our ultimate business, the worship of God. In a sense, this is *all* we are asked to do, to keep renewing life itself at its roots, at the deep springs of its being. Everything else follows from it — from a firsthand exposure to the presence and the power of God. How curious it is, then, that we are so easily led off into thinking that there are more important things for us to be doing! Take time, then, for a thorough scrutiny of your church's towline to eternity — its provision for the worship of God, both private and corporate.

Two fundamental assumptions lie behind our primary concern with worship in the life of a church. They are " given " quantities of the human pilgrimage.

The first is that we come into this life with a built-in affinity for unseen realities. The spiritual runs native to the grain, it is our natural habitat. The " spiritual life " is not an experience for saints, for a select few who by a lifetime of discipline have pried loose a few of its secrets. It is everyone's rightful inheritance; it is the sure ground beneath all of us.

Few people in our time have been able to talk about this fundamental fact more lucidly than Evelyn Underhill. She has written many lengthy and learned books about worship, the experience of mysticism, and other subjects. But I call your attention to and commend to your reading a small and simple volume which she calls *The Spiritual Life*. It comes from a series of radio talks given a few years ago in England. Let me share a few things that Miss Underhill has to say on this subject of the spiritual life.

"Any mature person looking back on their own past life," she writes, " will be forced to recognize the factors in that life which cannot be attributed to heredity, environment, opportunity, personal initiative, or mere chance. The contact which proved decisive, the path unexpectedly opened, the other path closed, the thing we felt compelled to say, the letter we felt compelled to write. It is as if a hidden directive power, personal, living, free, were working through circumstances and often against our intention or desire; pressing us in a certain direction, and molding us to a certain design.

"All this, of course, is quite inexplicable from the materialistic standpoint. If it is true, it implies that beneath the surface of life, which generally contents us, there are unsuspected deeps and great spiritual forces which condition and control our small lives. Some people are, or become, sensitive to the pressure of these forces. The rest of us easily ignore the evidence for this whole realm of experience, just because it is all so hidden and interior; and we are so busy responding to obvious and outward things. But no psychology which fails to take account of it can claim to be complete. When we take it seriously, it surely suggests that we are essentially spiritual as well as natural creatures; and that therefore life in its fulness, the life which shall develop and use all our capacities and fulfil all our possibilities, must involve correspondence not only with our visible and ever-changing, but also with our invisible and unchanging environment: the Spirit of all spirits, God, in whom we live and move and have our being. . . . The meaning of our life is bound up with the meaning of the universe. . . .

" When we consider our situation like that, when we lift our eyes from the crowded by-pass to the eternal hills; then, how much the personal and practical things we have to deal with are enriched. What meaning and coherence come into our scattered lives. We mostly spend those lives conjugating three verbs: to Want, to Have, and to Do. Craving, clutching, and fussing, on the material, political, social, emotional, intellectual — even on the religious — plane, we are kept in perpetual unrest: forgetting that none of these verbs have any ultimate significance, except so far as they are transcended by and included in, the fundamental verb, to Be; and

that Being, not wanting, having and doing, is the essence of a
spiritual life. . . ."[1]

And, Miss Underhill continues, " The practical life of a
vast number of people is not, as a matter of fact, worthwhile
at all. It is like an impressive fur coat with no one inside it.
One sees many of these coats occupying positions of great
responsibility. Hans Andersen's story of the king with no
clothes told one bitter and common truth about human nature; but the story of the clothes with no king describes a
situation just as common and even more pitiable."[2]

" The first question . . . then, is not ' What is best for my
soul? ' nor is it even ' What is most useful to humanity? '
But — transcending both these limited aims — what function
must this life fulfil in the great and secret economy of
God? "[3]

Few people have testified more simply or more elo-
quently to the intimate correspondence between the " spiritual " and the " ordinary " than Nicholas Herman, known as
" Brother Lawrence," a cook in a seventeenth-century mon-
astery. In his little book, *The Practice of the Presence of
God* (which, like Evelyn Underhill's, serves well as reading
and study material for a small group interested in this area)
Brother Lawrence writes of his finding the love of God in
even the most menial jobs in his noisy kitchen, as easily, he
said once, as if he were on his knees before the blessed Sacrament.

The second assumption behind our concern with worship is that of discipline. There are laws that operate just as
regularly in the spiritual realm as in the physical. By and
large, we reap what we sow, or reap little if we have sowed

[1]Evelyn Underhill, *The Spiritual Life.* Harper and Brothers, New York
   (Pp. 21–24.); Hodder and Stoughton Limited, London.
[2]*Ibid.,* pp. 28–29.
[3]*Ibid.,* pp. 34–35.

little. We draw dividends in proportion to our investment. Our inner life is rich and sturdy, or it is poverty-stricken and flabby, according to the amount of disciplined effort we have put into cultivating it. We finally become what we work away at becoming.

The familiar parable of the wild duck, attributed to Soren Kierkegaard, is very much to the point. The story is that there was once a wild duck that had become separated from his migrating flock and happened to land among a flock of domestic ducks in a farmyard. The wild duck joined them in eating the corn that the farmer was feeding them, and liked it so well that he lingered until the next meal, and the next and the next. He stayed a week, a month, two months. Finally the autumn came and his wild companions flew over the farmyard on their southward flight. Their familiar call reminded him that it was time to be away. He felt the old ecstasy within him again and he began flapping his wings in order to join them in the wide sky. But he could not get off the ground. He had grown too fat during those months of lazy existence in the barnyard. So he had no choice but to remain there. Every spring and fall he heard the call of his wild friends passing over, but each year their calls seemed fainter and less real until at last he no longer noticed them. The wild duck had become a tame duck.

This is an illustration of what may happen to a Christian who becomes so involved in the program of a local church that he loses his sensitivity to the spiritual realities and becomes satisfied with the routine of services and meetings. Somehow the church must prod its members into new life and continually challenge them to seek wider and higher horizons. Worship of the right kind can help do that.

As we think of the quickening of the spiritual life of its individual members as the root of the renewal of the church's life, we should consider the various elements that comprise the experience of worship.

Genuine worship picks a man up and takes him to the outmost rim of his life where he looks out into a mystery, where he faces the " wholly other."

This element of mystery, of the " other," of that which is not man, is often lacking in modern worship. There is a tendency to stress the ways in which man and God are alike instead of the ways in which they are different. God, some have said, is like a fellow-worker, a partner in business. Some people even get chummy with him; they speak of him in informal terms, like " the man upstairs," or the movie actress who referred to him as " a livin' doll! "

Some Africans in the bush came at the whole thing once in quite a different way. They referred with scalp-tingling awe to hearing something passing by through the trees at night, but they said, " We never speak of it."

The Bible puts it for us best: " My thoughts are not your thoughts, neither are your ways my ways, says the Lord " (Isaiah 55:8).

Let me report an experience I had recently which illustrates what I have in mind.

I was leading a group of high school young people who were discussing Christianity and its relationship to various forms of art. During the discussion we talked about the attempts of artists through the centuries to paint a likeness of Jesus. We examined two paintings in particular. One was the familiar head of Christ by Sallman; the other was the face of Christ by the French painter Georges Rouault.

We studied Sallman's work first. I'm sure you know it. Here is an extremely handsome Anglo-Saxon Christ: noble, virile features, a clean-cut jaw, high forehead, silken, wavy hair. Here is a tender, gentle Christ. Here is a satisfying Christ, restful to the eyes, a most pleasing composition of line, form, and color. Just the kind of picture, as one girl put it, that people like to have on their living room wall — easy to look at, easy to live with.

Then we turned to Rouault's work, grotesque, revolting at first glance: swirling, confused composition, broken lines, wide, staring eyes that almost burn through you, and all out of proportion to the rest of the face, eyes that shadow an unspeakable agony; the outline of piercing thorns.

"Never! " said a member of the group. "It would never do! People just wouldn't take it."

"But," said another, "it makes you think! "

If we had taken a vote then and there, the Sallman would have won, hands down. The Rouault painting would have been rejected by them and by most people. But I noticed one thing: the longer the Rouault portrait was in front of the group, the more individuals studied it and invested something of themselves in it, the more intriguing it became, the more it spoke to them.

You see, there are two widely different things in these two pictures. On the one hand we have a slick example of the illustrator's art: an attempt to show what Christ might have looked like, which, when you get down to it, is not terribly important. The result of the artist's attempt is, frankly, pretty much what we *want* Christ to look like, a reflection of our own easy-going kind of religion — a Christ who is nice to have around, "easy to live with." The Sallman painting does not take you anywhere; it leaves you right where many Americans already are, in a fairly cozy kind of world with a Christ whom they have been able to domesticate.

The other painting is a sensitive man's answer, not to the problem of what Christ might have looked like, but to what it really would be like to live with him if we were to take him seriously! This painting does take you somewhere. It takes you straight back to an honest facing of the fact that, although Jesus preached good news of rest and peace and joy, had a word of comfort for the heavy-laden, and wept with compassion over Jerusalem, nevertheless he could be, on occasion, a very difficult person to have around. He said hard and cutting things. He made extraordinary demands on those who wanted to follow him, told them that they would have to put their loyalty to him above the things they cared most about, even their families. He ended up on a cross, and, as someone has said, it's plain that he was not crucified for saying, " Consider the lilies of the field! "

More than ever now, in this disenchanted, neon-lighted culture of ours, in which we work so hard to eliminate the element of mystery, we need the experience that only genuine worship can afford, to be led to the border of the other world that impinges on ours, to that place where water from great deeps beyond our knowing floods the shallow little bays of our lives on an incoming tide.

Genuine worship is a two-way relationship: it is our seeking God, and, more important, it is God seeking us. The Bible talks about both, but, it has a lot more to say about the second. Generally speaking, we have preferred to talk about the first. After all, when you are the seeker you can set your own terms. You can pick the places where you will look — pleasant places, preferably — a quiet lake deep in the woods, a western slope at sunset, a hilltop beneath a glittering canopy of stars, the sweet face of a friend, a warm fireside in a home where love has lived for years. Which is all quite valid, of course. It is proper to speak of seeking and of finding God in true and lovely things, in gracious people, in moments of luminous beauty, in all ennobling experiences.

But there is another side that most of us know by experience — the kind of situation in which God is the seeker and we are running as fast as our legs can carry us to get away from him! We need to help people understand that kind of experience of God, too. Psalm 139 talks about it, you remember:

> Thou searchest out my path and my lying down,
>   and art acquainted with all my ways. . . .
> Whither shall I go from thy Spirit?

Or whither shall I flee from thy presence?
If I ascend to heaven, thou art there!
If I make my bed in Sheol, thou art there!
If I take the wings of the morning
    and dwell in the uttermost parts of the sea,
even there thy hand shall lead me,
    and thy right hand shall hold me."

(Psalm 139: 3, 7–10)

Genuine worship involves us, not always in renewing, exhilarating experiences, but often in long periods of waiting — creative waiting, if you will, as patient attendants upon the grace of God.

Waiting is not the easiest thing for us busy Americans to do. It strikes us as a waste of time, frankly. We would much rather organize, promote, and manage. But there must be for us, too, a " waiting on God,' and that does not mean falling back and doing nothing. It means taking the strain off; it means opening ourselves up, sweeping and garnishing the house of our spirit, and making it ready for a visitation.

Sometimes before we can experience God's presence we have to experience his absence, his silence, even what appears to be his indifference or his antagonism. There is a wasteland to be walked. I cannot say what it is in your life; I know what it is in mine. And I am sure that before I can know God, " enjoy him," as the saints put it, I shall have to know what life can be without him. We have all indulged too often in what Roger Hazelton calls " the terrible profanity in taking God too much for granted."

So, many times we simply wait, as other men wait. Yet, *not* as other men wait. For their waiting is beneath a barren tree, dead and fruitless; as the two tramps in Samuel Becket's play, *Waiting for Godot*,[4] wait in hopelessness.

[4] Samuel Becket, *Waiting for Godot*. Grove Press, New York, 1954.

But *we* wait with expectant hearts for one whose mercy endures forever, one who will come to renew our strength! He will not be hurried or coerced by all our fussy managing, by our insistence that he appear at stated times and in recognizable form. For the truth is that he is likely to appear at the oddest moments, in the most unlikely places! He picks his moments with care. He may corner a man deep in dialogue in a small personal group; he may move in on him midway in a formal service of worship, or catch him unaware as he kneels at the Lord's table.

You never know! But pray that you will recognize him when he comes.

Genuine worship, then, involves the open acknowledgment that God does things for us on his own behalf which we could never do for ourselves. It affords us in luminous, liberating moments of pure joy the knowledge that through our seasons of distress, all along God has been working away at our lives from his end of things. True worship implies the acceptance of the fact that whatever form of worship we use — the service of morning prayer in a cathedral, or the freest, most informal order of service in an open country church — it is at best only a clogged channel through which, we pray, God's Holy Spirit may come to visit us.

But he comes! That is the wonder of it, though half the time, looking about a congregation, one wonders if the people bowed in prayer really expect him to come, and if perhaps they would be struck dumb if they thought he had! Here again we hear Paul asking us the question he asked the Ephesians: " Did you receive the Holy Spirit when you believed? " Will we have to answer as they did? " No," they answered, " we have never even heard that there is a Holy Spirit! "

Sometimes we try to approach this experience of worship in the wrong way. We feel that we are not in the right mood to worship, that we are not worthy enough, and that surely we ought to work harder on our problem before we turn to God about it.

But that is to come at it backward, of course. As Evelyn Underhill says, this is the whole point of Jesus' story of the Pharisee and the Publican, the two men who were praying in the temple at the same time. She says: " The Publican's desperate sense of need and imperfection made instant contact with the Source of all perfection. He stood afar off, saying, ' God be merciful, be generous, to me a sinner! ' He had got the thing in proportion. . . . He knew he was an imperfect, dependent, needy man, without any claims or any rights. He was a realist. That opened a channel, and started a communion, between the rich God and the poor soul.

" But the Pharisee's accurate statement of his own excellent situation made no contact with the realities of the Spirit, started no communion. He was dressed in his own spiritual self-esteem; and it acted like a mackintosh. The dew of grace could not get through. . . . Osuna says that God plays a game with the soul called ' the loser wins '; a game in which the one who holds the poorest cards does best. The Pharisee's consciousness that he had such an excellent hand really prevented him from taking a single trick." [5]

Or, frankly, we simply expect too much when we worship. We forget that God often comes in homely, unpretentious ways! We need courage to act on the little intimations of faith which come to us from time to time. How tenuous they are; what fragile tendrils they offer! We are almost ashamed of them.

There is a moving scene in James Agee's novel *A Death in the Family*, from which the prize-winning play *All the Way Home* was adapted. Jay Follet has been killed in a highway accident. His young widow, Mary, is trying to work her way through her grief, trying desperately to make room

[5] Evelyn Underhill, *The Spiritual Life*. (Pp. 67–69.)

in her scheme of things for this senseless tragedy. She finally gropes her way to a tiny, bare spot of hope, where, at least, she can hold tight and not be engulfed.

" Whatever is, is," she says. " That's all. And all there is now is to be ready for it, strong enough for it. . . . Isn't that so? " she asks, turning to her Aunt Hannah, a woman of great understanding and compassion.

" That, and much more," said Hannah.

" You mean God's mercy? " Mary asked softly.

" What I mean, I'd best not try to say," Hannah replied. . . . " Only because it's better if you learn it for yourself. *By* yourself."

" What do you mean? " Mary asked.

" Whatever we hear, learn, Mary, it's almost certain to be hard. Tragically hard. You're beginning to know that and to face it; very bravely. What I mean is that this is only the beginning. You'll learn much more. Beginning very soon now."

" Whatever it is, I want so much to be *worthy* of it," Mary said, her eyes shining.

" Don't try too hard to be worthy of it, Mary. Don't think of it that way. . . . Just do your best to endure it and let any question of worthiness take care of itself. That's more than enough." [6]

Genuine worship implies a discipline. It is something to be worked at. To be sure, it does not mean as some people would imply, a rigid, chore-like routine to be grimly gone through on schedule. The saints never went at it that way. Worship is to be worked at slowly, in a relaxed sort of way, but worked at regularly. There are conditions to be met. There is work to be done. Jesus said that real faith could move even mountains, which means that those who possess it must know something about mountaineering.

[6]Reprinted from *A Death in the Family* by James Agee, by permission of Ivan Obolensky, Inc., 341 East 62nd Street, New York 21, New York.

For a long time I have had an absorbing interest in mountaineering in the Himalayas — at the armchair level, I admit, though someday before I die I hope at least for a chance to be in Darjeeling at the right time of the year, on a clear day, for a view of those smoking, white ramparts against the blue. At any rate, I have read dozens of books about the many attempts to climb Everest, earth's highest peak.

You may know that for years mountaineers were convinced that there was only one possible route to the summit — up the north face, just below the knife-like northeast ridge. All other approaches, particularly those from the west and the south, were considered wholly out of the question, utterly impassable. One after the other the expeditions failed, and with the coming of World War II were abandoned. Then in the spring of 1953 two members of an English expedition, building on the gallant efforts of the Swiss the year before, gained the summit and victory. Everest had been climbed, not by the north face at all, but up out of the Western Cwm and then up the cruel southeast ridge! Discipline did it: disciplined minds, disciplined bodies, disciplined wills.

Waiting did it, and an awesome sense of a great mystery beyond. And faith did it, faith that pocketed its doubts, shouldered its fears, lifted its face skyward, and dug hands and feet into the treacherous, icy slopes.

Everest is still there; but, in a profound sense, it got moved by faith.

So, said Jesus, it can be like that in the terrain of the spiritual life. If you will accept the risks, if you will settle for small advances, if you will work at it, mountain-moving power can be yours!

GOD'S PEOPLE AT WORSHIP

Obviously, the single most important thing a church does in a given week is to gather its people for the public worship of God. In one sense, it is the *only* important thing it does. For from that stems everything else; in worship everything is seen in true perspective. Without it, and unless it is conducted with infinite pains, with dignity, and with beauty, a church becomes merely one more society of earnest, conscientious people eager to do the right thing, but in danger of living truncated and trivial lives.

The renewal of a church's life will start here, with a fresh examination of the central meaning of corporate worship.

It is Sunday morning, on the drought-baked plains of North Dakota, in a quiet New England town, in a sprawling new suburb, or in an old urban neighborhood. One by one, the members of the congregation settle in their pews. A grandmother is first to arrive, and bows her head for a moment against the pew in front. Then come a middle-aged couple; three teenagers; a young mother. They come singly, in twos and threes, by the dozens, by the hundreds. . . . A prelude — by the organist or pianist — drops a veil between them and the clamorous world outside. . . . " I was glad when they said unto me, ' Let us go into the house of the Lord! ' " The minister enters. . . . Faces are turned upward, eager, hungry, hoping. . . . The words come, clear and reassuring: " They that wait upon the Lord shall renew their strength. They shall mount up with wings as eagles. They shall run and not be weary; they shall walk and not faint." The hymn begins. . . .

What is happening here? What *could* happen?

A worshiping congregation is the reminder of a truth without which we cannot live with any sanity or hope. It is the reminder that, all appearances to the contrary, there is a vast and changeless purpose overarching us, an indomitable will that holds its own surely and steadily through all the fitful changes of our little days.

The church is the only institution we belong to that keeps reminding us of the eternal dimensions of our lives. We have business with everlasting things but, were it not for the church, we might soon forget it.

You know the legend of the lost Atlantis, a whole continent that slipped beneath the waves of the sea — farms, homes, businesses, churches — and how on still nights sailors report hearing the sounds of it, hearing, for instance, the sound of church bells from depths far below them. Debussy has portrayed it musically in his tone poem " The Engulfed Cathedral." And, as one man puts it, this is exactly what the church keeps doing, reminding us of whole continents of our lives that we have lost, and almost forgotten. Above the noise of the world the church helps a man hear the pealing of his bells!

A worshiping congregation is, beyond this, a public victory celebration of what God has done for man, right out where people can see and hear it. It is the acting out of what it most deeply believes to be true: that in Jesus Christ God entered our human life to save us from destroying ourselves, to show us how life is meant to be lived, to break open new paths through the tangled underbrush of our human predicament. Christian worship holds this celebration regularly. It expects the people of Christ to be on hand each time it takes place, " not because they may," but quite the other way around, " because they must "; because unless God's mighty acts are celebrated regularly, with excitement and with the full participation of all who believe in them, we tend to focus on ourselves and to congratulate ourselves on how nicely we can manage with no outside help. But the whole point of Christian worship is the recognition that we cannot manage without such help. It is, essentially, a service of thanksgiving in which we pour out our hearts in gratitude for the undeserved gift of God's grace. " Liturgy," says a friend of mine, " is the shape of that which happens when people meet their

God in serious encounter." In worship this people remember
who they are, acknowledge their faithlessness, think back
over the long way they have come, recall the signs of God's
gracious presence along the way, and finally re-dedicate
themselves to the doing of his will in their time, in their particular corner of his vast kingdom.

They do all this through the hearing of God's word —
in the reading of scripture and the sermon which, really to be
called that, must be something more than the dispensing of
sound advice or some rousing words of encouragement, or a
pleasant discourse on the merits of religion as obviously a
good thing. They do it through the singing of Christian
hymns, the folk songs of the faith; through the voice of common prayer lifted to God in adoration, in confession, in
thanksgiving, in petition, and in intercession. They do it
through re-enacting Christ's own dramatization of his sacrifice, in eating his bread and drinking his cup at his own table.

Someone has said that in the early church, *every* Sunday
was Easter Sunday. Every gathering of Christians was the
occasion for them jubilantly to celebrate God's splendid triumph over everything that degrades and defeats life. In a
sense, this still is so: Each service of worship is the heralding
of this same victory, in the context and language of our own
day. In a sense, what each service of worship should an-
nounce, sometimes explicitly, always implicitly, is that God
has a grand strategy for dealing with situations, private or
social, which too often we are inclined to conclude are beyond hope.

What I mean is somewhat like the strategy adopted by
the United States Navy high command for the struggle in
the Pacific during the Second World War. In the end, we
knew, victory would involve the capture and surrender of
the enemy's homeland. That seemed an impossibly long way
off. Between Pearl Harbor and Tokyo stretched thousands
of miles of open sea, systematically spiked by heavily forti-

fied Japanese bases. Truk in the Carolines, for instance, was considered by many to be impregnable. The war could drag on forever if these fortresses were to be taken one by one.

But another strategy was settled on: to sweep daringly past these bases, to by-pass them and to press on toward the main objective, leaving Truk and all the rest for mopping-up operations later.

God works that way in human life. He sweeps past all the stubborn, nasty resistance we offer, breaking us out of some backwater in which we have let ourselves be trapped, setting our faces once more toward the open sea. This is his way of telling us to take heart, that he has already won the big victory, and that though there will always be mopping-up operations for us — a daily dying and being born again — victory can be ours, too!

Do you dare think what it could mean for someone in your congregation really to get hold of that idea next Sunday morning?

Put it this way: Corporate worship is a supreme attempt to get life in focus again, to see things clear and whole. And a man or woman coming into church on Sunday morning may need to have just that one thing happen to him: to have the focus of his life changed.

Photography and I have never been very close. I have mastered very little of the technique. But soon after I got my camera I learned one fundamental lesson. I learned that there are certain key adjustments in focus that have to be made if you are going to get any kind of picture at all. Most of the first few Kodachromes I took were pretty bad; one of them in particular. It was a distant landscape, terribly out of focus. I looked in the manual that came with the camera and discovered my error. I had snapped a scene covering five to ten miles, but had left the focus set for ten feet! " For distances of more than one hundred feet," said the manual, " use the infinity setting."

In times like these, feeling crowded and hemmed in, lost in demands of the present moment, that is what we need more than anything else — the perspective of infinity. In the worship of God, both in the private cloister of the heart and in the congregation of God's people, we find the right setting.

Chapter VI

A Ministry That Rings True

PEOPLE HAVE HAD a lot of fun and turned out a lot of pseudo art the last few years with the pastime of " painting by numbers." You know how it goes. You fill in a thousand little spaces, each with the paint of a designated number — four, sunset pink; eight, banana yellow; fourteen, forest green; and so on. You take special pains, of course, not to spill over the lines! Then, when you're done, you prop up your handiwork, stand back, take a good look, and for the first time see it for what it is — a plain, unadulterated fake!

That may be putting it a little strongly, perhaps, but you hear of a church now and then that is no more real or honest than that. It is synthetic. It is going through a lot of motions, but one can hardly see just what they have to do with the business of the church of Jesus Christ in the world.

Kierkegaard once said that there will be only one question asked of us in eternity. There you will be, he said, naked and alone, and a voice will be asking, " Were you honest in your relations with yourself as an individual? "

The same question, I'm sure, will be asked of a church. There will be a number of other things the Almighty will want to know about us, but this will be among the first things that he will say: " You may not have been a great church, but

93

were you an honest church? Was there an authentic ring about what you said and did? "

If you buy a cherry wood chest labeled " Genuine Colonial " from a reputable antique dealer you take it for granted that it is what it claims to be. If you enter a devil's food cake in the baking contest at the county fair, the judges assume that it is not a packaged mix, but a product which you made yourself, from the first sifting of flour to the last spreading of icing. How do you tell when a church is carrying on an authentic witness to Jesus Christ? Is it real, or is it phony?

We have already considered a number of marks of the authentic church, of course. It is a real church when it is proclaiming the gospel of Jesus Christ and not merely peddling good counsel, or urging people to be better than they are. It is a real church when in the way it conducts its life it demonstrates the kind of community it talks about. It is a real church when it understands itself as a mission operation, in touch with the world around it and serving it in Christ's name. It is real when it puts the worship of God at the center of its life. These are basic " norms "; these are the generally accepted marks of a church's authenticity. But there are others which have a particular relevance and meaning for these present years, and they deserve our attention.

LAYMEN FOR THE " OUTSIDE " JOB

One of the sturdiest and most promising signs of renewal in the church is the steadily increasing part that laymen are taking in its life. By laymen we mean, of course, both men and women. This is one of those instances where " renewal " means a return to primitive principles and practices. In the church that we read about in the New Testament there was no distinction at all between laymen and clergy. The " laity " in its original meaning — coming from the Greek word *laos* — included everybody; it meant " the chosen people of God," *all* of them. In the first centuries, the faith was spread by the unrecorded witness of a whole army of anonymous Christian laymen — fishermen, shopkeepers, craftsmen of all kinds, housewives. There were only a few " pros " among them, and the chief of those, the apostle Paul, always kept his standing as a layman.

But as the church grew and finally flowered into the massive institution of the Middle Ages, more and more power and authority came into the hands of the clergy who, initially, had been simply certain members of the " laity " set aside for specialized functions. Consequently, laymen, the rank and file members of the church, more and more became spectators.

The Protestant Reformation — in which, as Hendrik Kraemer says, laymen largely provided the driving force — restored the basic biblical concept with its emphasis on " the priesthood of all believers," the belief that every man is meant to be a priest to his neighbor. But, as Protestantism developed, it too tended to magnify the role of the ordained clergy and to minimize that of laymen, who generally have thought of themselves as " the flock " under the shepherding of a competent and " professional " pastor. It is significant that most of the organizing of laymen into effective instruments for witness and for training in Christian character, particularly during the nineteenth century, took place outside the church, in movements such as the Y.M.C.A., the Y.W.C.A., and the Student Christian Movement.

But now the church is rediscovering the central place of the layman. This marks one of the frontiers of the modern church, one of the places where we can look with real promise for genuine renewal in its life and mission. Here we have a reassertion of the forgotten concept that " ministry " includes both clergy and laity, that both have the same calling, and that the latter, to use Dr. Kraemer's phrase, are part of the " frozen credits " of the church.

For, as Dr. Kraemer puts it, laymen are " the dispersion

of the church." That is to say, far more than is true of most clergymen, they are the church in daily contact with the everyday world in the places where it does its business, where it meets its severest tests, where it is most frequently held up to ridicule, where, in a profound sense, it either sinks or swims. This is how all valid communication takes place, anyhow: when life testifies to life in the language and in the exchanges of every day; when heart enkindles heart; when a person is drawn out of brokenness and loneness into a fellowship of acceptance, and where the kind of understanding love he meets enables him to give himself in a response of trust. Professional standards, methods, and guidance are all important, but the moment of illumination, of clarification, takes place in a quite unprofessional way. To borrow the well-known phrase of D. T. Niles, the business of Christian witness is very much like "one beggar telling another where to find food." And, much of the time, it is a witness that only laymen can make because of their involvement in the affairs of community and business.

Robert Spike put it well in an address some time ago before a group at a General Assembly of the National Council of Churches. " I pray," he said, " for an upsurge of a new kind of a roving band of prophets, lay and ordained, who move through the mechanical jungle with their own personalized ministries in each profession, on intercontinental airplanes, in resort hotels, over the back fence. This is a plea for a new kind of lay response — one that is not bound up in Guilds and Brotherhoods — but that sees clearly the dealings of God with this generation, that can talk theology like it does baseball, that can love and not be shocked, that seeks no allegiance to a complacent patriotism, but holds up the glory of God in the midst of the world. . . . We need desperately not more churchmen, but more lay missionaries. We need laymen who have no patience with our restrained and genteel fussing around in mission ' programming.' We need a ' Third

Force,' an informed and committed laity that moves out and stays out." [1]

As we have said, the main-line mission of the church is outside of it, not inside, and the urgent need is for men and women to do this " outside job." As one man puts it well, laymen are the bridge between sanctuary and society.

Now, such a view of the role of laymen — that they, essentially and chiefly, are the means by which the ethical teachings, the insights, and the life-giving power of the Christian faith are going to be inserted into the life of the world — implies a sobering look at most of our church programs for them, our traditional women's and men's organizations, for example. There is really just one question that has to be asked about them: *Are they carrying out the work of God's people?* In other words, are they doing the real work of the church? Or are they simply reproducing, on a slightly higher level, perhaps, the typical pattern of community fraternal organizations?

At your next opportunity ask the officers of a women's organization in your church to take some time at a meeting to discuss this question: Are we actually furthering the mission of Christ's church in the world, or are we mainly a luncheon club with spiritual overtones? Ask the men's brotherhood to do some similar probing: Are we furthering the mission of Christ's church in the world, or are we largely a sort of ecclesiastical service club, long on fellowship and good cheer, but short on grappling with what it means to be a member of the church and to live a Christian life in this kind of world? Ditto for the Couples Club: Have we latched on to Christian mission, or are we just providing, as Georgia Harkness put it once, " a folksy place for folksy folk who want a folksy time " ?

The comment has been made that if a group's program is too " religious " people will not come. When you get down

[1] Robert Spike, in an address before the National Council of Churches.

to it, a remark like that makes about as much sense, in a way, as a member of a photography club saying, " If there's too much talk about photography, the people won't come," or someone in a choral group complaining, " There's altogether too much singing in this organization! " The real question, of course, has to do with what you mean by " religious " when you talk about programs. What *do* you mean? And how do *you* reply to the protest that's made about the content of church programs being too " religious? "

The plain fact is that we have some scratching around to do in our various church organizations in these changing times in order to find ways to make them more effective instruments for carrying out the work of the church. In our church, for example, some careful experimenting is going on in the matter of reaching the growing number of women who are working at full-time jobs. Fewer of them are able to attend the daytime luncheon meetings of our " Mayflower Fellowship," and to participate in its fairly elaborate organizational structure. But these women are in closer touch with the world and, therefore, have more chances to testify to the meaning of their faith than ever before. More than ever, they need the sustaining strength of deep Christian fellowship, of fresh insights into the meaning of their faith. Do these people understand that their function as Christians is to live in the world as salt or as leaven? And how can they be helped so to live and witness? Much of the time they feel quite inadequate and powerless. Some of them are finding the answer, again, in small personal groups, coming to grips with vital issues in informal, uncomplicated ways.

Now, the recovery of the idea that laymen are of as much importance as the clergy, if not more, has something to say, too, about the way in which we recruit and employ them for the work of the church. People must never be appealed to, says Dr. Kraemer, with the request to be so kind and good-willing as to help the church. Nobody, he says, thinks of speaking in such a way to the ministry or clergy. We can ask people to serve only in terms of who they are — the " people of God," sent into the world for mission and service.

And then, having once recruited them, it is important that we put them to work in the most efficient kind of organization we can devise. In many of our churches the organizational structure is complicated and clumsy. It may have just developed over the years, and the practical result is a snarl of uncoordinated boards and committees which a responsible businessman would not tolerate for a day in his organization. Many churches would benefit by a thoroughgoing project in self study, not only in clarifying their organizational structure, but also in getting a tighter grasp of their mission. Denominational resources are generally available for such a project. I have been minister of two churches that have carried out such projects, and I can vouch for their fruitfulness. Whatever else such a study may do, it helps a church ask the right questions about itself, and usually little progress can be expected in any enterprise until those questions are asked!

Also, if careful arrangements are made for the ordination and installation of ministers and for the recognition of other professional workers, it is just as important that there be a fitting acknowledgment, through public ceremony, as part of corporate worship, of the place and the functions of the officers and other lay leaders in a church.

THE ROLE OF THE MINISTER, AND THE IMAGE PEOPLE HAVE OF IT

Have you looked at your minister lately? Not just as he stands in the pulpit on Sunday morning, or calls at your bedside in the hospital; but in the totality of his office, the whole bone-wearying, impossible, but glorious job to which you and the other members of your church called him?

Well, if you have not studied him recently, other people have. In fact, there has been considerable investigation and surveying going on regarding the life and habits of that peculiar species known as the Protestant minister.

One piece of documentation and commentary in this field was a widely discussed article in *Life* magazine a few years ago. Its main point was that ministers are breaking down, right and left, because their churches expect them to do an impossible job. In his work the minister is expected to preach interesting, provocative sermons, conduct worship with taste and skill, study conscientiously, call diligently in the homes of the parish, tend the sick and bury the dead, counsel the distressed, baptize babies, marry young people, conduct study classes, administer a complex of boards and committees, sometimes supervise a staff, be reasonably astute in business and financial matters, attend denominational meetings, be active in community affairs, and through it all be a model husband and loving father. One minister reported that in a survey that he had made he asked his congregation how much time they thought he should give to the several aspects of his job. The result was an average work week of eighty-two hours! Another minister who conducted the same survey, found his people recommending a work week of two hundred hours, thirty-two more hours than there are in even the longest week!

Now, I may not get around as much as other people, but I do not find many ministers " cracking up." And when they do the cause of the collapse may not actually be the strain of an " impossible " job, but the inability to come to terms with unresolved tensions and problems within their lives, which they would have to cope with, whatever their vocation. There is, after all, a blunt and salty wisdom in Harry Truman's observation that if a man cannot stand the heat in the kitchen he'd better get out!

For all of that, I do find ministers who feel frustrated much of the time, working away at their jobs with a thin top-coat of guilt over everything they do, distressed that they cannot complete half of what they feel they should be doing. This, again, is partly an interior matter for the minister himself to handle, part of a private transaction between himself and God. But part of it lies in the need for a freer, more open understanding between a minister and the people of a church as to just what his role is. For the truth is that many times the feeling of frustration and anxiety that a minister has about his job lies in a disparity between what he considers himself called to be and the image which the community and his own congregation have of him. As one minister said, apparently what holds the modern minister together, much to his dismay, is his public role of responsibility for the external advancement of the congregation, or being expected to handle the Christian message in such a way that it will be instrumentally useful for attaining immediate goals.

How a minister conceives his role, as well as the image his people have of it, is of considerable importance to a church concerned about revitalizing its life. For the chances are that in most instances renewal will start with the minister himself. So writes James A. Farmer, Jr., minister of a west coast church in a fast-growing suburban area, that has recently gone through a heartening experience of renewal. What he has to say is important: "As renewal takes over his own life, [the minister] finds that he can settle for nothing less than seeing renewal come into the lives of his people, his church, and the community. As pastor, the minister is in a position whereby he may be able to initiate and direct such a widespread renewal. But before this can happen, he must make some decisions within himself as to how this renewal will be expressed.

" The pastor is faced with the dilemma in his ministry as to whether he primarily will seek to promote breadth or depth in the church. The pastor is tempted to seek the promotion of breadth, material strength, and size in his church first, hoping that he can work at depth and renewal later. But in this way, is he not running the risk of promoting and creating primarily a secular, religiously tinted social organization that is a ' mile wide and an inch deep ' at the center of the community? . . . Breadth without depth is dead.

" On the other hand, if the pastor chooses to stress depth and renewal exclusively at the expense of size, he may be influential in overly minimizing the church. In the midst of a rapidly expanding population, a church which limits itself to being a handful of deeply committed Christians not only can run the risk of becoming lost in the shuffle, but can also be shirking its opportunities and responsibilities to the surrounding people." [2]

Honest conversation between pastor and people about his job is needed, especially in churches where there has been pulling and hauling between them. It becomes quite properly part of a self-study project of which we have already spoken. The crucial question to be asked is this: Is the role of the minister so conceived and so accepted that he becomes the agent through which the mission of the *whole* people of God is grasped, is guided, is consecrated? The concept of the *whole* people of God being employed in the church's mission is crucial. As one minister, Robert C. Dodds, writes me, " This will mean a revision of our view of the ministry. Our present conception of the ministry may be blocking the laity from doing its essential work. I believe that we must re-examine our entire concept of the role of the ministry, its recruitment and its training, so that our full-time professional leadership in the future will be able to release, rather than to stifle, the immense spiritual and human resources which God has placed within his church."

[2] James A. Farmer, Jr. " Unshackling the Holy Spirit," *Union Seminary Quarterly Review*, March 1961. Copyright, 1961, by Union Theological Seminary. (P. 305.) Used by permission.

Here, as in other areas of the church's life, we have a lot of question-asking to do, a lot of probing and experimenting. There is no fixed formula. What works in one parish may not work at all in another. But one thing is very plain: However his job specifications may vary according to special needs or the place of his calling — open country, small town, suburb, or inner city — at the heart of every church there needs to be a consecrated, professionally trained, hard-working, winsome " man of God," an " enabler " of the Holy Spirit, as someone has described him, doing his best, in season and out, with humility and with a quiet mind, to release the enormous resources within the church.

THE " WHOLE PEOPLE OF GOD " — MINISTERS AND LAYMEN — MINISTERING AUTHENTICALLY

A new recognition of the central place of laymen in the life of the church; a re-examination of the minister's role and the renewal of his own personal life — these are starting points for Christian ministering that has the ring of authenticity and authority about it. Now let us consider some other marks of the same kind of ministering.

We could use much more spontaneity, a kind of bubbling, sparkling freshness in the way we do things.

This can be carried too far, obviously, but there is something to be said for the late James Thurber's point of view. He was talking once about his own work, and especially his inimitable drawings. " They have been described," he said, " as pre-intentionalist! That is to say, they were finished before the ideas for them had occurred to me." A lot can be said, too, for the offhand informality of the great conductor, the late Sir Thomas Beecham. I was saddened by his death. He left a rich bequest of music incomparably performed. We are the poorer, too, without his salt-and-pepper spirit, his puckish good humor and relaxed approach to life, even to its most serious matters. It is told how he once arrived in the

orchestra pit of Covent Garden in London to conduct the
evening performance. Bowing and smiling, he acknowledged the applause of the audience, then turned to the orchestra, but before lifting his baton leaned over to the con-
certmaster and whispered, " By the way, what opera are we
doing tonight? "

Thurber and Beecham, of course, were masters of their
craft, and back of their lightheartedness were the years of
unrelenting discipline and backbreaking work. The point is
that when they offered themselves publicly, they did so with
a lilt, with an infectious enthusiasm about what they were
doing that could not help attracting people. In church work
often we are piously solemn and heavy-handed. What we
do seems awfully tired and threadbare. What we say sounds
labored, lacks style and excitement.

Ministers, I think, are the worst offenders. They
usually have true and right things to say; but they say them
dully. A lot of their sermons, while most of the time on the
side of the angels, limp and plod, more in the style of an inter-
office memo than the heralding of great good news. Of
course, not every sermon, letter, or article has to be a piece
of deathless prose; but more often than they do, they could
exhibit a sharper sensitivity to words and a more effective
combination of them to give color and force to what is being
said. A minister can no more afford to be careless about the
words he chooses in a sermon than a surgeon can be about
his choice of instruments for an operation.

Nor is there any more excuse for laymen to be dull and
uninteresting. The trouble is that sometimes we do not dig
out and employ the rich talents waiting to be mined in the
lives of people. Instead, we rely on worn-out stereotypes.
Without a doubt, there are people in your church with unsuspected flairs for all kinds of things — decorating, writing,
organization, artistic layout of material, dramatic expression.
We need to keep looking for new forms of expression,

new ways to do and to say old things. As Dr. Kraemer says, we must find new ways to talk to the world, and, when necessary, to interfere in its affairs. This must be a time of experimentation in the church, with a readiness to try new things and to acknowledge frankly those experiments that fail.

One area where considerable experimentation is going on, and still more is needed, is in contacts with teenagers. Few churches really have their hands on that. Old stereotypes have gone by the board here. How do you get close to, let alone get inside of, the world of high-school youth, for instance? For most adults, even for many ministers, it is a bewildering, disorganized world of noise and restless movement. But this is where young people live, most of them with honor; it is their security, in part, against the broken, disorganized world into which they have been born.

Do they feel that their church really takes them seriously, or that the church is usually bemoaning their low standards, their irresponsibility, their poor taste? Does the church make any investment in the things that youth invest a lot of time in? Jazz, for instance. It may be a stiff dose for the oldsters, but it is part of the language of our time. Do we primly shut our ears against it? Rather, we should be exploring the implications of jazz as a voice of contemporary culture.

A new approach is needed, too, in the fundamental business of the preparation and the reception of adult members into the church. More and more churches are moving away from a brief, casual conversation between the minister and a prospective member, which is still the prevailing practice in many quarters, toward some form of serious orientation into the life of the church, its history, its essential beliefs, the obligations and privileges of membership, and so on.

Instruction in some churches involves several weeks of classes, whereas in other churches prospective members are merely asked to attend two or three carefully planned, skillfully directed sessions. Here, again, no standard formula can be expected. But there should be a serious attempt to make induction into the Christian church a more exacting and memorable experience than it frequently is. There comes to mind the story that George Webber tells of a conversation with a minister of a large suburban church. "And what are your problems? " Mr. Webber jokingly asked him. He answered, " Oh, we've got a really serious issue. We have no place for people to park on Sunday morning. If we just had better parking facilities, our membership could jump a thousand in six months! "

To assure renewal at a level where it makes a noticeable difference, a church has to let people outside know that it is one with them in sharing the stresses and strains of this age. Here again is the old business of involvement versus aloofness. We need men and women in our churches who can be links with the world outside its doors, for many of whom, as David Roberts said once, God is not a premise but a target.

Do you remember Casy, the preacher, in *The Grapes of Wrath,* John Steinbeck's unforgettable novel of the migrants from the dust bowl in the 1930's? The people were all moving westward. The chaotic conditions of the time tore up by the roots all the safe and familiar patterns for preaching the gospel. Shaken and dismayed, Casy explains: " I got to go where the folks is goin '. I'll work in the fiel's, an' maybe I'll be happy."

"An' you ain't gonna preach? " Tom asked.

" I ain't gonna preach."

"An' you ain't gonna baptize? " Ma asked.

" I ain't gonna baptize. I'm gonna work in the fiel's, in the green fiel's, an' I'm gonna be near to folks. I ain't gonna try to teach 'em nothin'. I'm gonna try to learn. Gonna learn why the folks walks in the grass, gonna hear 'em talk, gonna hear 'em sing.... Gonna eat with 'em an' learn.... All that's holy, all that's what I didn' understan'. All them things is the good things."

Ma said, "A-men."[3]

So will many others when they recognize something of this identification with life's brokenness in the outreach of a church, see, even, some of the brokenness in the lives of its people and its minister!

But if Christians, ministers and laymen alike, are to identify themselves with this brokenness of modern life, if they are to recognize it and serve it, they must come to grips with it in the deep places of their own lives.

Actually, we should give thanks that the situation of our time is as it is. For in it we have an unusual opportunity to communicate the faith that the church professes. As Paul Tillich has said, the situation the world is in has opened up many people in such a way that they are receptive to what the Christian gospel has to say to them; they are asking the questions to which Christians can give the answers.

And the answers will come, not because we have studied a catechism or read a book on how to achieve spiritual peace in six easy lessons. They will come because of the grace of God, and also because we have grappled with the questions ourselves. And however stumblingly the answers come, however many questions are still hedging them about, we must share them with others. Even partial answers from the heat of the heart's struggle are better than complete ones from the back of the book, or from a sermon. And you — especially if you are a minister — can be sure that the people who listen to you will know this, even if you do not recognize it yourself!

Why, do you suppose, do people come back to our

[3] From *The Grapes of Wrath*, by John Steinbeck. Copyright 1939 by John Steinbeck. Reprinted by permission of The Viking Press, Inc., New York, 1939. (Pp. 127–128.)

churches, once they have been there? Do they come back principally because they have been treated in a friendly fashion, because of the congeniality of a coffee hour after the morning service? Possibly. But we cannot sustain true Christian community through an unbroken succession of pleasant coffee hours or through planned friendliness. Eventually, people will return because down at a deep level of their lives where they can tell whether things are real or fraudulent, it has been made plain to them that here is a place where they can belong, where they have been listened to and accepted, where they can be rescued from their isolation.

Leslie Fiedler says of Simone Weil that nothing in religion ever came to her as a convention or a platitude; it was as if she were driven to reinvent everything from the beginning. This is what Kierkegaard meant when he said that the real question to ask is not "What is Christianity? " but "How does one become a Christian? " And John Ciardi, the American poet, critic, and teacher, says the same thing about a poem and its meaning; what you have to ask about it, he says, is not *what* does it mean, but *how* does it mean?

Take some time to ponder this yourself. Ask, not *what* does Christianity mean to me, but *how* does it mean what it means? Is the truth it represents what *I* have wrested from it while struggling with the powers of darkness?

All this is simply to say that a self-authenticating witness carries the most weight in the end, the kind that says: " Hear this — this is the gospel coming to you through me. I haven't found very many final answers; I'm still searching, and now and then my doubts seem to cancel out my faith. But what I have is mine, all mine, and I'd like to show you the way I've come! "

This is how for most of us an authentic Christian faith gets off the ground — with the courageous acceptance of ourselves, undiscouraged by obvious defects or crippling limitations. A cartoon in the *New Yorker* puts it well. The sketch shows a balding, middle-aged man peering anxiously into a mirror and saying, " You're all I've got! "

John La Montaine, the American composer, writing in the Sunday music section of *The New York Times* a couple of years ago, was talking about composers and how they are often asked what they must do to get ahead. " I doubt," said Mr. La Montaine, "... that many composers, especially those for whom their work is a true vocation, could answer. A serious composer is so deeply involved with a larger problem: how to get all that he has to say out of himself. . . . Can you imagine," he asks, " Schubert thinking of the publicity value of the ' Erlkoenig ' ? Of writing it, for example, in response to the demand for songs about death — so that he could get ahead as a composer? Get ahead! What is get ahead? A composer's job is to dig out of himself what is behind him, what lies deepest buried in his past. His own past. Not Bartok's, not Stravinsky's, not Beethoven's. Out of himself he has to make the music that he needs . . . not what critics . . . need. . . . Above all, he must not write what he thinks that they think they need."[4]

Or, as another critic said, this is the kind of testament every great musician comes to at last when he explains himself.

To explain yourself! This is the nature of authentic ministering. But more, it is to let Christ explain himself to another through you! For, after all, the *New Yorker* cartoon is not the whole truth. By the grace of God we are *not* all we've got. We have Christ. There is one who has us in his safe and holy keeping, and who will not let us go. What he asks of us is not easy. And in our faithfulness to him lies, at times, our anguish and our despair. But in it, also, lie our dignity and whatever glory our lives will wear.

" So we do not lose heart. Though our outer nature is

wasting away, our inner nature is being renewed every day
... because we look not to the things that are seen but to the
things that are unseen; for the things that are seen are tran-
sient, but the things that are unseen are eternal " (2 Corinthians 4:16-18).

A Pastoral Postscript

Nothing is more discouraging than summaries that do not summarize, conclusions that do not conclude, or last chapters that serve as a kind of catch-basin for all the brilliant but disappointingly unused notes gathered by the author.

What I have in mind, therefore, for these concluding pages is in no way an attempt to summarize what has been said. Nor is it a set of " rousements " or final " inspirational " thoughts intended, as Pooh Bah would say, " to give artistic verisimilitude to a bald and unconvincing narrative."

All I am interested in doing is to send this discussion on its way with a pastoral word of encouragement and of hope. For all the possible limitations of scholarship, profundity, and brilliance, there is a peculiar and indispensable quality to the pastoral. It is that point of view on the world, on man, and on the church which, though it has looked at their unloveliest, goes on believing in their capacity for the noblest.

In short, then, for those of us who believe in the church of Jesus Christ, who long to see it at its strongest, there are all kinds of reasons to be hopeful and expectant that it will meet the test of trying times. In many ways, some of them half-hidden and quiet, the church is beginning to reform itself — a kind of mid-twentieth-century reformation, if you will. And where this is taking place, certain inescapable facts are being acknowledged, certain unmistakable things are happening.

First, there is the frank recognition that we cannot go back to things that are gone for good. We cannot go back to New Testament times, for example. Too many things have changed. We have so much more information and knowledge about the world than people in those days had (though not necessarily more wisdom!). The Christian message, obviously, has to be put differently, to be re-stated in the language, the thought forms, and the style we know.

Nor, as someone has said, can we rebuild Christendom. That is, we shall never again have a world in which Christianity is the determiner of culture, as in Europe in the Middle Ages, or as in colonial New England.

Those days are gone, and their going poses serious questions which the Christians who are awake have to answer as best they can. We live in a time of rapid social change; everything is in a state of flux, few things are stable, and our wisest policy is to accept all this as a given quantity of our time, and to settle down to live with it and to stop stewing about it.

Second, we can accept another plain fact: that there are aspects of the Christian gospel that do not fit easily into society as we have organized it. The world is hostile to it. Christians are always getting into trouble. They are bound to because of who they are and what they believe. They are meant never to be fully at home in society; they are to be *in* it, but they never are to be wholly *of* it.

Third, we can avoid putting all our trust in a particular phase of the church's witness, as though it were the total answer to our needs. It is understandable how " emphases " come and go. They serve the needs of a particular time; they have often involved heroic testimony to neglected truth. The need for perspective on them is important, however. We cannot substitute them for the gospel itself, for the message

of Christianity in all its life-giving fulness. Unless we keep
perspective, these emphases can become " fads," easy short-
cuts, " packaged " answers.

*Fourth, we can cultivate, to some degree, an attitude of
detachment, a kind of sitting-loose-to-the-world.* We do not
mean cavalier indifference, but the kind of caring that does
not get tied up in knots, that looks at suffering and evil
squarely, yet with a quiet mind, without panic, and with a
sense that the ultimate treatment of it is in hands other than
ours.

It is the kind of caring that is stripped for action, with
the surplus fat and and the fancy parts of our church life cut
away. These days we need churches and Christians that are
mobile, flexible, triggered for action on any flank, at any
time.

*Finally, we can put our main accent on the things that
are essential and basic to the proclamation of the Christian
gospel:* a fresh understanding of the Bible; a more-than-
nodding-acquaintance with the history of the Christian
church, and the sense of how God works through all history,
particularly the history of our own time; facility in prayer,
and the nurture of the things of the inner life; an awareness
of the church as being essentially a mission operation, bringing the gospel to bear at those points in society where there is
ignorance, disease, injustice. So much of what we mean by
renewal means the recovery of things we have lost.

I think of that place in the book of Revelation (chapters
2 and 3) where the Holy Spirit speaks with shocking direct-
ness to the seven little churches of Asia Minor, suffering
under the whiplash of Roman persecution. To five of them
some blunt and biting things are said:

The church in Ephesus: This was the church that had
lost its first, warm love of the gospel; its enthusiasm had
dwindled. It was a faded copy of what it had once been.

The church in Pergamum: In its desire to be " liberal "

it had made room for all kinds of teaching, much of it false, and Christ had been displaced.

The church in Thyatira: Here the ways of the world had crept in and rampant immorality was its problem and its shame.

The church in Sardis: It looked all right on the outside. But appearances are deceiving; on the inside it was dead.

The church in Laodicea: This church was lukewarm. " Would that you were cold or hot! " But a lukewarm church! " I will spit you out of my mouth! " he says, rather inelegantly.

But for two of the churches the Spirit had only words of warm encouragement.

The church in Smyrna: " I know your tribulation and your poverty (but you are rich). . . . Do not fear what you are about to suffer. . . . Be faithful unto death, and I will give you the crown of life " (Revelation 2:9–10).

The church in Philadelphia: " I know your works. Behold, I have set before you an open door which no one is able to shut. . . . Because you have kept my word of patient endurance, I will keep you from the hour of trial which is coming on the whole world. . . . Hold fast what you have. . . . He who conquers, I will make him a pillar in the temple of my God. . . . and I will write on him the name of my God, and the name of the city of my God, the New Jerusalem. . ." (Revelation 3:8, 10, 11, 12).

To be sure, our churches stand in deep need. But they are God's churches; he loves them, and by his grace and by the power of his Holy Spirit they can and will be renewed!

Honor and majesty, dominion and power be unto him!